Decision Leadership

DECISION LEADERSHIP

EMPOWERING OTHERS TO
MAKE BETTER CHOICES

● ● ●

DON A. MOORE
AND
MAX H. BAZERMAN

Yale
UNIVERSITY PRESS
New Haven and London

Yale University Press books may be purchased in quantity for educational, business, or promotional use. For information, please e-mail sales.press@yale.edu (U.S. office) or sales@yaleup.co.uk (U.K. office).

Set in Gotham and Adobe Garamond types by IDS Infotech Ltd. Printed in the United States of America.

Library of Congress Control Number: 2021946781
ISBN 978-0-300-25969-8 (hardcover : alk. paper)

A catalogue record for this book is available from the British Library.

This paper meets the requirements of ANSI/NISO Z39.48-1992 (Permanence of Paper).

10 9 8 7 6 5 4 3 2 1

To Sarah, Josh, and Andy
D A M

To Marla and all of my coauthors on the journey
to learning the stuff in this book
M H B

Contents

Preface   ix

1   Leading the Decisions of Others   1
2   Guts vs. Brains   19
3   Be Investigator-in-Chief   44
4   Calibrate Your Confidence   62
5   Advice, Persuasion, and Collaboration   85
6   Recruiting the Best Evidence   105
7   Negotiate for One and All   124
8   A Higher Purpose   143
9   Nudging Toward Better Leadership   167
10   Designing a Better Decision Factory   182

Appendix: Decision Biases   195
Acknowledgments   211
Notes   213
Index   239

Preface

We collaborated on a book entitled *Judgment in Managerial Decision Making*, first published in 1986 (and revised several times). That book helped introduce what is now commonly called behavioral economics: using psychology to understand behavior of economic consequence. The book shared exciting developments in the study of human judgment and decision making, and it was directed at audiences of students and practitioners who could put that knowledge to use making better decisions in their lives and in their work. The ensuing thirty-five years have brought important research progress and a huge increase in the field's public profile. Behavioral economics is now regularly covered by the press and popular media, with several scholars achieving what counts as celebrity status (at least for the nerdy denizens of the academy).

Daniel Kahneman's book *Thinking, Fast and Slow* generated a great deal of interest in practitioners. Thaler's and Sunstein's *Nudge* allowed organizations, particularly governments, to think about how small changes in the environment could help people make better decisions. Dozens of fantastic scholars have conducted studies that demonstrate the powerful and useful application of insights from research.

As we considered writing a ninth edition of *Judgment in Managerial Decision Making*, we became convinced that rather than updating our existing book it would be more useful to connect the dots between decision making and leadership. Leaders not only make critical decisions themselves but also create and design organizations that influence the decisions of hundreds, thousands, or even millions. This book is for current and future leaders. We hope that you will use it to improve not just your decisions but also the decisions and lives of those around you.

Decision Leadership

1

Leading the Decisions of Others

Quarterbacks lead on the football field. They call the plays. They motivate their team members. And they lead off the field as well— they represent their teammates in talks with coaches and managers. On September 1, 2016, Colin Kaepernick, the starting quarterback for the San Francisco 49ers, decided to lead his team in a different way.

As the 49ers and the San Diego Chargers stood for the national anthem along with fifty thousand fans, Kaepernick took a knee; his teammate Eric Reid joined him. By kneeling, Kaepernick intended respectful protest against racial inequality and police brutality in the United States. In the 49ers' prior game against the Green Bay Packers, Kaepernick had sat on the bench during the anthem; afterwards, his teammate Nate Boyer, a military veteran, suggested that kneeling would better convey respect for the flag and the anthem while at the same time signaling defiance.[1] After the game Kaepernick spoke about his motivation: "I'm not anti-American . . . I love America. I love people. That's why I'm doing this. I want to help make America better."[2]

Kaepernick's actions drew both praise and criticism. "He can speak out about a very important issue," said New Orleans Saints star quarterback Drew Brees. "But there's plenty of other ways that you can do that in a peaceful manner that doesn't involve being disrespectful to the American flag." President Donald Trump condemned the protests: "Wouldn't you love to see one of these NFL owners, when someone disrespects our flag, to say, 'Get that son of a bitch off the field right now'?"[3] Yet several more players joined Kaepernick in taking a knee or raising a fist during the anthem, and the protests continued through the season. NFL viewership dropped 8 percent, with player protests being the most-cited reason.[4]

Kaepernick left the 49ers in March of 2017 in search of a team that would appreciate him more. However, he received no offers and did not play in a single NFL game in 2017. In October of 2017 Kaepernick filed a grievance accusing the teams of the NFL and their owners of colluding against him. The league bolstered his case by making him no offers in 2018. In February 2019 Kaepernick reached a confidential settlement with the league. But that settlement did not guarantee him a place on the field. Kaepernick did not play for the NFL in 2019 or in 2020.

While the NFL was treating him like a pariah, others celebrated Kaepernick's courage. In 2018, well after Kaepernick's on-field protests, Nike made Kaepernick the face of the brand by releasing an ad with the line, "Believe in something. Even if it means sacrificing everything." The ad, though controversial, was undeniably successful at increasing Nike's visibility. A year later Nike's "Dream Crazy" campaign featuring Kaepernick won an Emmy Award. Kaepernick also won awards for his activism, including accolades from *Sports Illustrated*, the American Civil Liberties Union, Amnesty International, Harvard University, and even, ultimately, the San Francisco 49ers.

After George Floyd's brutal murder at the hands of Minneapolis police in 2020 Kaepernick's profile rose again. At first Brees repeated his criticism of Kaepernick, saying, "I will never agree with anybody disrespecting the flag of the United States."[5] But as Black Lives Matter protests unfolded nationwide, public opinion coalesced around the need for change. Brees walked back his comments, confessing they were "insensitive and completely missed the mark."[6] NFL commissioner Roger Goodell publicly apologized for neglecting the concerns of African American players.[7] "Mainstream white America is going to reconsider Kaepernick at some point—the way it reconsidered Muhammad Ali years after he refused to go to Vietnam, the way it reconsidered Jackie Robinson and Jack Johnson," wrote Michael Rosenberg in *Sports Illustrated.* "Progress comes in fits and starts, and this country tends to punish those who urge it to move faster. The reconsideration of Kaepernick has begun."[8]

Was Kaepernick's kneeling an act of leadership? It certainly differed from a motivational speech, announcing a mission statement, or rallying the troops. And it isn't captured by Thomas Carlyle's "great man" theory of leadership. In 1840, the Scottish philosopher posited that great leaders are born, not made.[9] Endowed with the right mix of abilities, traits, and divine inspiration, great men, Carlyle believed, leave their marks on history. Although his theory held sway for more than a century, it turned out to be as vacuous as it was sexist; hundreds of studies seeking to identify the distinctive attributes of great leaders ended in disappointment. Eventually, universities quit teaching the concept, which had little supportive evidence and offered even less useful guidance to aspiring leaders. The great man theory has rightly withered, along with many other fads that have passed through the study of leadership over the past century, due to its lack of usefulness.

In this book we aim to define leadership in a new way, one grounded in the belief that leaders' success depends not only on their ability to make good decisions but also on their ability to help *others* make wise decisions. Colin Kaepernick used his high-profile position to direct the nation's attention to the discrepancy between our ideals and reality. His motivation was less immediate self-interest than the welfare of our diverse society. In doing so he sparked a movement whose ripple effects continue to spread.

We believe that leaders need to broaden their focus beyond making effective personal decisions to building teams, organizations, communities, and societies that empower everyone. In our view, great leaders create the norms, structures, incentives, and systems that allow their direct reports, the broader organization, consumers, investors, and other stakeholders to make decisions that maximize collective benefit through value creation. By this definition Kaepernick's kneeling was an act of leadership that fueled the protest movement of 2020, which in turn has inspired individuals and organizations to fight for changes aimed at promoting racial justice. Kaepernick's leadership was evident at protests in the summer of 2020 when protesters, rather than clashing with police, knelt before them.

Choosing Wisdom

We offer a few examples to clarify our definition of leadership. Consider the aptly named Jessica Wisdom, who has made wise choices at crucial junctures in her career. After completing an undergraduate psychology major at Brown University, Wisdom moved to Pittsburgh and joined Don at Carnegie Mellon University to successfully launch the new Center for Behavioral Decision Research. From there Wisdom entered the PhD program in CMU's unique and innovative Social and Decision Sciences Department, an interdisciplinary group of scholars from economics, psychology, political science, and history. For her dissertation advisers Wisdom chose the behavioral economist George Loewenstein and the decision researcher and health psychologist Julie Downs. Wisdom's dissertation tested the influence of calorie labeling and convenience on food choice. Her research examined consequences of the practice, mandated by law in some places, that menu options include calorie labels.[10] For instance, calorie labels at McDonald's reveal that a McDonald's Big Mac delivers 550 calories, more than a chocolate milkshake. As it turns out, simply providing this information has disappointingly small effects on calorie consumption.[11]

As she finished her PhD, rather than entering the academic job market, Wisdom accepted a position in Google's People Operations unit. There, she put to use the knowledge she had gained studying behavioral science to help Googlers (Google's employees) make better decisions. At Google Wisdom found herself in the role of decision architect: someone who structures decision environments to nudge others toward wise choices. Wisdom loved how quickly she was able to apply ideas, run studies, and get things done at Google. For example, she helped address a problem Google had created by offering its employees so much free food in the company cafeteria: weight gain. The company wanted to keep its employees healthy, but the availability of free, fattening foods was undermining that goal. Wisdom used her knowledge of behavioral science to help employees make healthier choices. To make them less tempting, for example, fattening desserts and snacks were moved from the front of the cafeteria to the back. They were still available but employees had to seek them out. Those who really wanted chocolate cake had to look for it at the back of the cafeteria in opaque containers. Googlers consumed fewer calories, gained less weight, and enjoyed better health.

Wisdom's boss at Google, Laszlo Bock, credits her for helping Googlers make wiser choices about food, retirement savings, hiring, and other consequential decisions.[12] In part thanks to Wisdom's and Bock's successes Google has been consistently rated as one of the best companies to work for in the world. Indeed, they were so successful that they saw an opportunity to take those tools beyond Google. Bock and Wisdom left Google to found Humu, a company driven to "make work better." Humu applies insights from behavioral science to help companies enhance workers' happiness and productivity. Humu begins by diagnosing a company's greatest personnel challenges and then designs interventions to remedy them. If the organization is missing the input of junior staff, Humu might suggest that meetings start with the input of the newest hires. If workers are unmotivated because they feel like cogs in a large machine, Humu might arrange for them to hear from colleagues or customers who depend on them. If employees are feeling unappreciated, Humu might remind managers to praise good performance when they see it. In short, Humu nudges organizations to make the work environment more supportive, inclusive, and productive.

Easy Virtue

Bruce Friedrich is another example of a leader who focuses on enabling others to make better decisions. Friedrich had long understood that if people ate less meat, fewer animals would suffer, human health would improve, carbon emissions would decline, and agricultural efficiency would increase. From 1996 to 2015 Friedrich devoted his life to advocating for social justice across species by teaching and working for the People for the Ethical Treatment of Animals (PETA) and the Farm Sanctuary, where he publicized the plight of farm animals.

Friedrich was not afraid to take bold action for the cause he championed. In February of 2000 he was arrested and charged with "criminal mischief" for throwing red paint on a fur coat during the Randolph Duke fashion show.[13] His mischief was part of a coordinated protest against the use of animal pelts that also included throwing a tofu-cream pie in the face of the designer Michael Kors. PETA justified the campaign by explaining that the paint was water-soluble and that the tofu pie was "a lighthearted way to bring attention to a serious issue." Ultimately, however, Friedrich concluded that there was a more effective path to reduce the suffering of animals. What did he do?

In 2015 Friedrich cofounded the not-for-profit Good Food Institute (GFI), a team of scientists, business analysts, and policy experts focused on accelerating the plant-based and cell-based meat industries. GFI informs consumers about the benefits of consuming less meat and about how to improve the environment, reduce animal suffering, and provide protein for the expanding world population. GFI also coordinates the efforts of scientists, entrepreneurs, and investors to develop new plant-based foods and so-called cultivated (also called clean or cell-based) meat grown from animal cells in a lab and produced without the need for animal torture and slaughter. Beyond Meat and the Impossible Burger are examples of meat alternatives that are appealing, affordable, and increasingly available in grocery stores and restaurants. Friedrich's leadership will soon bring many more such products to market.

Rather than preaching about the ills of eating meat, Friedrich is making it easy for people to choose virtuously by seeing to it that their grocery stores offer them substitutes that are tastier, safer, and cheaper. Consumption of meat substitutes has grown dramatically in the United States: about 20% annually in recent years, even as the percentage of people identifying as vegetarian has remained unchanged.[14] Rather than becoming vegetarians people are becoming flexitarians and reducetarians or are simply eating more food from plants. In so doing they are improving their health, reducing misery among farm animals, helping to conserve water and land, cutting carbon emissions, and reducing the risk of future pandemics caused by diseases transmitted from animals to humans.[15]

Decision Nudge

Cass Sunstein, a law professor, has also supported the rights of animals. In the introduction to *Animal Rights: Current Debates and Future Directions*, Sunstein considers, among other things, the legal standing of nonhuman animals as parties to potential lawsuits.[16] Some years later Senator Saxby Chambliss of Georgia zeroed in on this passage and cited it as a reason for putting a hold on Sunstein's nomination to head Barack Obama's White House Office of Information and Regulatory Affairs (OIRA). Chambliss opposed Sunstein's nomination because the law professor "has said that animals ought to have the right to sue folks."[17]

When Obama nominated him, Sunstein was on the faculty of the law school at the University of Chicago. One of the features of Sunstein's illustrious academic career is his spectacularly prolific list of publications. Given how much he has written, it should perhaps be no surprise that there was something in his extensive published record that Chambliss could find to object to. Sunstein's fifty-five-page resume lists something like nine hundred published articles, essays, and reviews. In addition, he has written or edited eighty-one books, including *Law and Happiness*[18] and *The World According to Star Wars*,[19] which explores the legal philosophy and timeless themes in George Lucas's science fiction saga.

Perhaps Sunstein's most important work, however, is his book *Nudge* (2008), coauthored with Richard Thaler.[20] The authors, a legal scholar and a behavioral economist, had originally planned to title the book "Libertarian Paternalism." The book presented ideas for how to use our growing understanding of human foibles, biases, and weaknesses to design systems that made it easy for ordinary people to make good decisions. The authors credits their editor at Yale University Press with persuading them to change the title. The year following the book's publication Sunstein overcame Saxby Chambliss's objection to his being confirmed by the U.S. Senate as head of the Office of Information and Regulatory Affairs. In that job he applied his knowledge of behavioral science to change rules in ways that improved food safety, highway safety, and air quality, to name just a few.

On January 18, 2011, encouraged by Sunstein, President Obama signed an executive order that called for cost-benefit analysis and scientific integrity in government policies, a review of ineffective regulations, and an increase in public participation in finalizing regulations. As Sunstein documents in his book *Simpler*, the order brought U.S. government rulemaking into the electronic age.[21] It nudged government toward policymaking based on evidence rather than on politicians' intuitions.

One behavioral nudge in Sunstein's toolkit is defaults: the choices implemented when people fail to make an active choice. Defaults are what happen automatically to people who fail to make an active choice. For example, Thaler's work shows that too many people fail to sign up for retirement savings programs, a mistake easily remedied by automatically enrolling people. (What makes this sort of paternalism libertarian is also making it easy to opt out of it by choosing not to save.) As the OIRA chief, Sunstein implemented many helpful defaults, including in the domain of retirement savings. Through a number of small and boring policy adjustments, Sunstein led millions of people toward billions of wiser decisions. When Sunstein left the Obama administration he returned to a faculty position at Harvard, where he wrote a few dozen more books. In 2021 Joe Biden nominated him to join the Department of Homeland Security.

Do the Actions of Kaepernick, Wisdom, Friedrich, and Sunstein Qualify as Leadership?

In 2013 Max helped create the Behavioral Insights Group (BIG) within the Center for Public Leadership at the Harvard Kennedy School of Government. BIG's goal is to connect Harvard's behavioral scientists to important problems via carefully crafted field experiments (also called randomized controlled trials, or A/B tests). Putting BIG under the umbrella of the Center for Public Leadership invited the question of whether behavioral insights could help teach leadership. That question came up in October 2013 during a panel discussion that explored how behavioral insights could improve government effectiveness. Each panelist, including the economist David Laibson and Cass Sunstein (back at Harvard Law School), gave a short presentation on the topic.

When the time came for questions, a Harvard professor who studied leadership raised his hand. He said the presentations were interesting, but he doubted they had anything to do with leadership. Since leadership, he said, was about changing the hearts and minds of followers, he was skeptical that decision making, behavioral insights, and nudging belonged on a panel hosted by the Center for Public Leadership. If you change behavior without changing people's hearts and minds, he asked, is that really leadership?

Sunstein responded by saying that effective leadership must affect what people do. Leaders succeed by changing the behavior of individuals, organizations, communities, or governments for the better. Sunstein noted the power of interventions to make wise choices easier and expressed his belief that these interventions were no less authentic than more costly (and less effective) persuasion attempts. David Laibson added that in the area of retirement savings, nudge-like interventions, tested through experiments, are able to change behavior ten times as effectively as any intervention that changed the heart or mind of the saver.

Max watched in stunned silence as Sunstein and Laibson made the case—better than he could have—that leaders are most effective when they guide others toward wise decisions. Too many leaders devote their energies to the difficult task of changing minds when a simple nudge can have a much more positive effect on behavior. Leadership is no more authentic when it is effortful and ineffective.

Colin Kaepernick did not try to change hearts and minds by giving a motivational speech to his teammates or to the world about racial injustice. Instead, he engaged in quiet protest and thereby became a powerful symbol of courage. For many, his willingness to risk his career was inspirational. Jessica Wisdom recognized how common it is for people and organizations to fail to follow through on plans that would benefit them. She devised simple systems to help people enact their values and improve themselves and their organizations. Bruce Friedrich thought about what it would take to get people to eat less meat and concluded that the answer was to make more plant-based foods available. He then started working on getting entrepreneurs and investors to bring such products to the market. Finally, Cass Sunstein used his knowledge about how humans make decisions to tweak federal regulations in ways that have improved the lives of millions of Americans.

None of these four individuals is a traditional leader, but all four meet our definition of effective leadership. All four have been enormously influential. All four have made decisions designed to steer people toward wiser decisions that create collective good. They have all acted as architects who helped better structure decision-making contexts for others. Throughout the book we will explore similarly effective and inspiring leaders and extract lessons that can help you become a better leader by making small adjustments with big effects.

The Power of the Situation

For one to understand how small adjustments can have big effects, it is useful to understand a debate that has raged for decades in psychology. The debate is about what determines human behavior: situations or dispositions. Personality psychologists defended the dispositional argument with evidence on the predictive value of personality traits. Obviously, they argued, people have different personalities from one another. Extroverts, for instance, talk more than introverts.

However, even the most loquacious extroverts are quiet when they ride in an elevator with strangers; at cocktail parties even the shyest introverts talk to others. The situationist argument notes how often situational effects swamp personality differences in accounting for behavior. You have no doubt noticed the ways in which your behavior changes in the company of different people, when you go from home to work, when you move between cultures, or when you travel between countries. In real ways, you are a different person in these different situations. Systematic analyses reveal that individual behavior differs as much across different situations as does the behavior of different people.[22]

The situationists pointed to the weakness of personality by noting its inability to predict behavior in any particular situation. For instance, studies that took the best personality surveys and used them to try to predict particular behaviors produced pitifully low correlations. Did conscientious students show up to meetings punctually? Did they submit their assignments on time? Correlations between traits and behaviors were usually positive and statistically significant, but they were modest in size, rarely exceeding 0.3.[23] In other words, conscientious personality was not the most important determinant of how conscientiously someone behaved in a particular situation. Instead, small differences in the situation could have powerful influences on behavior.

The person–situation debate in social psychology these days is largely regarded as being resolved.[24] The resolution notes that when aggregated over time and across many situations people's behavior is consistent in ways that highlight individual differences. The extrovert in the elevator is the one more likely to talk. But personality researchers have largely conceded to the power of situations to drive behavior. Even extroverts rarely strike up a conversation in elevators with strangers. Even the Google employee with the biggest sweet tooth eats fewer desserts when they are hidden in opaque containers at the back of the cafeteria. Even someone who has never given a thought to the suffering of farm animals will select a plant-based meat substitute when it is cheaper and more convenient than animal meat.

Leading others toward better decisions does not require changing hearts and minds. Often all it requires is for a leader to modify the situation to make wise choices a little easier or more convenient. One study underscoring the power of the situation examined the 38% of criminal defendants who fail to appear for their court dates.[25] The failure to appear for one's trial is a big deal. It can have exceedingly costly consequences, including additional charges and legal penalties. It can get you arrested. It is tempting to assume that only the most delinquent scofflaws fail to appear. The researchers introduced a small situational change by randomly assigning some defendants to receive text-message reminders ahead of their court dates. These reminders reduced the failure to appear from 38% to about 30%. This change occurred without changing the personalities, proclivities, or preferences of defendants.

Corporations capitalize on the power of the situation when they make it easy for their customers to do business with them. Amazon went so far as to patent its one-click buying feature. By contrast, companies are not so interested in making it easy for customers to return defective merchandise or end their subscriptions. So these actions are often inconveniently hidden and require long waits or annoying paperwork.[26] Companies have incentives to introduce these barriers. When they do so, they successfully exploit the power of the situation to produce behaviors they desire. But too often organizations inadvertently erect these sorts of barriers to effective decision making, thereby making bad decisions easy and inviting.

Leading from the Gut

In his book *Winning: The Ultimate Business How-To Book* (2005), the former CEO of General Electric Jack Welch affirmed the common assumption that effective leaders must have good instincts. Some of the decisions he made at General Electric were not amenable to easy quantification or rational analysis, he wrote, but rather relied on his gut: "Sometimes making a decision is hard not because it is unpopular, but because it comes from the gut and defies a 'technical' rationale. Much has been written about the mystery of gut, but it's really just pattern recognition, isn't it? You've seen something so many times you just know what's going on this time. The facts may be incomplete or the data limited, but the situation feels very, very familiar to you."[27] Welch elaborated, "The trick, of course, is to know when to go with your gut. That's easy when you discover, over time, that your gut is usually right. But such confidence can take years. . . . So when it comes to looking at deals, consider the numbers. But be sure your gut plays a big role in the final call."[28]

We agree with Welch that some big decisions are more amenable to quantification than others. But we disagree that this means that leaders must rely on intuition. Quantifying and analyzing qualitative issues can be challenging but is usually possible.[29] Moreover, thoughtful deliberation is perfectly capable of factoring in qualitative concerns. Welch is correct that experience often increases our confidence in our gut instincts and feelings of mastery. The problem is that those feelings may have more to do with familiarity than with true mastery. Experience or familiarity may enhance confidence more than it enhances accuracy, exacerbating overconfidence.[30]

Even if you believe that all of Welch's important intuitive judgments turned out well, that doesn't mean that "follow your gut" is useful leadership advice. The following chapters argue against intuition as a guide for decision making. Intuition's great flaw is not that it is hopelessly biased; in fact, it can be quite accurate. The fatal flaw of intuition is that you can't audit it. Because intuition emerges fully formed from the unconscious, there's no way to check its calculations or reflect on its inputs. Consequently, it's hard to tell when it is biased. You have a bad feeling in the pit of your stomach about a job candidate. Is it because your unconscious mind has picked up on an important warning sign? Or is it because the candidate speaks with an accent or looks different from you? Or could it be that your bad feeling is just your lunch disagreeing with you?

You might think your own intuition is above average. Perhaps it has benefited from the training and experience you have accumulated in life. Unlike most leadership books, this one will discourage you from being confident in your intuition. The fact is, for the vast majority of us our intuitions can be wrong even when they feel right. Even worse, decades of research have failed to provide useful guidance for improving intuition. Nevertheless, we can help you improve your own decisions and those made in your organization—often by showing you when to question your intuition and what to do instead of following your gut. Moreover, we will guide you to help your employees, customers, clients, and investors to make decisions that are justified by more than gut feelings.

A Guide to What Follows

The psychologists Richard Nisbett and Lee Ross famously captured the strengths and weaknesses of human capabilities in their book *Human Inference* (1980):

> One of philosophy's oldest paradoxes is the apparent contradiction between the greatest triumphs and the dramatic failures of the human mind. The same organism that routinely solves inferential problems too subtle and complex for the mightiest computers often makes errors in the simplest of judgments about everyday events. The errors, moreover, often seem traceable to violations of the same inferential rules that underlie people's most impressive successes. . . . How can any creature skilled enough to build and maintain complex

organizations, or sophisticated enough to appreciate the nuances of social intercourse, be foolish enough to mouth racist clichés or spill its lifeblood in pointless wars?[31]

We each have the capacity to make great decisions, yet we routinely fail to do so. This book will give you the tools you need to make better decisions as a leader. We will draw on the literature on behavioral decision research, now commonly called behavioral economics, to explore how you can anticipate predictable shortcomings in your judgment—biases and errors we all make routinely—before they trip you up in high-stakes decisions. We will also review research on nudges and decision architecture to give you tools to help others choose wisely, consistent with their own values and the best interests of their organizations, their communities, and the planet. These insights will position you to design systems that can direct people toward making better decisions. More generally, we will identify how psychological insights from social science can modify behavior more efficiently than trying to change hearts and minds.

In each chapter we will focus not only on how you can make great decisions, but also—more importantly—on how you can create environments that will prompt others to make great decisions as well. In chapter 2 we will focus on how leaders can move beyond intuition, recognize the value of deliberation, and set others up to do the same. Chapter 3 examines the common tendency to fail to notice critical information that leaders and their organizations need to make wise decisions.

Dissecting and dispelling the conventional wisdom that leaders must be confident, chapter 4 highlights the enormous advantages of well-calibrated confidence that avoids both the recklessness induced by overconfidence and the quicksand of under-confidence. We will also examine the hazards of leaders rewarding overconfident subordinates and offer insights on how to lead others to calibrate their confidence.

Chapter 5 will explore how leaders can best use the advice of others in reaching wise decisions. We will discuss ineffective and effective decision processes, ranging from Netflix's brush with death in 2011 to the Covid-19 pandemic of 2020. We will discuss the degree to which leaders should trust their own judgment versus the advice of others and also consider how to best integrate insight from experts.

In chapter 6 we will consider how leaders can foster a culture of experimentation in their organizations. Once a tool limited to the scientific world, in the new millennium experimentation has taken off as a useful decision-making tool in the business world. You can make a huge difference in your organization by showing others the value of methodically testing their ideas, products, and proposals.

In negotiation and many other workplace contexts people believe that what is good for them is bad for someone else and vice versa. As we'll see in chapter 7, this fixed-pie mindset is typically a myth: most of the time wise trade-offs can create value for all. Leaders have a special responsibility to facilitate value creation.

Chapter 8 will explore what leaders can do to create more ethical organizations. Most of us behave ethically most of the time. But we can each remember times when we have fallen short of our ethical standards. As we will explore, our ethicality is affected by our environments. It's up to leaders to create environments that promote ethical behavior, and we'll explain how you can do just that.

Chapter 9 provides guidance on how leaders can influence others to make wise decisions by using nudges and decision architecture. In addition to discussing the psychology and economics of reward systems, norms, and decision structures in organizations, we will summarize what we have learned from more than a decade of research on how to use choice architecture to nudge others toward better decisions.

Chapter 10 integrates the lessons of this book into memorable and useful tactics that aspiring leaders can put to use in their lives and their organizations right away. These lessons can help you empower yourself and those around you to make choices more consistent with your values, improving the effectiveness of teams, groups, organizations, our society, and the world.

2

Guts vs. Brains

Your firm needs to hire a new executive for a critical post. Following an extended search, you have reduced the list of 143 candidates to 2 finalists. They have met with all members of the senior team in your office as well as select members of the rest of the organization. Your executive team is in agreement on how the two finalists, Mina and Anu, compare. Mina has a better set of work experiences, has stronger recommendations, has accomplished more, and is generally the stronger of the two on paper. One key member of your executive team argues that what she has accomplished over the last ten years makes her the stronger candidate. In contrast, another executive argues for Anu, who wowed the whole team during her visit with her confidence, personality, and charisma. As this member of the management team put it, "Whom do we want to hang out with for the next few years?"

Which of the two would you hire?

Many organizations attempt to employ a systematic approach to hiring, yet we have seen many hiring decisions swayed by appeals to intuition like the argument in favor of Anu. We are most familiar with the hiring process for university faculty. University departments publicly announce an available position and collect applications. Faculty on the recruiting committee review all applications, reduce the group under consideration to a short list, send those files to a larger group of faculty, and then bring each of the top three or four candidates to campus for a daylong visit. Each visit consists of a series of meetings with individual faculty members, a presentation of the candidate's work, and a group dinner. These visits provide some additional information on top of the extensive information available from candidates' résumés, letters of reference, and research papers. Most social scientists agree that academics have a tendency to overweight the interviews, despite the better predictive value of candidates' multiyear record of accomplishment. Our decisions also overweight the ninety-minute research presentation due to its salience and the fact that it is our department's shared exposure to the candidate. We agree on all of this when we're not in the middle of interviewing and recruiting. However, each year we return to our old form of trusting our intuition and valuing the impressions we gather during the ninety-minute presentations over the multiyear records of accomplishment.

Now imagine that you are a job candidate who has received two job offers. Before getting the offers you created a spreadsheet that lists the job attributes you care about: the type of organization you want to work for, your responsibilities, the location, salary, vacation time, etc. You carefully thought through how much you valued each attribute. Now you have assessed both jobs on each of the attributes and created a logical tool for aggregating your assessment. The result is that Job A gets a higher score than Job B. The only problem is that your intuition favors Job B. When presented with this hypothetical problem, most people say that they would take Job B.

As these hiring scenarios illustrate, we clearly trust intuition a great deal.[1] Whether we are choosing among job candidates, careers, romantic partners, houses, or vacation destinations, most of us rely on our intuition. If you have relied on your intuition in the past, rest assured that you are not alone. Steve Jobs, the founder of Apple, once said that intuition is "more powerful than intellect." Richard Branson, the founder of Virgin Group, prefers intuition to data.[2] And in chapter 1 you read praise for intuition from Jack Welch.

The Siren Song of Intuition

Before explaining why you should question intuition, we acknowledge that the nature of life—and, even more so, the nature of leadership—requires leaders to use intuition for the vast majority of their decisions. Leaders are so busy that it would simply take too long to engage in careful deliberations over every decision they make in a day. This is true for us non-CEOs as well. The cost of search overwhelms the importance of each of the dozens of decisions you will make in the twenty minutes that you are in the grocery store. But our focus in this chapter is on important decisions, those in which the stakes are so high that any small improvement in decision quality would justify even substantial increases in effort. Even here many of us are still tempted to trust intuition.

It's easy to find popular support for trusting intuition. In his book *Blink* Malcolm Gladwell describes intuition, or "thin-slicing"—using split-second impressions to guide decisions. He suggests that such intuitions are often as good as—or even better than—more deliberative decisions. In beautiful prose Gladwell shares a wide range of examples from medicine, science, sales, dating, and war to showcase intuition at its best. He also highlights the risk that a surplus of information can interfere with the accuracy of a judgment, such as when a preponderance of interesting but irrelevant details leads a doctor's diagnosis astray. Gladwell's compelling anecdotes reinforce readers' inclination to trust intuition. It just happens to be terrible advice.

It is easy to find examples of intuition leading to good decisions, because it often does. It is even easier to identify catastrophes caused by trusting intuition over science and other forms of objective data. Leaders who trust their feelings over the facts can be like the airline pilots who trusted their feelings more than the plane's instruments and ended up dead. By reasoning through anecdote Gladwell risks being convincing and misleading at the same time. While he admits that intuition can go wrong, *Blink* enthusiastically celebrates the success of intuition, despite systematic evidence showing the strength of deliberation over intuition for important decisions.

"It is ironic that Gladwell (knowingly or not) exploits one of the greatest weaknesses of intuition—our tendency to blithely infer cause from anecdotes—in making his case for intuition's extraordinary power," wrote the psychologists Chris Chabris and Dan Simons.[3] Richard Posner, a judge and law professor at the University of Chicago, argued that Gladwell makes a variety of unsupported assumptions and mistakes in his characterizations of the evidence.[4] Gladwell seamlessly moves from the accurate argument that we use our intuition regularly to inaccurately claim the superiority of intuition over deliberation. "Malcolm Gladwell does not believe that intuition is magic," concludes Daniel Kahneman, a Nobel Prize winner.[5] "But here his story has helped people, in a belief that they want to have, which is that intuition works magically, and that belief is false."

We believe that people regularly rely on intuition, that the pace of leaders' lives necessitates it, and that intuition frequently results in good decisions. But intuition is not perfect, and it errs in predictable ways. By relying on our intuition, therefore, we risk making substantial errors. The inclination to blindly trust intuition and to be convinced by anecdotal evidence of its effectiveness can be enormously harmful.

Bringing Science to the Intuition/Deliberation Debate

Prescriptive models of decision making encourage us to think rationally so that we can make the best decisions possible to maximize whatever we wish to maximize (profits, happiness, efficiency, etc.).

The essence of rational decision making is simply to choose the option with the highest expected value at every opportunity. Expected value simply multiplies an option's value by its probability.

In our previous book, *Judgment in Managerial Decision Making*, we outlined the following logical steps for rational decision making:[6]

1. Define the problem
2. Identify the relevant criteria
3. Weight the criteria
4. Generate alternatives
5. Rate each alternative on each criterion
6. Compute the optimal decision.

Step 1, "define the problem," seeks to identify why you need to make a decision. Usually, that is because the path forward is uncertain. How should you proceed? It can be easy to breeze past potential branches on the path of life without ever considering our alternatives.[7] We pass on opportunities to form potentially close, lasting relationships. We decline to pursue job openings. Or we forego opportunities to start new businesses. Pausing to clarify the actual problem that you are trying to solve may open your mind to broad vistas of possibility.

Step 2, "identify the relevant criteria," invites you to consider what you value. What exactly do you seek to maximize, improve, change, or achieve? Usually it is obvious what brought you to the decision in the first place. Suppose you're looking for housing in a new city. Think broadly about issues of concern, including the potentially unforeseen consequences of your choice. There may be many neighborhoods and homes to consider. What are the opportunity costs of your choice? For example, will buying a home keep you from considering international job assignments that come your way later? What other opportunities will you forego by making a choice? How will your choice affect others and their likely behavior? What if others also chose as you did—would that lead to a desirable outcome? For example, what are the consequences for the city in which your company is headquartered when employees choose to live in distant suburbs? Are there ethical implications in your decision, such as pollution, traffic congestion, and payment of local taxes to cover the infrastructure you use?

Step 3 puts a weight on each criterion, allowing you to think through the trade-offs that you would make across them. If you are seeking a home with both the lowest price and the best location for you, one simple solution would be to treat these criteria as if they were equal in value. But if you reflected on them you might find that you weigh one consideration more heavily than the other. For example, exactly how much more money are you willing to pay for a home that would reduce your daily commute by fifteen minutes?

Step 4 requires you to generate alternatives: to think broadly about the full set of possibilities. If you are looking for housing you could consider the homes currently listed by real estate agents. There are other alternatives. You could rent a place from one of the many landlords who have posted rental vacancies. It is also possible to consider homes not currently on the market. The real estate website Zillow, for instance, allows homeowners to specify a "make me move" price: a price so attractive it would make the owner want to sell. Maybe you could build your own home. Or if there is a rental you want badly enough you could buy the current tenant out of their lease.

Step 5, "rate each alternative on each criterion," compares the options generated in Step 4 using the expected values from Step 3. This stage highlights the need to assess each of the alternatives on each criterion. Your own views are an essential input, but often others—

family members, colleagues, or experts—have useful perspectives too. Research on the "wisdom of crowds" (which we will discuss in detail in chapter 5) highlights the fundamental value of others' views. When it comes to estimating something uncertain, such as the market value of a house, collecting guesses from several people and averaging them may provide a more accurate estimate than trying to pick one expert. Assessing alternatives may also include considering their probabilities. If you are deciding how much to offer to pay for a house you should consider how likely it is that a low offer might be rejected.

Step 6, "compute the optimal decision," can be as simple as selecting the option with the highest expected value. If you have been systematic in Steps 1 through 5, computing Step 6 will be so simple that you can easily automate or delegate it. In fact, that is precisely what people do when they employ an algorithm to support them in their decision making. One simple decision algorithm with a proud track record is the linear model. A linear model simply computes the value of each of the various alternatives, multiplies their values by their probabilities, and selects the alternative with the highest expected value.

These six steps can help you organize your thoughts and make an informed decision. Yet if we asked you if you regularly follow such steps when making important decisions, we are confident that you would respond, "Of course not." If you methodically moved through each of these steps for every decision you made at the grocery store you'd be there for hours. Following these steps makes sense when you're facing important decisions, but even in this realm most of us are far from implementing such formal logic.

To understand how our brains process information it is helpful to consider a distinction between System 1 and System 2 thinking, first articulated by the psychologists Keith Stanovich and Richard West.[8] System 1 comes first because it's part of every decision. It is fast, automatic, effortless, implicit, and emotional. For instance, when we interpret verbal language or visual information we do it automatically and unconsciously. When we react to a person, a product, or an idea with either an instantaneous positive or negative feeling, that's System 1. By contrast, System 2 employs more deliberative reasoning. It is slower, conscious, effortful, explicit, and logical. In most of life System 1 is sufficient; it is speedy, efficient, and often quite accurate. It would be impractical to invest the time and attention of System 2 deliberation for every trivial decision we make. The busier you are, the more you will rely on System 1 to make decisions.[9]

The problem comes when we rely too much on System 1 thought. Decision making is complex, and any methodical System 2 process will include inputs from System 1. One example is when top executives at the Swedish retailer IKEA realized in the mid-1990s that children were making some of its Indian rugs. If IKEA viewed the problem only from a financial perspective it likely would have done nothing, as child labor was helping it keep production costs low. But profiting from child labor conflicted with the company's values. Difficulty in quantifying beliefs, preferences, and ideals did not detract from their importance. IKEA sought to address the problem, in part, by helping to improve the financial independence of women (the children's mothers) in India's "carpet belt."[10] System 1 inputs helped the company make reasoned decisions that better reflected the company's larger interests beyond the profitability of carpets.[11] System 1 and 2 frequently work well together.

System 2 thinking can take a variety of forms. It can simply mean going through a structured decision-making process like the one detailed above. It can mean playing devil's advocate when you're tempted to go with your gut. It could mean delaying a decision until the time pressure, stress, or emotions you're feeling subside. Or it might mean asking a smart friend, partner, or colleague for advice or a critique of your thinking.

The fields of decision making, decision analysis, economics, and computer science also help us develop successful formal strategies for guiding our System 2 thinking. As described above, one form of System 2 thinking involves using an algorithm to reach a quantitative prediction. Linear models, among the simplest algorithms, make decisions that outperform those of experts across an impressive array of domains, including in university admissions, parole, consumer choices, and many more.[12] For example, making admissions decisions with a linear model would quantify the various factors, including standardized test scores, high school grades, letters of recommendation, application essays, extracurricular activities, and more. These scores could be standardized, weighted, and summed to compute an overall score.

One way to standardize and compare would be to compute z-scores for each factor. A z-score puts each measure on a similar scale. To compute a z-score for, say, SAT scores, simply compute the average score for all applicants. From each individual's score subtract the average. Then, because different measures are on different scales, divide each by its standard deviation.[13] The result is a distribution of values with a mean of 0 and a standard deviation of 1. This makes different factors comparable, and averaging across them produces a standardized score.

Some who object to reliance on linear models argue that they fail to take complex interactions between factors into account. For instance, if an applicant's good grades came from an elite private school with notoriously lenient grading, they should be discounted. When human admissions officers attempt a holistic judgment including all these considerations, they ought to be able to consider these interactions. Do they? Evidence is not encouraging. Even when they get clear evidence of lenient grading at some schools, human judges still favor applicants with high grades, suggesting that they fail to discount their interpretation of grades using knowledge about grading leniency.[14]

But a simple linear model can easily solve the problem by standardizing grades relative to the institution or by relying on class rank instead of grade point average. More generally, linear models can help decision makers overcome many of the decision-making pitfalls that we will highlight throughout this book. Much of the field of artificial intelligence and machine learning is devoted to using more modern techniques to make such models even better.

A different System 2 strategy consists of taking an outsider's perspective on the decision—that is, imagining how someone who has no stake in the outcome would view it. For example, most people who renovate their homes underestimate the cost and time it will take to complete the job; by contrast, many of their friends, with a little outside perspective could make more accurate estimates. Distancing oneself mentally from a situation makes it easier to think more logically and avoid being carried away by intuition.[15] Taking an outsider's perspective reduces decision makers' overconfidence in their knowledge, the time it would take to complete a task, and their odds of achieving entrepreneurial success. Asking someone not involved in a specific decision for their view is likely to help decision makers improve their judgments.[16]

We have been focusing on the shortcomings of intuition, but we also acknowledge that we can't write it off completely. How can intuition contribute to making your decisions better? For example, when you're weighing two or more job offers does intuition have constructive input to offer? What should you do if Job A performs better in the formal scoring system, but your gut prefers Job B? Before Stanovich and West wrote about System 1 vs. System 2, Howard Raiffa suggested that when our intuition and deliberative processes diverge, each process should audit the other. Perhaps the deliberative self can confront your intuition about what you might be overweighting intuitively. At the same time, Raiffa conceded that your intuitive response might elucidate an error in how your deliberative self formulated the problem. Perhaps your calculations omitted an important consideration because it was difficult to quantify. In sum, even one of the most enthusiastic advocates for deliberation believed that intuition might be a good check on your deliberative processes.

Heuristics and Biases

Successfully consulting your intuitive processes is most helpful when you can appreciate both the strengths and the weaknesses of intuition. Thanks to decades of research, we know a great deal about intuitive processes and their vulnerability to bias. The evidence suggests that intuition relies on a number of heuristics to simplify the processing and interpretation of complex information. These heuristics provide good rules of thumb for making decisions quickly and efficiently, but they are not perfect. Their predictable imperfections leave them vulnerable to bias. This book's appendix offers a detailed consideration of four powerful heuristics, the study of which has provided deep understanding of how they work. Here, we describe them succinctly.

One important heuristic leads us to rely too heavily on information that is most readily available in our minds. The availability heuristic leads us to overestimate the likelihood of recent, vivid, or memorable events. For example, following the terrorist attacks of September 11, 2001, Americans dramatically overestimated the likelihood of future attacks. We do too much to protect ourselves and our families from vivid threats like terrorism, kidnapping, and home invasion. Meanwhile, we do too little to protect ourselves from mundane threats that represent greater risks than terrorism, such as obesity and diabetes.

A second heuristic is intimately related to the first. The confirmation heuristic simplifies our search for information by focusing on affirmative cases and supporting evidence. Confirmatory information then makes it easier for us to uphold our beliefs than to question them in the face of new evidence. In part because the human mind is better at identifying the presence of something and thinking of affirmative cases, we find supportive evidence more cognitively available. Our default mode of thinking asks, "Is my belief correct?" or "Is my hypothesis true?" Seeking supportive evidence allows us to confirm that we are good people, that our business ideas are promising, and that our political party's positions are the right ones. Because it is so counterintuitive to ask, "How might I be wrong?" we often stand to benefit from deliberately trying to consider the opposite.

A third important heuristic predisposes us to believe in causes that are similar to their effects. Kahneman and his longtime collaborator Amos Tversky dubbed this the representativeness heuristic. It produces a number of logical fallacies and errors that are attractive because they are so intuitively compelling. We assume outcomes are representative of their underlying causes, leading us to neglect the powerful role that chance plays in business, sports, and life. When an entrepreneur or an athlete encounters a string of successes, we are too quick to infer that they're hot, and we are thus perennially surprised when the hottest performances are followed by disappointing results. Rookies of the year frequently have a disappointing sophomore year. The intuitive appeal of the representativeness heuristic blinds us to the statistical power of regression to the mean.

A fourth heuristic leads us to assess gains and losses relative to a reference point, usually the status quo, and as a result be affected by the framing of the problem. To assess whether something is a gain or a loss, good or bad, we evaluate it relative to some comparison standard. We are sensitive to changes near the reference point, especially losses. It is painful for us to give things up, and we will often fight hard or endure risk to avoid losing. People dislike having to pay additional tax, and when they are completing their tax returns will often engage in tax avoidance until they have reduced their additional tax due to zero.[17] On the other hand, gains of similar size feel less important, and we are less willing to accept risk in their pursuit. People do not continue to pursue additional tax avoidance to maximize their tax refunds. The problem is that the reference point is often arbitrary.

If these brief descriptions of cognitive heuristics and the biases they produce are unfamiliar, see the appendix. It reviews evidence of the vulnerabilities of human intuition, providing background for the advice we'll offer on how to make wiser decisions.

Leading Deliberation across the Organization

Leaders have a great deal of influence over the processes people use to make decisions in their organizations. By implementing the following strategies, you can encourage others to make wiser decisions and thereby improve the effectiveness of your organization.

Maximize expected value.[18] Would you accept a new project that, without disrupting your existing business in any manner, would give your firm a 50% chance of improving its profits by $11 million but give it a 50% chance of losing $10 million? Despite the attractiveness of this risky decision on an expected value basis—an expected gain of $500,000—most people would pass on this risk.[19] In other cases, as evidenced by the popularity of casinos, people sacrifice expected value to take risks. They know that they are unlikely to beat the house but are willing to sacrifice expected value in order to *increase* their risk.

Most people, including economists, treat risk as a personal preference. How you balance your desire for more money (on average) with risk is up to you, most would argue. But the work of the behavioral economist Matthew Rabin demonstrates that most of the time your colleagues and coworkers deviate from risk neutrality the result will be bad for your organization—whether they are risk-averse or risk-seeking. As a leader, you generally ought to discourage such divergent risk preferences and instead promote decisions that maximize your organization's expected value.

Our System 1 intuitions lead us to avoid risks in the domain of gains and to accept risk in the domain of losses. This is evident in a problem that Max adapted from Kahneman and Tversky:[20]

> *Problem 1.* A large car manufacturer has recently been hit with a number of economic difficulties, and it appears as if three plants need to be closed and 6,000 employees laid off. The vice president of production has been exploring alternative ways to avoid this crisis. She has developed two plans:
> *Plan A:* This plan will save one of the three plants and 2,000 jobs.
> *Plan B:* This plan has a ⅓ probability of saving all three plants and all 6,000 jobs but has a ⅔ probability of saving no plants and no jobs.

Which plan would you select?

You might consider many factors. What will be the impact of each action on labor relations? How will each plan affect the motivation of retained employees? As you think about this problem in isolation, it might not be obvious that the way it is framed—in terms of *saving* jobs—leads most people to avoid risk and choose Plan A.

Now reconsider the problem with the exact same two plans framed in terms of losses:

> *Plan C:* This plan will result in the loss of two of the three plants and 4,000 jobs.

Plan D: This plan has a ⅔ probability of resulting in the loss of all three plants and all 6,000 jobs, but has a ⅓ probability of losing no plants and no jobs.

Which plan would you select?

Most people choose D over C, although careful examination of the two sets of alternative plans shows that this choice is inconsistent. Saving one of the three plants and 2,000 of 6,000 jobs (Plan A) is the reverse presentation of losing two of the three plants and 4,000 of 6,000 jobs (Plan C). Plans B and D are also identical. However, over 75 percent of respondents choose Plan A in the first set and Plan D in the second set. Framing the description of the outcomes in terms of savings versus losses shifts the dominant preference from risk-averse to risk-seeking behavior.

In an attempt to explain such common and systematic deviations from rationality, Kahneman and Tversky (1979) developed prospect theory, which shows that:[21]

1. People evaluate gains and losses relative to the current state of affairs.
2. People tend to be risk averse when facing risks framed as gains.
3. People tend to be risk seeking when facing risks framed as losses.

As Rabin notes, some moderately simple arithmetic makes it clear that leaders should want to discourage such divergent risk preferences in the vast majority of organizational decisions. Acting with risk neutrality, or avoiding divergent risk preferences, is the same as maximizing expected value, or what you will achieve on average. Risk aversion means that you are willing to accept a lower expected value in return for reducing your risk. Thus, in the example above, when you avoid a project with 50/50 odds of gaining $11 million or losing $10 million, you are acting in a risk-averse manner. By contrast, if you took a risk with a negative expected value (a 50/50 bet of winning $10 million or losing $11 million), your choice was risk seeking. Thus most casino bets are risk seeking, and that is how the house ensures that it will make a profit. In contrast, investing $1 million with a 20% chance of obtaining $10 million (and an 80% chance of winning nothing) is risky, but it is not risk seeking since it has a positive expected value. A leader who has the goal of maximizing expected value would take this bet.

Perhaps you are still reluctant to accept the bet that introduced this section—the project with an expected gain of $500,000—even though you understand expected value? We might be able to persuade you to take the bet by using more manageable numbers, drawing on an example from the Nobel Prize–winning economist Paul Samuelson. In 1963 Samuelson reported that he offered a colleague a bet involving a coin flip, in which the colleague would have a 50% chance of gaining $200 or losing $100. The colleague said no but said also that he would accept 100 such bets (flipping the coin 100 times and taking all of the losses and all of gains). Samuelson concluded that if his colleague's risk preference was to turn down the bet on a one-shot basis, accepting the aggregate bet was a mistake. Rabin and Bazerman conclude just the opposite. Unless losing $100 would devastate your finances, you should take the one-shot bet and enthusiastically take the 100-trial bet.

Follow a Good General Policy. The attractiveness of the aggregate bet should be clear. On average you will win half of the time and lose half of the time, resulting in an expected net gain of $5,000 (you would win $200 fifty times and lose $100 fifty times). In addition, you are projected to lose money only across all 100 trials one time in every 2,300 plays.[22] Yet most bets come to us one at a time, rather than with an offer to take the same bet 100 times, and with such good expected value. What's wrong with being risk averse to these one-shot bets? Consider that across your lifetime you will make an enormous number of risky decisions of minor consequence. Across all of those minor decisions you will be better off abiding by a policy to accept all positive-expected-value options and reject all negative-expected-value options, avoiding both risk aversion and risk seeking. Let aggregation work for you, and don't get too upset when the small losses occur—as they will.

Note that when you invest in stocks you do so in the knowledge that the stock market has a good history of performance. The wise investor does not expect that stocks will necessarily go up tomorrow. Rather, wise investors expect that over many years the average of all stocks will do well. In fact, investors are better off not paying attention to daily market returns, as this leads them to suffer too much on down days. Working through the aggregation of small bets, we hope to convince you that you should choose to maximize expected value, even when that means accepting the possibility of losses in some of the small- to medium-size risks that you confront.

The argument in favor of pursuing a policy of risk neutrality is even stronger for organizations because they are large; they have both greater financial cushion and greater borrowing ability than most individuals have. Yet virtually all firms sacrifice expected value to risk aversion. In fact, many organizations have departments where risk aversion is the norm, including legal, credit, and compliance. Organizations forego expected profitability due to risk aversion by passing on projects with excellent expected, but risky, returns; they hedge too much, buy too much insurance, and so on. Too often departments like legal and compliance are blamed for losses but not for foregoing profitable opportunities as a result of their risk aversion. By contrast, salespeople tend to be risk seeking, booking sales even with a risk of nonpayment. There is no sense in which clashing risk preferences within the company balance each other out. Instead, they expose a company to inconsistent risk and decrease its expected performance.

Consider Rabin's and Bazerman's adaptation of a classic set of problems from Tversky and Kahneman:[23]

> Imagine you work for a firm with a capitalization of $1 billion. One division needs to pick between two strategies, which will lead to either:
>
> a. A sure profit of $24M, or
>
> b. A 25% chance of gaining $100M and a 75% chance of gaining nothing. What choice do you think most firms would make?
>
> Now consider a different division facing a choice between:
>
> c. A sure loss of $75M, or
>
> d. A 25% chance of losing nothing and a 75% chance of losing $100M.

Most executives choose "a" in the first set and "d" in the second set. This is entirely consistent with the literature on framing discussed earlier. A majority of executives would choose a sure profit of $24M in the first decision due to the common propensity to be risk averse concerning gains and positively framed questions. And most would choose a 75% chance of losing $100M in the second decision because of the common human tendency to be risk seeking concerning losses and negatively framed questions.

Now let's aggregate the two options chosen and the two options not chosen:

> e. A 25% chance to gain $24M and a 75% chance to lose $76M
>
> f. A 25% chance to gain $25M and a 75% chance to lose $75M.

Most people prefer (f) to (e); (f) is objectively better. Yet when you combine (a) and (d) (the preferred choices above), (e) results, whereas when you combine choices (b) and (c) (the rejected choices) earlier, (f) results. Let's explain.

Adding choices (a) and (d) produces option (e). To combine (a) and (d), add $24M to each of the risky outcomes in (d). Here's the formula for computing that:

$$(100\%)(\$24M) + [(75\%)(-\$100M) + (25\%)(\$0)] = (25\%)(\$24M) + (75\%)(-\$76M)$$

Adding choices (b) and (c) produces option (f). To combine (b) and (c) just subtract the $75M loss from each of the risky options in (b). Here's the formula for that:

$$[(25\%)(\$100M) + (75\%)(\$0)] + (100\%)(-\$75M) = (25\%)(\$25M) + (75\%)(-\$75M)$$

As you can see, when we move away from risk neutrality and act with divergent and inconsistent risk preferences, we are costing our organizations, often without realizing that we are doing so. Leaders guide thousands of decisions in their organizations every year. When some employees make risk-averse decisions and some make risk-seeking decisions, your organization is collectively giving away expected profit. With rare and recognizable exceptions (generally, catastrophic risk), risk aversion is a mistake.

One intriguing documentation of risk aversion by lawyers comes from a study by a Harvard Law School student, finding that Harvard Law School students generally advise clients to avoid downside risk at the expense of maximizing client profitability.[24] Law students are more risk averse than Harvard Business School students, and their risk aversion increases during their time on campus.[25] Obviously, lawyers have a responsibility to advise clients about their legal risks. But, we argue, lawyers also need to facilitate clients' success given their legal risks. Wise counsel should balance risk reduction with other goals, such as innovation and profit.

Companies would be more profitable if they followed a general policy to make the vast majority of their decisions with the goal of maximizing expected value and discouraged individual employees and units from engaging in risk aversion (or risk seeking). A risk-neutral firm—one where every manager and department aimed to make risk-neutral decisions—would maximize the firm's expected value.

The benefits of risk neutrality in for-profit businesses is even stronger from the perspective of shareholders. Given that shareholders typically hold stock in many firms, a risk that affects only one firm is unlikely to pose much risk to their total portfolio. So when a CEO passes on the opportunity to take a 50% chance of increasing corporate profits by $11M (that comes with a concomitant 50% risk of decreasing profits by $10M) rather than treating this as a risk-prudent decision, we need to understand that by passing on the opportunity, the CEO just reduced the firm's expected profits by $500K!

There are times to be risk averse, but they are fewer than our intuitions would dictate. Risk aversion, Rabin and Bazerman argue, should be limited to contexts where you or your firm cannot afford the downside of the risk (e.g., risks in which losing would threaten lives or the broader community). This means that many of us should be taking higher deductibles on our insurance and, at times, declining insurance (such as extended warranties, car rental insurance, and travel insurance). There may also be good reasons for risk aversion in contexts where large numbers of lives or jobs are at stake, as in the example of a supplier offering a price below the expected-value-maximizing price to ensure that it does not need to close a factory.[26]

Reward Good Decisions, Not Good Results

Leaders routinely pay too much attention to outcomes while neglecting information about individuals' decision-making processes and the uncertainty that surrounds their decisions, a phenomenon known as the outcome bias.[27] What happens when an employee makes a good decision that turns out poorly? If she is punished, she's likely to be risk averse in the future. In the days when IBM was the leading computer supplier, known for selling reliable but expensive machines, the phrase "No one was ever fired for buying an IBM" was common in organizations. This simplistic slogan ignores the possibility that paying the extra cost for an IBM computer may not have been the best decision.

How can leaders promote risk-neutral decisions that maximize expected value? First, they can train key employees in basic decision analysis, including a lesson in how deviation from risk neutrality makes the firm less effective. Second, they need to accept that some good decisions will inevitably lead to bad outcomes. Leaders ought to reward wise decisions with positive expected values, even when they get unlucky results. This will be easier if the company documents expected values ahead of important decisions rather than relying on outcomes perturbed by chance.

When the only available data are outcomes, it is important to look at a large portfolio of outcomes. That's why Samuelson's friend wanted one hundred bets rather than one. Third, leaders should make risk neutrality part of the organization's culture. They need to view deviations from risk neutrality as likely mistakes rather than as personal choices. Everyone should make decisions that maximize long-term expected value. Fourth, leaders can encourage wise risk taking by rewarding well-intentioned failure. In other words, you should not punish people for unlucky outcomes on smart bets with positive expected value.

Promote joint, rather than separate, evaluation. Steps 1 and 4 of our rational decision outline require that decision makers compare the many alternatives before them. Nevertheless, companies regularly make high-stakes "whether" decisions. Companies decide *whether* to go public, *whether* to pursue an acquisition, *whether* to declare bankruptcy. Too many of these "whether" decisions fail.[28] Instead, you should make your "whether" decisions into "which" decisions between alternatives. Expand your thinking from evaluating a single option to considering all of the possible alternatives open to you. This is basically encouragement to think big about Step 4 in the logical decision-making process by generating alternatives that offer differing possible courses of action.

As a leader, you might be looking for ways to hire better people and discriminate less in the process. In a study with the economists Iris Bohnet and Alexandra van Geen, Max identified a tool that can help you meet those goals: joint decision making.[29] We found that when people are evaluating employees one at a time their System 1 thought processes tend to dominate. As a result, they tend to rely on nonpredictive gender stereotypes and to hire men for mathematical tasks and women for verbal tasks. They rely on fit similarity and neglect diversity. In contrast, when people compare two or more applicants at a time they focus more on job-relevant criteria and treat employees equally, regardless of gender. This more deliberative hiring improves organizational performance.

Why does joint, or comparative, decision making lead to more deliberation and better results? When we evaluate one option (one product, one potential employee, one job offer, one possible vacation) at a time, System 1 has a powerful influence on our decisions. But when we compare multiple options simultaneously, the comparison process activates deliberation about how the options differ. That is, comparison is more likely to trigger System 2 processing. As a result, we are less biased, more rational, and more ethical when we operate in joint-decision-making mode. As a leader, you can not only engage in joint decision making yourself but also encourage others in your organization to adopt this more effective mode.

In one experiment, Max and his colleagues asked graduating MBA students whether they would accept a particular job offer from a consulting firm.[30] Condition A participants were told they would receive the same moderate salary offered to all rookie MBA hires (Job A). Condition B participants were offered a job (Job B) with a slightly higher salary than was offered to participants in condition A, but they learned that some other new hires were being offered even more. MBA students who evaluated Job A *or* Job B rated Job A as more attractive, even though Job A offered less money. Feeling it was unfair for similar candidates to be paid more for the same job, participants in Condition B had a strong negative emotional reaction to Job B.

Now let's look at what happened when we presented MBA students with *both* offers, Job A and Job B, and asked them to choose between the two. The comparative process prompted the students to override their negative emotional reaction and focus on the fact that Job B would pay them more than Job A. We give the emotions triggered by social comparisons more weight when evaluating a single option than when comparing two or more options at the same time. The emotional reactions prompt more intuitive thinking.

The psychologists Ilana Ritov and Daniel Kahneman found similar inconsistencies in people's evaluation of the importance of addressing various environmental and social issues.[31] People read about environmental crises, such as birds being threatened by toxic pollution, and indicated their support for remediation. Those who read about just one remediation plan and indicated how much they would be willing to support it gave similar answers regardless of whether the plan would save 20, 200, or 2,000 birds. However, those who considered all three plans at once were, unsurprisingly, more enthusiastic about the plan that would save more birds. Basically, intuitive emotional reactions drove their decisions of whether to support a particular remediation plan. However, when they chose which of several different plans to support, it was obvious which plans were more effective, and participants' level of support better reflected plans' actual effectiveness.

Turning to a different context, Edward Chang and colleagues examined hiring decisions.[32] In one study they examined how people selected guest speakers for a conference. The conference needed speakers for each of five different topics. When the job was to select a single speaker, women constituted 32% of those chosen, even though the pool of potential speakers was evenly split by gender. By contrast, when participants selected speakers across all five topics collectively, on average, 46% were women. Although cognitively the participants generally endorsed the value of gender diversity, joint selection decision enabled decision makers to better consider diversity as a decision criterion.

Leaders can facilitate better decisions in their organizations by encouraging others to make comparisons when facing important decisions. Comparisons can be particularly relevant in the realms of hiring, choosing an acquisition target, and deciding which project to fund or which supplier to use.[33] Comparison steers us toward System 2 thinking, greater deliberation, and better decisions.

Benefits of Deliberation

Biases limit the quality of our decisions. Many biases are stronger when we employ System 1 thinking rather than System 2. Leaders need to be able to activate not only their own System 2 processes, but others' deliberative thought about important decisions. Joint decision making and structuring for expected value maximization provide two areas where leaders can effectively intervene to overcome intuition and improve the quality of an organization's decisions. Both are useful for making choices that maximize the outcomes valued by you and your organization.

When should you, as a leader, encourage costly and effortful deliberative decision processes? Not always. For routine, low-stakes decisions, intuition may serve well enough. Better yet, consider establishing organizational routines or algorithmic systems that obviate the need for human judgment altogether. But when the expected improvement in decision quality can outweigh the costs of effort and delay, then it is time for deliberation. This may be as simple as asking people to compare the various alternatives by estimating their expected values. Even an imperfect attempt to explain the decision process and compare expected values must engage deliberative processes that can sidestep intuitions and reduce bias.

3

Be Investigator-in-Chief

Robert Maxwell hated his job as an analyst for Telefilm Canada. What he loved was cooking. He envied chefs who got paid for doing what he loved to do. He indulged his creativity by thinking about new recipes, subscribing to cooking magazines, and buying expensive kitchen equipment. In 2011 he successfully applied to operate a booth at the Toronto Underground Food Market, a festival featuring talented amateur cooks. His mini panko-crusted codfish cakes, gourmet pork belly sandwiches, and wild mushroom and black pudding hash sold well. "I fed 400 people, and they liked my food," he later wrote in a *Toronto Life* article. "Several local bloggers wrote about my dishes. It was an adrenalin rush like no other. I lost money, but I didn't care. My dream was gnawing at my insides."[1]

Maxwell had a wife and two children. They owned a house in Toronto worth around $500,000 and had a $400,000 mortgage loan. When Telefilm Canada eliminated his job, he passed up a lateral move and instead took an opportunity to withdraw $60,000 from his $130,000 in retirement savings. While Maxwell knew that most new restaurants lose money, he thought his culinary skills and enthusiasm were better than most. He accepted a friend's offer for a lease on what had been a grungy dive bar in an out-of-the-way neighborhood in Toronto. Maxwell recounts what it was like:

A cloud of fruit flies congregated around the beer taps. . . . The whole place stank—a feral smell, like dirty hamster bedding or, more likely, rats. A swinging door led into the kitchen, and that's where the strongest whiff of rat hit me, but it was buried under the stronger and, if it was even possible, more offensive smell of old grease. The kitchen ceiling was water damaged and sagged limply. The extraction hood loomed over the stove at an uneven angle—like it had been installed without the benefit of a level. The kitchen floor and appliances were hidden beneath a veneer of toffee-coloured grease.[2]

Maxwell filled two industrial dumpsters with junk, including sixteen liters of expired relish. He hired commercial cleaners, who told him that, with the exception of the vent hood, nothing else was worth cleaning. He had it all hauled away for $475, then spent several thousand dollars on new appliances. He hired a pest control company to deal with the rats. Three thousand dollars went to a lawyer to transfer the liquor license. Fire suppression equipment cost another $2,000. The beer taps added another couple of thousand. Repairing water-damaged walls, laying subfloors, replacing wiring, installing fixtures in the bathroom, and rebuilding the front façade cost about $20,000. Maxwell spent fifteen-hour days renovating the restaurant, with help from his wife.

He named his new restaurant the Beech Tree. As the opening of the Beech Tree approached, Maxwell was running out of money. A friend who believed in his dream offered to invest $20,000 to help see him through. Never having cooked in a restaurant professionally, Maxwell hired a chef to execute his ideas. The restaurant opened and, after a slow, rocky start, started to attract customers who liked the chef's cooking. But the ordeal had taken its toll on Maxwell, who looked and felt terrible. He had grown a grizzled beard and had dark circles under his eyes. He had lost twenty pounds, even as he found himself indulging in the restaurant's readily available beer too frequently and too early in the day. He rarely saw his two young daughters, who were asleep by the time he got home.

When he couldn't make payroll, he was forced to beg his mother-in-law for a loan. When that wasn't enough, he cashed out $25,000 of the remaining $70,000 in his retirement account, forfeiting $7,000 in after-tax penalties for the early withdrawal. The remaining $18,000 lasted six weeks. Only then did he recognize that his prices were too low, and, in his words, he "clearly didn't have a head for business."[3]

When alcohol wasn't sufficient to quell his mounting anxiety, Maxwell started topping it off with sedatives. In 2014 he and his wife sold their house to pay off his debt. After receiving a glowing review in the *Toronto Star* the Beech Tree seemed to be on an upswing, but Maxwell got behind on bills again by making the "rookie mistake" of closing for a week in the summer. A series of subsequent catastrophes culminating in an unexpected $23,000 tax bill led Maxwell to conclude around the Beech Tree's first anniversary that it was time to cut his losses. He sold the business to a partner.

By the end of his restaurant misadventure Maxwell had lost his house, most of his retirement savings, and his good credit rating. He was deep in debt. He recovered from his addiction to booze and pills, got a nine-to-five job, and started a cooking channel on YouTube—"a low-cost, low-risk outlet for my passion," he calls it. Despite his fears, his wife did not leave him. So things could definitely have been worse. But Maxwell acknowledges that he never should have entered the restaurant business. He told his cautionary tale in an article for *Toronto Life:* "If I knew back in 2013 what I know now, I wouldn't have done it."[4] "Stick to your dinner parties," he advises other would-be restaurateurs. "You'll be better off."

Maxwell knew that restaurants were generally not great investments and that 80 percent of first-time restaurateurs fail. Focused on his passion for cooking, however, he ignored these facts as well as clear obstacles to his success:

- He was a novice at most areas crucial to running a business.
- He didn't think through the business model, start-up costs, and cash flow before starting the business.
- If he had inquired, he would have learned that $60,000 was far short of a reasonable budget for starting up a restaurant.
- He didn't know in advance that he lacked the credentials to qualify for a bank loan and was unlikely to secure funding from angel investors.
- He ignored warnings from his mother-in-law (who later loaned him money) and others that opening a restaurant might not be a good idea.
- He didn't grasp what a difficult and lengthy process getting a liquor license would be.
- He was overoptimistic that a restaurant in a marginal location would thrive.
- He assumed the old equipment in the former dive bar would be usable.

The astonishing thing about Maxwell's story is how common it is. Lots of people start businesses built on passion and optimism. Such optimism enables entrepreneurs to envision success while overlooking key information that is worth noticing: the strength of the competition.

These days entrepreneurs flock to new business models in the sharing economy, hoping to get rich quick. The Boston area (where Max lives) is filled with young people, heavy automobile traffic, and an aging mass transit system. Even before the 2020 pandemic local governments invested in creating bicycle lanes. Many entrepreneurs saw the opportunity for bike sharing. Ofo, Ant, Spin, Lime, Zagster, and Bluebikes soon entered the market. By the end of 2019 all but Lime and Bluebikes were gone; by early 2020, Lime had quit the bike-share business as well.

Bike sharing was indeed a good idea. But as they considered entering the market, entrepreneurs should have noticed that what seemed like a good idea to them would also seem like a good idea to others. Because markets have limited customer demand, competition matters. People are too often insensitive to the quality of their competition, a phenomenon called *reference group neglect*.[5] More broadly, entrepreneurs focus more on themselves—their strengths and weaknesses—than on the competition, Don's research demonstrates.[6] This self-focus makes people too eager to enter easy contests and too reluctant to enter difficult competitions, as Don has found in his work with the Yale professor Daylian Cain.[7] As a result, the rate of entry into industries like restaurants, bars, hobby shops, liquor stores, and clothing retail is persistently excessive. People think about what they do well without realizing that they need to do better than the competition. Sizing up the strength of the competition before entering a new market seems like an obvious step, but too many businesses neglect to take it.

When we think about why businesses succeed or fail, it is easy to think through just half the equation, focusing on *absolute* performance and failing to notice the *relative* nature of business performance. In his book *The Halo Effect* the IMD Business School professor Phil Rosenzweig writes about business delusions such as reference group neglect. He notes that it is not sufficient for established companies to get better at what they do over time. In order to succeed they have to get better faster than the competition. Kmart was once one of America's leading retailers but now is a mere shadow of its former self.[8] The story of Kmart's fall often focuses on the company's failures. In fact, Kmart was innovating, improving, reducing prices, and getting better at satisfying customer demand even as it was being crushed by Walmart. Kmart lost not because it was getting worse but because Walmart got better faster.

Although considering the competition seems obvious, the failure to notice is distressingly easy. All professionals need to be aware of competitors, but even the most sophisticated investors can fall victim to reference group neglect. And reference group neglect is only one of many focusing errors to which leaders are vulnerable. Leaders are responsible for noticing critical information before making key strategic business decisions, such as entering new markets. Leaders are also responsible for noticing and investigating the potential misbehavior of those they oversee, including close allies and trusted deputies.

In this chapter we will offer a few deceptively simple recommendations that will increase the chances you will notice problems before they become crises. First, we will encourage you to take responsibility to notice non-salient potential problems. Second, we will highlight that it is the responsibility of leaders to create environments that increase the noticing capacity of the larger organization. Third, we will explore the psychological challenges to noticing critical challenges that may soon confront you. Finally, we will provide advice on steps that leaders can take to become first class noticers.

Noticing Suspicious Details

Bernie Madoff was a crook. Over three decades he stole billions of dollars from his investors. Madoff's investment organization received most of its investments from feeder funds: other investment organizations that either advertised their access to Madoff or claimed their own exotic investment strategy. These funds typically did nothing other than invest with Madoff and take a small percentage of the funds invested plus 20 percent of any investment returns. Madoff claimed to provide a consistent record of success, and the feeder funds profited. In late 2008, after his sons turned him in, Madoff confessed that it had all been an elaborate Ponzi scheme and went to prison.

In her book *Wizard of Lies* Diana Henriques eloquently recounts the story of how Madoff descended into his grotesque fraud.[9] For our purposes the most interesting aspect of the story is that dozens—perhaps hundreds—of people around Madoff failed to notice the obvious. Madoff's fund outperformed the market for over nine years with essentially no volatility in performance. When the market went up, so did the Madoff fund; when the market went down, the Madoff fund still went up. His customers loved the consistency of his fund's performance so much that they failed to notice what should have been blatantly obvious: it is impossible to consistently outperform the market without volatility. There has never been—and there never will be—an actual investing strategy that could produce the returns that Madoff claimed. While it is possible that some noticed this fact but decided to play along with the fraud because they were making money, most of the evidence suggests instead that intermediaries (such as feeder funds) had hints that something was off but failed to ask hard questions. In the words of the author Upton Sinclair, "It is difficult to get a man to understand something, when his salary depends on his not understanding it."

Refusal to notice early on puts you at risk of a more painful reckoning later. To take one example, René-Thierry Magon de la Villehuchet, the CEO of Access International Advisors and Marketers, invested his own money with Madoff as well as his family's money and money from his clients. He repeatedly rejected warnings that something was fishy about Madoff's returns. When he finally came to terms with Madoff's fraud, de la Villehuchet was so overcome with self-recrimination and regret that he killed himself.[10]

We cannot pay attention to every potentially relevant piece of information in our environment. Moreover, it is often difficult to determine the relative importance of various pieces of information. For this reason we filter information, often unconsciously, automatically, and inefficiently. We can wind up neglecting useful information while paying attention to irrelevant information. The aware leader can do better.

The Special Demands on the Leader

In August of 2019 WeWork was preparing for its initial public offering of stock. The company heralded the future of flexible work, embodied by the airy, inviting work spaces it rented out. Having a well-dressed, hip staff, WeWork received generous financial support from Japanese SoftBank and its eccentric CEO, Masayoshi Son. Son favored big bets on the ventures he backed, endowing start-ups with the resources to vastly outspend and outpace their rivals. SoftBank poured billions into WeWork, an investment that contributed to WeWork's lavish $47 billion private valuation.[11]

The company's flamboyant front man was its dynamic young CEO, Adam Neumann. Neumann cultivated the company's hipster party vibe, seeing to it that the company's lounge provided unlimited beer, wine, and kombucha; his private jet was generously stocked with marijuana. The CEO's grandiose vision for WeWork—in its IPO filing, its stated mission was to "elevate the world's consciousness"—fed enthusiasm about the company.[12] At one point Neumann told reporters than he would like to see WeWork expand on Mars; he also wanted to become a trillionaire, leader of the world, and live forever.[13] Although analysts at SoftBank initially dismissed WeWork as overvalued, Son decided to invest after meeting with Neumann. Following their half-hour meeting, Son declared that he detected in Neumann the same "animal smell" that had inspired Son's successful investment in Jack Ma and his company, Alibaba.[14]

In fact WeWork was a glorified real estate broker, renting office buildings and subletting to commercial tenants. Outsiders were skeptical of WeWork's business model or even that it counted as a technology firm. "They have nothing," groused Larry Ellison, the CEO of Oracle. "WeWork rents a building from me, and breaks it up, and then rents it. . . . They say, 'We're a technology company, and we want a tech multiple.' It's bizarre."[15] Looking back, some employees confessed that the business model was built more on hype and wishful thinking than on reality: "In retrospect, there's no way this could have worked," one software engineer told the *New Yorker.*[16]

The financial documents WeWork released ahead of its planned IPO revealed what few on the inside had acknowledged: the emperor had no clothes. The market reaction was so negative, in fact, that WeWork withdrew its planned IPO. The company's valuation collapsed by over 90 percent, and investors had to write down the value of their shares.[17] Neumann was forced out as CEO and investigated by the New York attorney general. Among the charges was that Neumann had engaged in self-dealing when WeWork paid him $5.9 million for the trademark "We."[18]

"There was always this assumption that, behind Adam, there was someone intelligent—a group of people—who were watching and making the practical, financial decisions," said one WeWork employee. "That someone was taking care of it."[19] That job belonged to the people on WeWork's board of directors, those who represent the company's owners and supervise its managers, including the CEO. This was a strikingly homogeneous group. The board was all male and mostly white, despite WeWork's claim to promote a "culture of inclusivity." They represented WeWork's investors, including SoftBank, Benchmark Capital, Rhône Group, and Hony Capital. Instead of providing adult supervision, these men willingly drank Neumann's Kool-Aid. "You're not selling coworking, you're selling an energy I've never felt," Bruce Dunlevie, who represented Benchmark Capital, WeWork's first venture capital investor, told Neumann.[20] One WeWork executive marveled, "Adam was probably the best salesman of all time."[21]

Criminals like Madoff and hucksters like Neumann will always be with us. Most observers believe that WeWork started off with sincere enthusiasm and that a shortage of responsible oversight allowed Neumann's vision to carry the company away. Why didn't investors, business partners, and, most important, WeWork's board of directors take notice of the clear mismanagement? We believe they could have noticed; it was also their fiduciary obligation to do so. Their failure to notice cost WeWork's investors billions of dollars.

The members of the WeWork board were leaders from a different era—the youngest was fifty-six years old, and some were over seventy. WeWork is a story of how a smart, deceptive, and charismatic leader kept a bunch of rich old guys from noticing problems that should have been obvious. The board overlooked information about the company that simply didn't make sense. They had a legal fiduciary obligation to be sufficiently engaged in WeWork's business to effectively supervise its managers. Multiple alarms sounded, but no one was listening. Even Masayoshi Son had to admit later that he had allowed his intuition to cloud his judgment. When, in December of 2019, Jack Ma praised Son's investing guts, Son had to respond with chagrin: "Too much guts, sometimes I lose a lot of money."[22]

Leaders have an obligation to provide the oversight needed to detect and act on potential problems. Too often, though, when leaders confront information they can't fully explain, they fail to ask questions and instead focus on issues they understand better. These shortfalls describe many corporate scandals. We could tell parallel stories about Theranos, Deutsche Bank, Volkswagen, Barings Bank, Tyco,

Parmalat, Adelphia, Goldman Sachs, J.P. Morgan, Satyam, and Enron. In each case a few criminally unethical actors created a problem. In each case a corporate board enabled their crimes by abdicating its oversight function, ignoring obvious hints that something was wrong. Board members are typically paid large fees and are informally approved by the CEO. But this enviable position comes with responsibility. Too often board members fail the company's stockholders and society at large by turning a blind eye to corporate wrongdoing.

Why Don't Leaders Notice?

Sometimes noticing uncomfortable truths leads to immediate pain, embarrassment, or loss. For WeWork board members to have reckoned with Adam Neumann's mismanagement, they would have had to speak out against Neumann, WeWork leadership, and their fellow board members. They would have had to answer difficult questions about why they had failed to speak up earlier. And their investments in WeWork would have immediately dropped in value.

This so-called motivated blindness can lead to overly charitable interpretations of misbehavior by family members, friends, and coworkers. Motivated blindness explains why leaders in the Catholic Church, at Penn State, at the Boy Scouts, U.S. Olympic gymnastics, and in other organizations failed to notice and act on the crimes of known sex offenders. Ample evidence shows that our motivated blindness affects how we interpret information, even when we believe we're trying to be objective and impartial.[23]

Together, we have studied the U.S. auditing system.[24] Auditors have strong incentives to please their clients: happy clients are more likely to hire them again and perhaps purchase additional services. This motivation is at odds with the auditor's obligation to provide impartial, independent audits. Quite simply, auditors stand to make more money if their client is happy than if they provide an honest audit. But even after repeated corporate scandals that audit firms missed—most notably, the corrupt practices at Enron on which its auditor Arthur Andersen signed off—the U.S. government has failed to fix this corrupt institution.

Motivated blindness is just one explanation for leaders' failure to notice unethical and even criminal behavior in their organizations. Here are three more:

Ambiguity. Important leadership decisions often involve complex trade-offs and substantial ambiguity. A leader may get hints that something is wrong but initially lack convincing evidence. For example, a subordinate might tell a leader that they think they saw someone in the company doing something unethical. Motivated to see only the best in their people, the leader might discount this uncertain report. Optimistic leaders may prefer to hear, repeat, and convey good news. Knowing this, subordinates may be reluctant to provide bad news or disconfirming information, or they may soften its delivery to avoid implicating colleagues. Yet leaders often need to disambiguate information to clarify what's going wrong in their organization. Getting such information requires active investigation by a diligent leader.

The slippery slope. It can be hard for leaders to notice gradual slippage of ethical behavior within their firm. This slippery slope can account for why Madoff fooled so many investors. He began his fraud when he lost a relatively small amount of money. Believing he could make up the losses, he "temporarily" lied on his reports of the investments' actual performance. When additional losses meant that repaying the lost funds wasn't possible, he escalated by drawing in more investors. Madoff's ethical behavior deteriorated gradually. Many, many people who should have known better failed to notice, in part because his early returns were plausible and only became implausible over time.

Madoff's story matches the results of controlled experimentation. In their research Max and his Harvard colleague Francesca Gino asked study volunteers to play the role either of estimators or approvers. Estimators were asked to estimate the total value of pennies in a series of glass jars and were rewarded for providing higher estimates—the more inflated their estimates, the more they got paid. Approvers were charged with noticing when an estimate seemed too high. Approvers were less likely to flag overestimation by those who gradually inflated their estimates over time than those who corrupted their estimates in one bold move. Francesca and Max conclude that when ethical behavior deteriorates along a slippery slope, others are less likely to notice.[25] Similarly, Professor David Welsh of Arizona State University and his colleagues have shown that people engaging in unethical conduct are more willing to continue doing so if they have the opportunity to gradually increase their level of unethicality.[26]

Misdirection. David Copperfield is one of the most famous magicians in the world. Perhaps his best-known trick involved making the Statue of Liberty disappear, that is, disappear from the perspective of a large live audience and millions more on television. How did he do it? The live audience didn't realize this, but they were sitting on a rotating platform. The statue was observable through a pair of pillars, which were also on the rotating platform. A large curtain was lowered between the pillars, eliminating the Statue of Liberty from their view. The entire platform—including the audience, the pillars, and the television crew—rotated so slowly that the movement was undetectable. Moreover, Copperfield staged his trick after dark in a location lacking other visual landmarks. The platform rotated so that the statue was no longer in view, the curtain opened, and the Statue of Liberty was gone. Then the whole process was reversed to restore the Statue of Liberty.

Copperfield, like most magicians, took advantage of the fact that viewers' minds were occupied by other information—information that Copperfield created. He bantered about the benefits of independence and how precious liberty is. Helicopters flew through the area where the statue should have been located. Massive beams of light directed the attention of the viewers, and dramatic music played throughout. This misdirection was entertaining; it also kept the audience from noticing the rotating platform. Magicians are not alone in hoping their audience won't figure out the trick. Leaders are surrounded by people who want to misdirect their attention. Con artists, opponent negotiators, and politicians use similar techniques. Leaders need to be aware of the deceptive motives of these other parties.

Max once worked with a corporate client that was involved in an important negotiation to sell another company access to its intellectual property. The CEOs had an oral agreement about the terms of the deal. As the lawyers were writing up the agreement, the buyer's side claimed it needed continued rights to use the seller's intellectual property beyond the scope of the project that the two companies were developing. The seller wasn't clear why the other company was raising this issue of broader access to its intellectual property. At the same time, the buyer was suggesting it might walk away from the $100 million contract without the extended access. Why had this new issue sprung up at the last minute?

While the lawyers engaged in a dialogue over the issue, a negotiator from the buyer's side accidentally copied the seller on an internal email. The email revealed that the other firm had already criminally violated the seller's intellectual property rights. This clarified that the unusual additional request was an effort at misdirection. Negotiating for this extended use was an attempt to cover up past wrongdoing. The seller caught a lucky break when it received the errant email. But when someone makes a demand that doesn't make sense, it is a mistake for you to assume they are acting irrationally. Rather, ask yourself what you might not know that could explain their actions.

Toward Being an Aware Leader

Many of the anecdotes in this chapter could be accused of what academics describe as selecting on the dependent variable. That is, we look back with the benefit of hindsight and point an accusatory finger at the leaders who failed to prevent tragedy. It is true that the failure to notice is easier to identify in retrospect, and in most of these cases we can only speculate about how a more aware leader might have changed the outcome. A leader who notices a threat and prevents disaster can claim credit only for a nonevent. The absence of tragedy makes for a less memorable story than the failures, scandals, and calamities we document in this chapter. If WeWork's board members had exercised more effective oversight, the company would not have fallen victim to Adam Neumann's mismanagement, and we would not have re-counted its tragic fall.

The leadership guru Warren Bennis argued that the best leaders are "first-class noticers."[27] They pay close attention to critical information and overcome obstacles to awareness. They look at data objectively rather than seeing what they want to see. They strive to avoid being misdirected by people who want to deceive them. They notice when something is too good to be true. First-class noticers think about the future decisions and actions of others—they think several steps ahead.

We offer four concrete action steps you can take to move toward being a better noticer. First, acknowledge your responsibility to be more aware and develop a tendency to notice. Ask the difficult questions others are not. Too often executives defend themselves after an ethics scandal by saying, "No one could have predicted that." Later, we read about all of the hints that leaders ignored. Noticers view it as part of their duty to pursue clues of malfeasance and neglect. Recall a recent event that surprised you or your organization. If you were telling a friend about it, how would you explain what happened? Would you call it an unpredictable surprise or a freak accident? Would you say it wasn't your responsibility to notice the problem or claim it was impossible to predict which of many low-probability problems could eventually explode? Or would you answer like this: "I failed to consider what threats were confronting our organization," "I didn't consider how other parties would act," "I didn't ask what data were missing," or "I didn't search hard enough to develop the right options"?

The first group of explanations are external attributions; they focus on factors outside your control. The second group are internal attributions; they focus on what you could have done to anticipate and prepare for the surprise. Most of the time, both internal and external factors underlie any surprise. It's human nature to generate internal attributions for our successes and external attributions for our failures.[28] In contrast, first-class noticers focus on what they could have done differently. By acknowledging your role, you can learn from experience and become a more aware leader.

Second, leaders need to take an outsider's perspective. When organizations hire outsiders like Max or Don to help them address problems and we offer new ideas, we frequently hear in response that things just aren't done that way. Often this is because the industry or organization developed a bad habit that needs to be changed. One sales-team leader expressed disappointment with how many customers simply didn't pay their bills. We asked how employees were rewarded. It turns out that commissions were based on booked sales rather than collected sales. Thus salespeople were getting bonuses whether or not the customer actually paid for the goods provided. The leader then saw what was obvious to any outsider—that the incentives encouraged salespeople to ignore customers' credit problems. Outsiders can sometimes notice issues that insiders have simply accepted as normal practice. Unfortunately, too many leaders trust their intuitions and are overconfident in their wisdom, traits that prevent them from benefiting from outside perspectives.

Third, leaders should audit their organization to identify key threats and challenges it faces. Think about how decisions are currently made in your organization and whether the right decision architecture is in place to enable you and others to notice key threats and opportunities. Michael Lewis's *Moneyball* documents how the Oakland Athletics' general manager Billy Beane transformed sports leadership by auditing the intuition of baseball professionals.[29] He observed that their judgment was biased in systematic and predictable ways—specifically, it was self-serving and ignored objective data. Once he audited the system then in place, it became clear to him that future performance could be predicted better by measuring past performance rather than using a scout's intuitive assessment. Relying on tradition and trusting intuition had led teams to neglect the obvious. What conventional wisdom in your industry deserves to be questioned?

Fourth, aware leaders think multiple steps ahead. Game theory is a branch of economics and applied mathematics that focuses on the theoretical actions of rational actors in competitive contexts. While game theory is conceptually quite elegant, it can be criticized for being overly mathematical and for the problematic assumption that everyone behaves rationally. An important strength of game theory that is particularly relevant to leaders, however, is its guidance to actively think about the decisions of other parties when making one's own decisions. Even if others do not behave rationally, that need not prevent you from striving to do so. Adopting the propensity to think about other actors can make leaders aware of potential actions by others that they need to anticipate—often before others have taken any action.

We close this chapter by reiterating that we recounted the stories in this chapter with the benefit of hindsight. We don't know that the board members at WeWork or leaders at the Catholic Church, Penn

State, the Boy Scouts, Volkswagen, Barings Bank, Tyco, Parmalat, Adelphia, Deutsche Bank, Goldman Sachs, J.P. Morgan, Satyam, or Enron would have noticed and acted on the information they missed had they heard a lecture from us on being an aware leader. But the leaders of these organizations had the duty to notice, and they failed to do so. We hope that the tools described here will help you avoid similar failures in your own spheres of influence.

4

Calibrate Your Confidence

On January 15, 2020, a thirty-five-year-old Seattle tech worker returning from a visit to Wuhan, China, became the first person to test positive for the novel coronavirus in the United States.[1] Seattle soon became the epicenter of the first U.S. outbreak. A week later, at the World Economic Forum in Davos, a reporter asked Donald Trump if he was concerned about the coronavirus. "No, we're not worried at all," he replied. "And we have it totally under control. It's one person coming in from China."[2]

While China, Germany, New Zealand, and South Korea were rapidly ramping up their testing capacity and investing in contact tracing to help track disease outbreaks, Trump continued to tweet optimistically: "I think we have it pretty well under control" (January 30), "It's going to be fine" (February 10), "The Coronavirus is very much under control in the USA. . . . Stock Market starting to look very good to me!" (February 24).[3] Lulled by Trump's confidence, the federal government offered no coordinated response to the coronavirus. Too little testing made it difficult to track the spread, and blaming China distracted from infections brought by travelers from Europe.

Trump assured Americans on March 10, "We're doing a great job with it. And it will go away. Just stay calm. It will go away." Other populist leaders around the world shared Trump's optimism. Andrés Manuel López Obrador, the president of Mexico, encouraged his citizens to continue shopping, traveling, dining out, and hugging. "This crisis is passing, transitory," he assured them. "Soon normality will return."[4] "There are no viruses here," boldly declared President Aleksandr Lukashenko of Belarus. "Do you see any of them flying around? I don't see them either." Jair Bolsonaro of Brazil comforted his people by saying, "God is Brazilian. The cure is right there."[5] And shortly before he himself fell ill with Covid-19, Boris Johnson of Great Britain insisted, "I am absolutely confident that we can send coronavirus packing."[6]

By contrast, on March 3 the South Korean president Moon Jae-in announced grimly that "the whole country has entered a war against the infectious disease."[7] At a cabinet meeting in which everyone was wearing facemasks, Moon spoke plainly: "The economic situation is grave." Moon acted aggressively to identify outbreaks using extensive testing. By March 17 South Korea had tested a quarter of a million people for the virus. The United States, by contrast, had tested one-tenth that number, despite having seven times the population of South Korea.[8]

In New Zealand, Prime Minister Jacinda Ardern took action to restrict travel and prohibit large public gatherings. "We have a window of opportunity to stay home, break the chain of transmission, and save lives," Ardern told the nation on March 25. "It's that simple."[9] The next day New Zealand entered a strict, nationally coordinated lockdown. The director-general of health warned that the nation could see thousands of new cases before the outbreak was under control.

At the same time, Trump was talking about wanting to lift restrictions imposed by some states: "I would love to have the country opened up and just raring to go by Easter."[10] Even after that goal proved overly optimistic, Trump continued to push U.S. states to open up to commerce, at one point asserting that he had total authority to force an economic reopening.[11] When U.S. states did indeed resume more economic activity, coronavirus infections quickly followed. Due in part to the absence of any helpful, nationally coordinated strategy Americans' usage of face masks was sporadic. Social gatherings in bars and churches facilitated the spread of the virus, and neither God nor alcohol stopped it.

By July New Zealand was virtually free of the coronavirus. The nation was able to lift restrictions on commercial and social exchange, and life returned to normal. South Korea reported zero new cases about a year before the United States managed a partial resumption of economic activity.

Noticing Threats

What accounts for the differences in nations' responses to the threat of Covid-19? Some noticed the threat sooner than others. South Korea in particular may have been primed to notice the threat thanks to its brush with disaster in 2015. That year a sixty-eight-year-old South Korean man returned home after a visit to the Middle East with a new and highly contagious infection. The disease, which came to be known as MERS, Middle East Respiratory Disease, caught the South Korean government off guard. The first carrier quickly infected 186 others, 38 of whom died.

South Korea learned from its mistakes in 2015 and began preparing for future outbreaks of new diseases.[12] Those preparations proved useful when, on January 20, 2020, the governments of South Korea and the United States each confirmed their first case of Covid-19. Well aware of the risks of under-responding to a pandemic, the South Korean government met with medical supply companies, developed testing kits, and started mass production of all needed equipment. Leaders swiftly implemented widespread testing, began tracing the contacts of anyone infected with the disease, and provided quarantine facilities for those with even mild disease symptoms. They also developed a plan for communicating openly and honestly with an anxious public.

Public health experts studied the world's close call with the MERS outbreak in 2015.[13] The U.S. National Security Council created a special unit focused on pandemic risk. But Donald Trump disbanded the unit in 2018.[14] And when the coronavirus spread in China, Trump brushed off warnings from intelligence agencies that, without preventative action, it was likely to spread to the United States and cause considerable damage. Moreover, the Trump administration's refusal to adhere to the advice of scientists contributed to the spread of the virus in the United States. The U.S. wound up with a per capita fatality rate almost fifty times that of South Korea—despite a health-care system that spends more money per citizen than any other developed economy.[15]

Leaders are better able to take effective action when they notice threats early. An article published in June 2020 by the Harvard Business School professor James Sebenius and his son Isaac measured the benefit of noticing by asking the question, "Had American leaders taken the decisive, early measures that several other nations took when they had exactly the same information the U.S. did, at exactly the same time in their experience of the novel coronavirus, how many of these Covid-19 deaths could have been prevented?"[16] At the time they wrote, 120,000 Americans had lost their lives to Covid-19.[17] Their analysis examined how thirteen public-safety policy responses (including lockdowns, border closings, and tests) affected fatality rates in countries around the world. A conservative reading concludes that over 90 percent of deaths could have been avoided had the United States responded more like South Korea.[18]

Balancing Optimism and Honesty

Optimism is often touted as essential to effective leadership. "One of the most important qualities of a good leader is optimism," Disney CEO Robert Iger wrote in his memoir, *The Ride of a Lifetime*. "People are not motivated or energized by pessimists."[19] And the celebrated venture capitalist Randy Komisar advised, "Entrepreneurs need to believe, irrationally, that they are immune to the forces that defeat the normal every day and that they can succeed where a host of others have failed."[20] "Force yourself to think positively and encourage others by being optimistic" wrote Rebecca Knight in the *Harvard Business Review*.[21]

As Iger and Komisar know well, when leaders express optimism in their companies they help to attract investors, employees, and customers. Steve Jobs wooed loyal Apple fans with his promotion of "insanely great" products.[22] Donald Trump promised voters, "We're going to win. . . . We're going to win so much, you're going to be so sick and tired of winning."[23]

Optimism can represent one form of overconfidence—an overestimation of one's potential, ability, or future performance. Indeed, confident optimists are more likely to be elevated to positions of social status and leadership, as Don's research shows.[24] In a paper he published together with Professors Cameron Anderson (of UC Berkeley), Sebastien Brion (of IESE Barcelona), and Jessica Kennedy (of Vanderbilt University), they found that confidence inspires trust by signaling what one can achieve. In times of crisis the yearning for confident leaders is particularly poignant. We want people who can guide us out of our predicament. "We shall fight," Winston Churchill told the British people in the depths of the Second World War. "We shall fight on the seas and oceans, we shall fight with growing confidence and growing strength in the air, we shall defend our island, whatever the cost may be." But Churchill was also forthright about the grim challenges ahead: "We have before us an ordeal of the most grievous kind. We have before us many, many long months of struggle and of suffering." In his view, action was preferable to despair.

As guides, mentors, and decision makers, leaders have a special responsibility to be honest. The leader who gives false hope can be exposed as hypocritical, incompetent, or delusional. When Donald Trump told the nation in February that "this virus is going to disappear," his confidence did not motivate constructive action—quite the opposite. The more assured you are of victory, the less you feel you need to work for it. If you are certain you're going to ace an exam, you don't need to study. If you know you're going to win an election by a landslide, you don't need to waste your time campaigning. If you believe your firm's marketplace dominance is assured, you needn't bother improving your product or service.

Business history is littered with the carcasses of wealthy, powerful companies that were overconfident of their continued dominance. Even more numerous are the confident entrepreneurs who falsely believed they were immune to the forces that defeat others. And there are many confident politicians who misjudged their electoral prospects. If you would like to avoid their fates, then you should seek well-calibrated confidence over delusion. But if you are concerned that honesty might put you at a disadvantage in contests for leadership, we can offer hope.

Research by Professors Celia Gaertig (of the University of Chicago) and Joe Simmons (of the University of Pennsylvania) offers guidance on how to express confidence while telling the truth. They compared the credibility of different approaches to communicating uncertainty.[25] Participants in their studies received advice from different sources regarding the likely outcomes of future events like athletic contests or deaths due to infections from Covid-19. The least credible advice came from those who claimed certainty about an uncertain future, predicting game scores or number of fatalities with precision.[26]

They found that the most credible advice confidently recognized the inherent unpredictability of an uncertain world: "I am confident the Warriors have a 60 percent chance to win the game" or "There is a 95 percent chance that the number of confirmed deaths due to Covid-19 in the United States on August 1, 2020, will be between

141,000 and 168,000." A well-calibrated adviser is fully informed about the risks and honestly reports uncertainty when offering advice. This result identifies a useful approach for leaders who aspire to be both honest and credible. Prime Minister Jacinda Ardern of New Zealand walked the line between confidence and honesty in her press conferences and online speeches. "If community transmission takes off in New Zealand," she warned on March 23, 2020, "our health system will be inundated and tens of thousands of New Zealanders will die. There is no easy way to say that, but it is the reality that we have seen overseas and the possibility that we must face here. Together, we must stop that from happening, and we can."[27]

Acceptance of uncertainty is a bellwether of a leader's trustworthiness. All of us should want—and ultimately need—leaders with the courage to confront uncertainty and factor it into their decisions. Mapping uncertainty allows you to place smart bets that maximize expected value or minimize expected losses.

To estimate probabilities associated with an uncertain future, you will need to collect the best evidence available and analyze it dispassionately. Even with the best information, you will not be able to say with absolute certainty what will happen. Being honest about what you know and what you don't know is essential for identifying risks and choosing the path forward. "You gain more respect as a leader when you admit you don't have all the answers," says Steve Kerr, the coach of the championship Golden State Warriors basketball team. "It can actually add to your credibility."[28]

This is even true for entrepreneurs. In 1995, as the World Wide Web gained popularity, Jeff Bezos correctly foresaw the potential of electronic commerce. Pitching his idea for an online bookstore to anyone who would listen, he won some investors by describing the vast market awaiting retailers who could make it easy and convenient to buy online. But Bezos also cautioned that Amazon's success was not guaranteed. His road to profitability would be long, and he estimated his company had a 70 percent chance of failure.[29] Bezos advised potential investors they should not give him money they could not afford to lose. At the same time, he argued that investing in Amazon had positive expected value: if it succeeded, the potential rewards could be substantial. You can acknowledge, like Bezos, that there are many ways to fail, even as you pursue the actions most likely to succeed.

If you are worried about the perils of admitting to uncertainty, imagine how your credibility could suffer if you feigned certainty. One of Donald Trump's greatest liabilities heading into the 2020 presidential election were his vacuous assurances than the coronavirus would disappear and the economy would rebound. His overconfident claims echo what he wrote in his 1987 book *The Art of the Deal*: "A little hyperbole never hurts."[30] As it turns out, it can hurt, as those who have lost loved ones to the coronavirus know too well.

Leaders' confidence is most useful when based on reality. Demagogues, fools, and charlatans may pretend they know exactly what the future holds. But the future is best thought of as a distribution of possible outcomes, some more likely than others. Mapping that uncertainty allows you to place smart bets that maximize expected value or minimize the expected loss of life. As a leader, this is how to sharpen your thinking and messaging. You should be the type of leader with the courage to admit uncertainty and use it to make wise decisions. Even so, leaders face difficult decisions about how ambitious they can be.

You Can Handle the Truth

In his book *Perfectly Confident* Don encourages readers to approach decisions with an appropriate level of confidence by calibrating their beliefs to reality.[31] You are perfectly confident when your beliefs accurately reflect your achievements, abilities, and potential. Because the future is uncertain, assessing your potential is probably the most challenging of these. How can you assess the odds of future success? There is a clear, unambiguous, and useful answer: think probabilistically about expected values. That is, consider the probabilities associated with future outcomes. For example, before committing to some sales forecast for your new plant-based burger, think about the whole range of possibilities. What's your best forecast for sales next year? How likely is it that sales will be less than half of forecast? How likely is it that sales will be more than double your forecast? Break the distribution of possibilities up into bins and estimate the probability of each, seeing to it that they sum to 100 percent.

Acceptance of uncertainty is a cornerstone of rationality, as Julia Galef writes in her book *The Scout Mindset*. Galef is a rationalist who cofounded the Center for Applied Rationality, which offers guidance to people who want to be more rational decision makers. She has served on the board of the New York City Skeptics and the Northeast Conference on Science and Skepticism, and she is the host of the podcast *Rationally Speaking*. In *The Scout Mindset* Galef considers how different mindsets can affect confidence calibration.[32] She contrasts the scout mindset with that of the soldier. The soldier pursues a mission. Even if you don't have actual soldiers in your organization, those in marketing and sales may serve as the foot soldiers in a sales campaign. Before the soldiers know which direction to march in, your organization needs good scouts. Scouts gather the best information they can and use it to inform decisions around goals, strategy, and tactics. What product formulation is most likely to succeed in the market? Which market segments will be most interested in your product? Which potential customers should you pursue first?

These decisions require accurate information. What is the likelihood of success? What is the probability that a potential retail distributor will place an order with you to buy and distribute your product? Galef encourages readers to practice translating their subjective feelings of uncertainty into a numerical quantification of probability. Most of us need practice attaching numbers to that subjective sense of likelihood. Fortunately, we can all improve our calibration skills through practice, learning from clear, accurate feedback.

Here's a simple calibration exercise: name the twenty-seven member nations of the European Union as of November 24, 2020. Write down twenty-seven guesses. Then, next to each, write your estimate of the probability that the specific nation is correct—that is, how likely is it that each country you listed is, in fact, a member of the EU? Then check your answers against the list provided in the endnotes.[33] For how many of your entries were you correct? Compare your average confidence with the percentage of responses you got right. How did you do?

Please stop and attempt this exercise now. We mean it. The only way to calibrate your confidence judgments is with practice and feedback. Taking five minutes to test yourself will deepen your understanding of what follows and will increase the likelihood you will benefit from the lessons this book has to offer. Go ahead. We'll wait.

[Reader attempts to name the twenty-seven member nations of the European Union here.]

If you're like most people, your calibration leaves something to be desired. Like all of us, you are prone to overconfidence—in this case, being too sure your guesses were correct. With practice, you can learn to do a better job of assigning well-calibrated probabilities to your feelings. You can learn, for instance, that when your feelings make you want to say you are 90 percent sure of yourself, you are correct only 60 percent of the time. This is a valuable lesson for improving your decisions.

Keep Track and Keep Score

You can help the people who work for you better calibrate their confidence judgments by encouraging them to get specific about their forecasts and goals and then check after the fact to see how well they met them. Some organizations even institutionalize the record keeping of claims and outcomes. Bridgewater Associates, by some measures the world's most successful hedge fund, scores people's credibility based on their track record of prior claims, projections, and achievements.[34] Those whose forecasts have proven accurate and who reliably achieve their goals earn greater credibility than reckless optimists who talk big but fail to deliver.

In Don's research lab we have a project tracker that lists timelines associated with task completion. Each milestone along the route gets a planned deadline. But because there is always uncertainty about our ability to meet those deadlines, we also estimate the probability. Ambitious project timelines come with lower probabilities of success than do more realistic plans. Each individual is responsible for updating project timelines in light of the best available information. Overconfidence in planning reveals itself in the need to push back project timelines—a useful lesson for project planners, who learn to make more accurate forecasts.

As a leader, you must often rely on information and advice from others to help you make your decisions. If you don't hold them accountable they may be able to get away with puffery and exaggeration. Worried about the possibility that an overconfident poser might dupe you? Ask for evidence. Have they delivered on their promises in the past? What commitments, predictions, or forecasts have they made, and how have those worked out? Every corporation publishes regular earnings forecasts, and many companies collect internal forecasts of sales, revenues, and profits. How accurate have those forecasts been? Because people may be tempted to highlight their successes, be sure to analyze *all* of their forecasts, not just their successes. That entrepreneur who promises that their new product will produce enormous profits? Pin them down: what is their prediction for sales the first year? The first six months? Is it possible to get some preliminary test data that could inform a decision on a larger investment? If an adviser or consultant claims they have a plan to turn your company around, find out exactly what that plan entails and how quickly they expect to see results. How do they expect to measure that turnaround? Are they willing to make your payment to them contingent on the accuracy of their forecasts?

Politicians, wary of being held accountable, often avoid making verifiable commitments. When Donald Trump promised his supporters, "We're going to win so much, you're going to be so sick and tired of winning," he did not specify what "winning" meant. Presumably he did not mean that a global pandemic would kill more people in America than in any other country. Did he mean that U.S. unemployment would be lower than in other countries? That U.S. GDP would grow faster than in other countries? That more Americans would wear red "Make America Great Again" caps?

You can help those who work with you improve their own calibration by helping them keep track and keep score. Before they make any major decision, encourage them to write down the key components of their decision-making process. Every decision depends on a forecast of what will happen, so write these forecasts down. Discipline your own confidence by following this helpful practice yourself. It is useful both for assessing expected values at the time of a decision and for scoring the accuracy of forecasts later on.

Big, Hairy, Audacious Goals

In 2011 American Airlines chief executive Gerard Arpey lit a fire under the aircraft manufacturer Boeing. Although American had been a loyal Boeing customer for over a decade, American was considering placing an order with Boeing's archrival, Airbus. Airbus was moving faster to deliver its next-generation aircraft, Arpey informed

Boeing CEO James McNerney that day. Boeing stood to lose American's business if it could not compete.

McNerney responded to the threat by ditching Boeing's plan to develop a completely new airplane model, which would have taken a decade to design, test, certify, and produce. Instead, Boeing decided to update its existing 737, which had an airframe already certified by aviation authorities and regulators around the world. Moreover, in its race against Airbus, Boeing set ambitious deadlines to produce the updated 737. Managers pushed engineers to submit technical drawings and designs in roughly half the time they would normally take. "This program was a much more intense pressure cooker than I've ever been in," reported Rick Ludtke, a nineteen-year Boeing veteran.[35]

"Stretch goals" may be one of the most important ways in which managers manifest optimism. By encouraging workers to reach beyond what they have previously achieved, stretch goals imagine a bold future and express confidence in the possibility of achieving it.[36] Stretch goals entail extreme difficulty and build on the well-documented effectiveness of goal setting. The most basic result from goal-setting research is that setting a specific goal can elicit greater effort and performance than the instruction "do your best."[37]

Jim Collins and Jerry Porras famously preached the value of "big, hairy, audacious goals" in their business best seller, *Built to Last*.[38] They told compelling stories of visionary goals and the companies that achieved them, like the story of how Boeing overtook McDonnell Douglas in the 1950s to become the world's leading aircraft manufacturer. Prior to that, Boeing had not been a major player in commercial aircraft. Companies like Douglas Aircraft dominated the market with their propeller planes. Boeing committed to the audacious goal of flying to the top of the commercial aircraft market with its new jet airplane, the 707. And Boeing succeeded. "Boeing has a long and consistent history of committing itself to big, audacious challenges," wrote Collins and Porras.

Great ambitions frequently precede great achievements. The best leaders inspire us to raise our sights and elevate our game. They persuade us that we can accomplish more than we thought we could. In the early 1960s, as it grew its presence in commercial air travel, Boeing challenged its engineers to build a new aircraft that could do what no existing aircraft could. If they built a plane that could fly nonstop from Miami to New York with 130 passengers and land within the short 4,860 feet of runway #4-22 at La Guardia, they would have a customer in Eastern Airlines. The engineers answered with the Boeing 727, a plane that went on to become the workhorse of many airline fleets.[39]

How ambitious should a goal be? It stands to reason that if goals improve performance, then the more ambitious, the better. Taken to its logical conclusion, this line of reasoning would suggest that goals should be infinitely ambitious. Could James McNerney have maximized Boeing's performance if he had demanded the production of an infinite number of new aircraft instantaneously? Obviously, even the most audacious stretch goals represent a compromise between ambition and realism.

In principle, a leader would want to set a goal at that point that maximizes performance. McNerny sought the deadline, somewhere between tomorrow and a decade hence, that would have maximized Boeing's performance delivering its next-generation aircraft. This identifies the challenge of quantifying performance: what exactly should Boeing have sought to maximize? There are many outcomes that Boeing ought to have been concerned with, including speed to market, production cost, quality, customer appeal, worker health and safety, pollution, legal compliance, and product safety. In setting goals for the new 737 Max, Boeing behaved as if speed to market was the key performance metric. In doing so, it neglected other legitimate concerns, including product safety. The result, we now know, has been devastatingly costly.

The U.S. Federal Aviation Administration supported the aircraft's speedy delivery to market by letting Boeing take the lead in testing and certifying safety.[40] Boeing sped through its safety testing and decided against taking the time to create guidance for pilots on the new automated flight system in its new 737s. The pilots of Lion Air flight 610 and Ethiopian Airlines flight 302 were unaware of the 737's new maneuvering characteristics augmentation system (MCAS) and thus did not know how to respond when the MCAS system malfunctioned. They and their passengers paid the ultimate price when the planes crashed in 2019. The consequences have also been colossally costly to Boeing, which grounded all its new aircraft and halted production while searching for a solution to the design flaws of the 737 Max.

As the crisis of the 737 Max vividly illustrates, delusional, ambitious goals can lead people to cut corners, in addition to increasing stress and burnout. The biggest stretch goals also come with a substantial probability of failure. Failure can be exceedingly costly for the company, its customers, and those who worked so hard yet fell short. If you have taken the lessons of chapter 3 to heart, you will be better able to notice the risks of excessively ambitious goals. You will anticipate their potential downsides and think ahead to consider the risks and benefits of various different possible goals. How likely are you to achieve each of them and how good would it be? Multiplying the probability by the value of each possible goal level can help you see which goal has the highest expected value.

It is worth reflecting on how Collins and Porras selected the stories they recount to support the benefits of stretch goals. Like the companies they profiled, they focused on success. But when we focus on goals achieved and ignore those that failed, we see an incomplete picture and can easily reach the wrong conclusions. "Selecting on the dependent variable" is one of the most basic threats to the validity of scientific research results. If researchers study the effectiveness of setting big, hairy, audacious goals by only considering successes, they are likely to get a misleading picture of the goals' effectiveness. If you want to learn how to succeed, it might be tempting to study successes. However, unless you compare them with their equally talented and ambitious counterparts, it can be difficult to identify what distinguishes those who triumph from those who do not.

Wanna Bet?

One way to test someone's confident claim is to propose a bet. In her book *Thinking in Bets*, the poker pro Annie Duke recounts how players invite each other to back up the claims, forecasts, and promises they made away from the poker table by putting money on the line.[41] When the high-stakes poker player Phil Ivey claimed he could be a vegetarian, a fellow poker player, Tom Dwan, challenged him, betting $1 million that Ivey could not maintain a vegetarian diet for an entire year.[42] Ivey's vegetarianism lasted only three weeks. Tempted by a plate of meat, he called Dwan to negotiate. Ivey bought out of the bet by paying Dwan $150,000. Ivey did not report afterward whether he thought the chicken was worth it.

Omnivorous poker players aren't the only ones whose overconfidence gets them into trouble. It is common for businesspeople to make excessively rosy predictions of their prospects for success. When entrepreneurs offer overly optimistic forecasts, their investors end up disappointed. It is worth noting, however, that investors can contribute to this problem when they encourage founders to be optimistic. Venture capitalists often push founders to set big, hairy, audacious goals. When potential investors demand a promise of glorious revenues in five years, founders often oblige.

Let's consider the dynamics created by these incentives. For simplicity, imagine that one investor (an individual investor or a venture capital firm) is considering dozens of potential start-ups for a single $1 million investment. Using the information provided by the entrepreneurs, the investor assesses the expected value of each investment option. Now think of each assessment as having two parts, signal and noise. The signal is the expectation that arises from an objective evaluation of useful information. In addition, there is also noise or error that comes from the optimistic bias of the entrepreneur, their selective provision of information about uncertain events, and potential exaggerations and other distortions provided by (some) founders. The investor chooses the start-up with the highest apparent expected payoff. The start-up with the most grandiose profit projection is likely to have been biased upward by noise, leading the investor to overestimate its value.

Now let's turn things around and imagine a start-up founder who manages to start a bidding war between potential investors. The founder is seeking $1 million and wants to give up the smallest percentage of the firm possible in return for the $1 million. You are one of ten potential investors. Due to your willingness to accept the lowest percentage of the firm in return for your $1 million, the founder agrees to the investment terms that you offered. Should you be happy?

Max's research suggests that you should limit your celebration because you may have just become the most recent victim of the "winner's curse."[43] When many parties bid on a target of uncertain value, the winner typically pays more than the target is worth. Winning is thus more of a curse than a blessing. Not only is the "winning" investor in such an auction likely to be the one who placed the highest valuation on the firm, but they are also likely to be the one who most overestimated the value of the firm. If this happens to you, you may ultimately end up cursing both your misfortune and the noisy signal that fooled you into overestimating the benefits of winning.

People typically fall prey to the winner's curse when they fail to take into account the information present in others' bids. The very fact that other interested bidders are not willing to pay as much as you are suggests they reached lower estimates of the target's value. If those cautious bidders have useful information, then outbidding them is dangerous as that increases the risk that you will overpay. The more rivals you outbid, the more likely you are to have paid too much. Winning against a large number of well-informed rivals strongly suggests you have overpaid. Thus bidders on uncertain commodities competing against many other bidders should lower their bids accordingly. However, most people ignore this consideration or even bid more aggressively as the number of bidders goes up.

Newly minted MBAs compete fiercely for jobs at venture capital firms, lured by legends of outsized returns from early tech investments. VCs closely guard the decision-making strategies they use to identify those few start-ups whose fortunes will land in the long right tail of the distribution. Yet a 2012 study by the Ewing Kaufmann Foundation found that the average venture capital fund barely broke even.[44] Why is actual performance so weak? The winner's curse provides part of the answer: venture capitalists tend to invest in the most extravagantly overoptimistic start-up founders. Just think of Adam Neumann's infectious optimism and how much venture capital backing it won WeWork. Collectively, investors reward founders for providing low-quality, upwardly biased forecasts.

Even if skeptical investors discount entrepreneurs' forecasts, they will have difficulty knowing the extent to which founders have exaggerated their claims. Access to better information would enable VCs to make better investment decisions. How can they get it? One idea, used too rarely, allows founders to bet on their forecasts. Negotiators call this a contingent contract. To illustrate, let's return to the case of the start-up seeking $1 million in funding on a valuation of $5 million. A standard contract might provide the $1 million for 20 percent of the firm. Assume that the founder has made some quantifiable and measurable forecast based on revenues, profits, or future valuation within a specific timetable. As the investor, you could then make an offer in which the percent of the firm that you own for $1 million depends on the founder's ability to meet their claims.

For simplicity's sake, imagine that the founder predicts the company will be worth $10 million in two years, at the next round of funding. Instead of offering $1 million now for 20 percent of the start-up, you could offer $1 million in exchange for

1. 15 percent of the firm if a new round of funding leads to a valuation of $10 million or more within two years,
2. 20 percent of the firm if a new round of funding leads to a valuation of $8–$10 million within two years, or
3. 30 percent of the firm if the firm's valuation does not exceed $8 million within two years.

Notice that when the founder believes her claim, this offer will be more attractive to her than an offer of $1 million for 20 percent of the firm. But if the founder has exaggerated the estimate, she will become less interested in your offer. Her reluctance reveals valuable information. If the founder declines your contingent contract in exchange for someone else's more generous investment offer, you can feel good that you have reduced your exposure to the winner's curse.

More broadly, leaders can think about how to create an environment that will lead others to provide accurate information by allowing people to bet on what they say they believe. This same solution can apply to internal funding. Too often leaders reward employees for their optimism rather than holding them accountable for their predictions. Establishing incentives for accuracy can be a useful tool for helping others reduce bias. The result is better decisions—for leaders, employees, the organization, and the broader society.

Persistent Optimism about the Benefits of Optimism

We have done our best to make the case that you should strive to be accurate and honest, to acknowledge uncertainty, and to insist on accountability when making predictions. But we cannot blame you if you still suspect, just maybe, that there can be times when talking yourself into being more confident could help you. You may be thinking of times when self-confidence preceded great achievement, giving you the courage you needed to overcome risk aversion. Without disagreeing, we offer three caveats. The first is to note how easy it is to confuse correlation with causation. In life we routinely observe instances of confidence preceding success. It is tempting to conclude that confidence caused the success, neglecting the possibility that both confidence and success resulted from ability, practice, and preparation. Experiments that attempt to manipulate confidence while holding those other factors constant have failed to find a benefit of confidence alone.[45]

The second caveat is that if you actually succeed, then your belief in yourself was not overconfident. If you believe, as did Winston Churchill, that your scrappy island nation can, with its allies, defeat Nazi Germany in a world war, and you do, then your belief was accurate. Having the courage to enter a competition that you will win is not overconfidence. This is an important point because it underscores the importance of judging beliefs relative to a standard of accuracy.

The third caveat is a reminder that selecting on the dependent variable can produce misleading results. You cannot focus only on confident successes if you want to understand how confidence affects performance; you also have to consider confident failures. Remember the confident managers at Boeing whose stretch goals for the production of the 737 Max resulted in the loss of two airplanes, the deaths of the 346 people aboard, and the grounding of the entire fleet. Remember the many entrepreneurs, sure of their success, whose small companies crashed and burned. Remember Donald Trump's confident response to the coronavirus and the national tragedy that followed.

There is special danger in being the leader who peddles overconfident ambition. Aspiring leaders can gain credibility and an advantage over rivals by cloaking themselves in the mantle of confidence. To pick a biological analogy, animals sometimes exaggerate their strength. When challenged, they will stand tall, fluff their fur or feathers, and appear as large and intimidating as they can. By playing tough they can sometimes scare off stronger challengers.

Exaggerated displays of confidence are all the more intimidating when we fool ourselves into believing we're as strong and capable as we pretend to be, writes the evolutionary biologist Robert Trivers in his book *The Folly of Fools*.[46] But overestimating our strength can draw us into losing battles. Believing you can bring your airplane to market faster than ever before can lead you to cut corners on safety. And believing in bogus cures for Covid-19 can be dangerous for the citizens you lead. The Brazilian president Jair Bolsonaro touted the curative powers of hydroxychloroquine, an antimalarial drug he incorrectly claimed could protect against Covid-19.[47] He ordered the Brazilian government to produce and distribute the drug, despite its failure to prevent or treat Covid-19 in well-designed experimental studies.[48] Bolsonaro was taking the drug when he himself contracted Covid-19. Meanwhile, Aleksandr Lukashenko, the authoritarian president of Belarus, advised his people to protect themselves from the virus by working hard and consuming lots of vodka: "When you come out of the sauna, not only wash your hands, but also wash your insides with 100 milliliters [of vodka]. . . . You just have to work, especially now, in a village. Tractors will cure everyone! The field heals everyone!"[49] Trump, for his part, considered the possibility of disinfecting one's insides by injecting bleach.[50]

Maintaining our delusions may require us to actively avoid the truth—with potentially devastating consequences. The nations that responded successfully to the threat of Covid-19 invested in testing and contact tracing, which they recognized as critical to containing infection. They were guided by scientific facts and the advice of experts in public health. Trump instead tried to hide the facts. He confessed that, while Americans desperately sought widespread testing, he resisted it: "When you do testing to that extent, you're going to find more people, you're going to find more cases. So I said to my people, 'Slow the testing down, please.' "[51]

A Warning

As you advance in your career, your confidence in yourself and your decision-making ability will grow. Some of that may be a useful signal that reflects your greater abilities, hard-won through practice, experience, and effort. But some of it will be noise. Those who get ahead are usually lucky in addition to being talented.[52]

You will be tempted to misattribute your good fortune to your abilities. For the privileged, a belief in a just world can assuage concerns about the inequality and unfairness of compensation and promotion systems.[53] Loyal supporters, sycophants, and supplicants who praise your talents and seek your favor will bolster this belief. The higher you rise, the more of these people you will encounter and the more tempted you will be to drink in their praise.

As you advance, remember that you likely were not the most talented, capable, or promising of the rivals you overcame. Be grateful for your good fortune and resolve to do what you can to earn your privilege. Listen to your critics; try to address your greatest weaknesses. When you can, support those less fortunate. Develop systems that maximize everyone's chances to make the most of their talents, whatever they may be.

Remember as well that others are also vulnerable to the biasing influence of praise and flattery. You can help them make wiser decisions by questioning their proposals and highlighting potential flaws. Challenge their rosy forecasts by asking, "Wanna bet?" and by helping them work through the logic, forecasts, and calculations that justify important decisions. Keep track of their predictions so they can learn from experience to improve their calibration. Hold premortems to consider how a new project might fail.[54] Appoint a devil's advocate or assemble "red teams" whose job it is to find flaws, infiltrate secure systems, or attack popular assumptions.[55]

If you are reluctant to commit to numerical forecasts or open yourself up to criticism, it will undermine your credibility. Like the entrepreneur who declines a contingent contract that bets on her future success, your reluctance suggests you don't actually believe your own claims. Courageous leaders gratefully accept wise counsel. They will accept bets on claims they truly believe. They seek out advisers who may disagree with them and bring their confidence down to earth. And they empower others to make wise, well-informed decisions that consider all the facts and are based on well-calibrated confidence. If Donald Trump, Jair Bolsonaro, and Andrés Manuel López Obrador had been more receptive to the warnings of their public health experts, the Covid-19 pandemic might not have been so cataclysmic.

5

Advice, Persuasion, and Collaboration

In 2011 Reed Hastings made the biggest mistake of his career. Hastings was the CEO of Netflix, a company that rented DVDs (digital video discs). For a monthly membership fee of $10 Netflix sent you DVDs in the mail. After watching the movie, you would mail it back to Netflix and the company would send you the next movie in your queue. But Hastings glimpsed the commercial potential of offering online streaming video and anticipated that it would one day eclipse the DVD-by-mail business. So he proposed that Netflix focus on streaming content and announced that members who wanted to keep getting their DVDs in the mail should sign up for separate accounts at Qwikster, a new subsidiary. Members who wanted both DVDs and streaming would need to get two accounts and pay two eight-dollar monthly fees.

When Netflix announced the change, public outcry was swift. Unhappy customers left in droves and the company's stock dropped 75 percent. "Everything we'd built was crashing down because of a bad decision," Hastings wrote later.[1] He posted an apologetic video in which he acknowledged the company's mishandling of the situation.[2] Public ridicule followed, including mockery on *Saturday Night Live*.[3] One technology columnist wrote, "Qwikster was a dumb idea. Dumb, dumb, dumb. It should certainly be a first ballot entrant into the Bad Decision Hall of Fame."[4] Shortly thereafter, the company undid the change, dissolving Qwikster and again allowing customers to get streaming content and DVDs with one membership.

It is worth understanding how Netflix stumbled into the Qwikster debacle. Reed Hastings failed to benefit from the knowledge and insights of those around him. He failed to solicit their views ahead of the decision. He did not hold a premortem discussion in which he invited his best people to anticipate Qwikster's potential failure and try to think through its greatest weaknesses. He failed to conduct an experiment to market-test his idea with Netflix customers. Instead, Hastings fell in love with his own idea and promoted it with passion. His energetic advocacy silenced opposition and cowed dissenters. That wasn't because he had a ruthless, dictatorial management style. On the contrary, Hastings was loved and respected by his colleagues. He was a charismatic leader with an impressive track record of successes at Netflix. He just fixated too early on one plan and failed to seek input from those who disagreed with him.

When making decisions, leaders begin with what ought to be an enormous advantage: their followers, who are available to provide useful input, feedback, and correction. Any group contains more knowledge than an individual member—even the smartest member. This is especially true if the group brings diverse perspectives, backgrounds, and assumptions. But leaders need to know how to get the most value from those they lead, and it is easy to miss such opportunities. These failures can result when leaders don't hear the ideas of others or aren't open to their advice.

Hastings advocated so enthusiastically for Qwikster that others inside the company were reluctant to challenge him. Only afterward did the doubters speak up: "I knew it was going to be a disaster, but I thought, 'Reed is always right,' so I kept quiet."[5] One vice president at Netflix later confessed to Hastings why he had suppressed his objections to Qwikster: "You're so intense when you believe in something, Reed, that I felt you wouldn't hear me."[6] As a result, Hastings made a bad decision without gaining useful insights from his closest advisers.

The Qwikster debacle parallels one of the worst decisions made by any president of the United States. In 1961 a young John F. Kennedy decided to support a plan to overthrow the communist regime of Fidel Castro in Cuba with an invasion starting at the Bay of Pigs on the island's southern coast. The new Kennedy administration was brilliant, young, confident, and inexperienced on military issues. Kennedy did not invite disagreement or encourage dissent. According to Kennedy's adviser Arthur Schlesinger, "Our meetings were taking place in a curious atmosphere of assumed consensus, not one spoke against it." Those who harbored misgivings "never pressed, partly out of a fear of being labeled 'soft' or undaring in the eyes of their colleagues."[7]

Attempting to understand how good leaders like Kennedy and Hastings make bad decisions, the Yale psychologist Irving Janus developed the concept of groupthink.[8] Groupthink is a drive for consensus that suppresses dissent, often marked by pluralistic ignorance: dissenters' silence leaves them in ignorance of others' doubts.[9] They infer from others' silence that everyone must support the plan, neglecting the obvious fact that they too are silent, despite their own opposition. One Netflix employee said of Qwikster, "We thought it was crazy, because we knew a large percentage of our customers paid the ten dollars but didn't even use the DVD service. Why would Reed make a choice that would lose Netflix money? But everyone else seemed to be going along with the idea, so we did too." Another confessed, "I always hated the name Qwikster, but no one else complained, so I didn't either."

Hastings came to realize he had failed to solicit input from those who disagreed with the Qwikster plan. Hastings made an effort to learn from his mistakes. He apologized and resolved to do better. Netflix has become a company whose culture empowers people to take responsibility for decisions and speak up. And Hastings has grown as a leader. The lessons of the Qwikster debacle are embodied in the first step of the Netflix innovation cycle: "If you have an idea you're passionate about, do the following: 1. 'Farm for dissent' or 'socialize' the idea." Leaders should actively seek out criticism of their ideas. Netflix strives to make decisions that incorporate diverse inputs and collective wisdom. And the company has recovered from its brush with disaster in 2011, when its stock fell from $42 per share to $9.12. Netflix stock has rebounded, and as of our writing now trades at about $500 per share.

Weighting of Advice

The Qwikster debacle, the subsequent success of Netflix, the Bay of Pigs, and the Covid-19 pandemic all highlight the importance of leaders using available advice wisely. Successful companies from Google to Netflix seek to make the most of the intelligence and wisdom of their employees to facilitate wise decisions. Ray Dalio, the founder of the hedge fund Bridgewater Associates, attributes the fund's success to its being a meritocracy for ideas. The firm encourages open debate and fact-based argument that allow the best ideas and most accurate judgments to win the day.[10] And Amazon's long string of business successes is at least in part attributable to the organization's culture of respectful disagreement and evidence-based decision making.[11]

However, the scientific literature on advice taking demonstrates how hard it is to listen to and learn from others. We routinely neglect or discount useful advice in favor of our own views.[12] In a typical study, participants estimate some quantity (such as the weight of someone in a picture) and are paid based on their accuracy. They then get advice and have the chance to revise their initial estimates. These studies then compare people's initial and revised estimates against the right answer. Again and again, researchers find that people's revised estimates are better, but that they underweight advice from others and overweight their own opinions.[13]

A common measure that researchers assess is weight-on-advice (WOA). It is easiest to understand through an example. Imagine that a company's CEO wants to estimate next year's sales. Her first estimate is $14 million. The VP of sales offers a $16 million forecast. If the CEO revises her estimate to $15.5 million, her WOA is 75 percent, since she moved 75 percent of the way from her own estimate to that of the sales VP's estimate. Had she revised her estimate to $14.5 million, her WOA would have been 25 percent. WOA typically averages between 20 to 30 percent, depending on the situation, even when people are getting advice from others who are, on average, as wise and well-informed as they are. But average WOA is an oversimplification. The Duke University researchers Jack Soll and Rick Larrick showed that people often either choose one of the two estimates (theirs or the other person's, for a WOA of 0 or 100 percent) or use an equal-weighted average (WOA of 50 percent); the 20–30 percent mean results from a combination of these three responses, with a WOA of 0 percent being the most common.[14] In contrast, study participants would have done better and earned more money, on average, by equally weighting their own estimates and the advice they receive.

Of course, your optimal WOA depends on the quality of your knowledge relative to your adviser's. If Don is asked what his age is, he knows the answer, and it would be reasonable for him to ignore information provided by others. But for most forecasts a leader doesn't have such perfect knowledge. And when forecasting the future it is easy to see the general wisdom of averaging two estimates from equally knowledgeable people. Consider the example above, in which one executive forecasts next year's sales at $14M and the other at $16M. Let's assume that neither party has an ulterior motive and both are just trying to get as close as possible to the truth. The average of their estimates is $15M. If sales turn out to be $14.75M next year, the executives will be off by $.75M and $1.25M, respectively, and their average error will be $1M.

In contrast, the average ($15M) is off by only $.25M, with the high and low estimates bracketing the correct answer and the errors offsetting each other. If sales ended up being $13.5M, with both executives overestimating (by $.5M and $2.5M, respectively), then the average error would have been ($.5M + $2.5M)/2 = $1.5M, which matches the error of average between the two of them ($15M–$13.5M). Thus when we have two people with similar levels of knowledge, the average is better than the random choice of one of their estimates. We improve when the true answer is bracketed by the two estimates, and we break even (in comparison to randomly listening to one of them) when the true answer is not bracketed. Even when one executive is better informed about the domain than the other executive, unless the more-informed executive is sure of their answer, it makes sense to place a WOA greater than zero on the assessment of the less-informed executive.

Given the benefits of combining judgments, why do leaders put so much weight on their own estimates? Larrick and Soll argue that people incorrectly assume that averaging judgments leads to mediocrity.[15] That is, people tend to believe that the average judgment is no more accurate than the average judge—which, as the prior paragraph illustrates, is wrong. And part of the problem is overconfidence, as documented in our chapter 4 and in Don's book *Perfectly Confident*.[16] People are routinely too sure their views are correct. Overconfidence in our judgments may result in part because we are more aware of the reasoning behind our own judgments than those of others.

Although people typically underweight advice, this is not always the case. In fact, we tend to be underconfident in difficult domains. This tendency generalizes to advice taking. Don's research with Professor Francesca Gino shows that while people underweight others' advice in domains where they feel competent, they tend to overweight advice when making more difficult judgments.[17] Leaders tend to seek out advice and input on difficult decisions, hoping that high-priced consultants can provide answers. However, when no one knows much about a particular topic, it is dangerous to defer to a consultant who claims to have all the answers. Problems that are hard for leaders to solve are often hard for their advisers too. When leaders know little, rather than seeking an expert, their limited knowledge should motivate them to consider getting more advice and tapping the group's wisdom.

Group Wisdom

Periodically, the *Wall Street Journal* (*WSJ*) asks about fifty economists from different institutional backgrounds to predict key economic outcomes for the coming year. There is typically substantial variation in the predictions of these experts, more variation than most of us would intuitively expect.[18] Daniel Kahneman and his colleagues note that in most professional business forecasting the variation is typically about five times what executives expect.[19] The *WSJ* later publishes the results of the competition among economists. The first question most people want to ask is whose forecast is most accurate. Indeed, seeking the top expert is a time-honored practice. The Greek philosopher Socrates advised as follows: "First of all ask whether there is any one of us who has knowledge of that about which we are deliberating? If there is, let us take his advice, though he be one only, and not mind the rest."[20] A different approach relies on the wisdom of crowds, a term popularized by James Surowiecki in his 2004 book.[21]

Surowiecki recounts the story of Sir Francis Galton's visit in 1907 to the West of England Fat Stock and Poultry Exhibition. There, some eight hundred spectators estimated the weight of an ox.[22]

Galton averaged their estimates and found that the average was off by just a single pound. Galton kicked off a history of scholarship on opinion averaging, which finds that the benefits of averaging improve as the group size grows. Extensive evidence shows that simple rules of aggregating judgments within a group, including using a mean or median or majority vote for yes/no decisions, typically outperform more complex decision-making strategies.[23]

When making decisions, do you tend to rely on advice from the most knowledgeable person you can find, or do you aggregate the opinions of a larger group? Many people have a negative intuitive reaction to the idea of averaging lots of opinions. Average opinion, after all, includes some ill-informed opinions that could work against accuracy. Identifying the most qualified experts might help avoid fools. While that may be true, it is also true that many people, including leaders, underestimate the value of aggregating others' opinions and overestimate their ability to distinguish experts from fools.

Rick Larrick and his colleagues argue for combining the benefits of selecting experts with the statistical benefits of averaging with what they call the select-crowd strategy.[24] The select-crowd strategy involves choosing a small number of individuals based on their ability or expertise and then averaging their opinions. While choosing to follow one person's advice based on their prior accuracy works well in some domains, and averaging advice from a large crowd works well in other domains, the select-crowd strategy performs well across many judgment environments. In addition, their research finds that while many people are distrustful of simply averaging many opinions, they respond more trusting of select crowds than to simple averaging. Returning to their analysis of the *WSJ* competition, Larrick and his colleagues find that averaging the estimates of all of the economists is a better strategy than selecting the estimate of a random economist or the best predictor from the previous year. But averaging the top five predictors from the previous year outperforms a simple average all of the economists' opinions.

If we have convinced you that leaders should value the wisdom of crowds, it is important to think about who belongs to the crowd. Obviously, you want better-informed people providing input. In addition, substantial research highlights the benefit of having diverse perspectives in a group. When a group is composed of similar experts, they share biases. By comparison, people from diverse areas of expertise bring a variety of perspectives to the decision as well as different biases. Their different biases often cancel each other out. Imagine that you work in a firm with offices in the Bay Area and Boston and that the Golden State Warriors are playing the Boston Celtics. You want to predict who will win and by how much. There is a good chance that any estimates you gather from San Francisco will tilt toward the Warriors, and estimates from Boston will favor the Celtics. If you aggregate the estimates, the two biases may cancel each other out. The same may be true if the diversity found in a group is rooted in the function of the employees (such as sales vs. legal) or demographic differences (such as race or gender). When the group lacks diversity, they may share "correlated errors," making the homogeneous knowledge of different people redundant—the knowledge of one individual is redundant with another's. As diversity shrinks, so do the benefits of the wisdom of crowds.

It is easy to mistakenly interpret uniformity of opinion as evidence of consensus. If everyone in the group agrees, it can be tempting to take the matter as settled. However, every leader should worry about the risk of being blinded by groupthink. That is why Netflix encourages its leaders to seek out and cultivate dissent. Chapter 2 encouraged you to consider joint versus separate evaluation. One of the enormous advantages of considering the full menu of options is that it opens your eyes to the value of diversity in backgrounds and perspectives. Compose your team to take advantage of the wisdom of the crowd. You don't just want people whose similarity to each other makes it easy to see how they fit together. Teams with enough diversity that they disagree are more likely to bracket the truth and less likely to fall victim to groupthink.

You may have noticed that we have been talking about the knowledge found within groups while neglecting to discuss how people interact within those groups. Before the Covid-19 pandemic, when we pictured a decision-making group, we generally imagined a bunch of people sitting around a table. During the pandemic we got used to meeting in groups on videoconferencing platforms like Zoom. Whether they're meeting in person or virtually, it is common to think of a group as people who interact synchronously. Maybe one member of the group, sometimes the leader, offers an opinion about the job candidate, the start-up under consideration for funding, or the sales forecast for next year, before allowing members to offer their own judgments. Ample research documents that this first opinion expressed, particularly if it comes from someone with authority, is likely to bias the estimates of many of the other members of the group.[25] Thus the very nature of typical group meetings undermines the crowd's wisdom. The logic of averaging estimates across many experts depends on having uncorrelated errors. Interpersonal influence compromises independence, along with some of the wisdom of the crowd. Independence requires that each individual assess the question on the table separately from the other participants.

It is possible to structure interaction to help the group members learn from one another. This aim led Olaf Helmer and Norman Dalkey of the Rand Corporation to develop the Delphi method of group decision making.[26] A facilitator solicits independent opinions or estimates from a group. The facilitator then shares the anonymous inputs with all group members and allows each member to revise their estimates. This process can go through multiple rounds until the group converges on a decision. In the original formulation, this process occurs without the group actually meeting in person (or on Zoom). Variations of the Delphi process include allowing participants to include explanations or justifications for their opinions, discuss them, estimate again, and discuss again (estimate—talk—estimate, and so forth), until the group converges. The process allows for both independent estimates and synergistic interaction.

Let's return to the decision to hire a new faculty member, discussed in chapter 2. (Feel free to imagine hiring someone for a position in your organization.) You may recall that we mentioned that a ninety-minute presentation is core to the academic interview process for the final candidates. We now want to share with you what happens in the fifteen minutes after the talk. The candidate heads off to another one-on-one interview with one of our colleagues. Then a bunch of the remaining faculty gather informally, and someone says, "What did you think of the talk?" An opinionated colleague answers and, in so doing, contaminates others' independent judgments. We have advocated, with some success, that while it might be unrealistic to use a formal Delphi-like process, we could at least form independent assessments before we start hearing the opinions of others. This suggestion is counterintuitive, even for social scientists who know the research.

We are not recommending the elimination of social interactions within groups. Rather, we recommend that leaders accept the advantages of gathering insights from multiple experts, value the benefits of diversity, and aim to gather independent initial assessments to the degree that is practical. We also want to note how easy it is to overestimate the value of the group interaction. Although belief in the value of discussion is widespread, evidence substantiating that belief is weak. Research frequently documents the downside of group interaction and the possibility of one dominant individual biasing the views of others; there is little evidence that group decisions are better than the average of their parts.[27] Often the group can make a better decision without meeting to discuss: simply average everyone's ratings of the options and choose the option with the highest ratings.

Leading Others to Provide Better Advice

So far this chapter has primarily focused on seeking help from advisers who have every intention of providing the best advice possible. Sometimes, however, advisers will have personal incentives that clash with your goals. Advisers may care more about being selected (hired) to provide advice than about giving you the best advice you could possibly obtain. One group of advisers that corporate leaders rely on a great deal is consultants. Accordingly, we ask whether leaders ought to be more skeptical of advice from consultants.

This question comes from two people (ourselves) who often serve in the role of consultant or in the broader category of adviser. Our students and former students ask us for advice. Our junior colleagues ask us for advice. Corporate leaders ask us for advice. We both have spent many days working for corporations, outside of our university obligations. Some of this work has involved teaching classes for specific organizations, but much of it entails consulting on specific problems an organization is facing. So when a former student contacts us and clarifies that they are seeking advice, here are a couple of easy predictions. First, something has already gone wrong. Few leaders call to say, "I have a negotiation that is going pretty well, but I thought you could help it go better." Rather, they call after the situation has blown up. Second, they call us with hard problems, not the easy problems we hear about at cocktail parties where the storyteller is a hero.

In our experience, though, leaders often don't want to be reminded that their problem is a hard one without an easy answer. They don't want to hear that even the best strategy we can propose comes with risks, either because of uncertainty about the future or because there is no way to create a positive result. They aren't interested in hearing about a process that would take time to implement, such as running an experiment or market-testing the different options.

Too often leaders demand that advisers act as if they know the best solution, even when this demand is not reasonable. Sometimes leaders get recklessly overconfident advice because that is the type of advice they reward. The tendency to be overconfident in easy domains and underconfident in hard domains results in leaders thinking that they will perform comparatively better than they actually do in easy domains, and that others will do better in hard domains. Consequently, leaders seek advice on hard problems because they think others will have better answers than they do.

Yet, when leaders do seek advice from consultants, they tend to seek advice that tells them what they want to hear. The Nobel Prize–winning economist Richard Thaler jokingly and somewhat cynically suggested forming a consulting firm called "Yes Associates" that would respond to all assignments by telling the clients who hired them that all their ideas were great. Yes Associates would affirm the company's current plans and ways of doing business, assuring leadership that everything was going just fine. To speed up report delivery and guarantee satisfaction, Yes would allow clients to write the final report themselves so that they could be sure it said everything they wanted it to say. Thaler went on to imagine that the success of Yes Associates might create a business opportunity for a second firm, Devil's Advocate & Company. Devil's Advocate's business model would be the opposite of Yes Associates. The company's consultants would critique the client's plan and point out its many vulnerabilities. Which of the two firms would provide more useful advice? Clearly, Devil's Advocate, since Yes Associates provides no novel information.

Ultimately, however, Thaler predicted that both firms would fail: few companies would pay to hear their plans maligned by Devil's Advocate, and Yes Associates already has too much competition from existing firms.

Management consultants have learned there is money to be made from telling corporate leaders what they want to hear. Leaders' desire for affirmation is so powerful that they will pay people to agree with them. The famous investor Warren Buffett articulated his skepticism and dislike of consultants at a shareholder meeting of his company, Berkshire Hathaway. Buffett had particular disdain for compensation consultants, whose job it is to tell their client companies why they should pay their executives high salaries. Buffett threatened that "if the board [of Berkshire Hathaway] hires a compensation consultant after I'm gone, I will come back."[28] Buffett was similarly skeptical of hedge fund managers, whom he described as being "compensated on the basis of something that in aggregate cannot be true"—that is, that their investments will outperform the market.[29] Like Buffett, we are skeptical of advice from intermediaries, including real estate brokers, fund managers, and consultants, who are often better at selling their services than at delivering real value.

Buffett aside, plenty of other leaders rely on the advice of consultants. Management consulting firms have thrived for decades, perhaps none more so than McKinsey & Company. James McKinsey founded the firm in 1926, but it was Marvin Bower, the managing director from 1950 to 1967, who grew the firm into a prestigious powerhouse.[30] Many regard Bower as the father of modern management consulting. In 2019 the company Bower led reportedly had annual sales of $10.5 billion, 27,000 employees, and over 100 offices in more than 50 countries.[31] These days it charges $67,500 for a week's services of one junior McKinsey business analyst.[32]

In 1953 McKinsey became the first management consultancy to focus on hiring recent business school graduates instead of experienced business managers.[33] The firm cultivates a reputation for hiring the very best graduates from the top MBA programs in the world. In 2018, 800,000 candidates applied for 8,000 jobs.[34] Its elite status is central to the image it presents to clients.

McKinsey claims to tackle its big clients' hardest problems, but the firm's track record is somewhat less positive than its public image.[35] The Enron Corporation was a McKinsey client that paid about $10 million a year in fees. McKinsey was working on about twenty different projects at Enron when the journalist Bethany McLean began reporting on the convoluted financial arrangements through which Enron hid liabilities from its balance sheet.[36] At the time, McKinsey "fully endorsed the dubious accounting methods that caused the company to implode in 2001."[37] Subsequent to Enron's spectacular collapse, McKinsey denied giving Enron advice on financial-reporting issues or suspecting that Enron was using improper accounting methods.

The journalist Duff McDonald documented McKinsey's role in advising major Wall Street banks in the lead-up to the 2008 financial crisis.[38] McKinsey consultants actively supported the securitization of mortgage-backed securities that were central to the credit meltdown. McKinsey also advised the pharmaceutical company Valeant before the SEC started investigating it in 2015 for improper accounting practices and predatory price hikes.[39] "Valeant's downfall is not exactly McKinsey's fault, but its fingerprints are everywhere," the *Financial Times* concluded.[40] The *New York Times* alleges that McKinsey advised leaders of the pharmaceutical firm Purdue Pharma on best practices to "turbocharge" their sales of OxyContin "to counter the emotional messages from mothers with teenagers that overdosed."[41] Purdue Pharma's success at turbocharging opioid sales contributed to tens of thousands of deaths during the opioid epidemic.[42] McKinsey wound up paying over $600 million for its role in the opioid crisis.[43]

McKinsey has also been willing to advise repressive authoritarian governments across the globe, including China, Turkey, and Saudi Arabia, as well as controversial agencies like the U.S. Immigration and Customs Enforcement.[44] Others see these criticisms as overstated, saying that McKinsey didn't cause the credit meltdown or the Enron blowup, but there are many hints in such stories that McKinsey played a supporting role by encouraging the avarice of greedy, irresponsible leaders.

The harmful consequences of McKinsey's work highlights the need for leaders to scrutinize the advice they receive from consultants and others. When you are asking for solutions to tough problems, treat any advice you receive—especially when it is simple or optimistic—with a healthy dose of skepticism. Just because advice comes from smart people with fancy graduate degrees does not make it ethical or even likely to promote the long-term health of your organization.

Prediction Markets

Another tool for aggregating opinions to obtain integrated advice is a prediction market. A prediction market is any collective of people betting on an event—for example, predicted sales, election results, commodity prices, movie receipts—and establishing a prediction based on a market price. In *Wiser*, an insightful book on group decision making, Cass Sunstein and Reid Hastie trace the logic of prediction markets to the Austrian-British economist Friedrich Hayek and his views of why free markets are so effective.[45] Hayek argued that markets are effective at aggregating dispersed knowledge because they offer market participants incentives for accuracy. If the price of a stock is too high, sellers will sell, and the price will go lower. If the price is too low, buyers will jump in and push the price up. By aggregating dispersed knowledge, markets set accurate prices. When new information arrives, supply and demand adjusts, and the market moves to adjust.

Recently, tech firms have taken to the idea of prediction markets. Specifically, firms are aggregating knowledge by creating artificial markets that allow people, often employees, to bet on their forecasts. For example, Google employees have opportunities to bet on future events that Google would like to forecast: when products will actually be ready to go to market, how successful those products will be, or when the company will open offices in cities around the world.[46] At Google and other companies employees invest virtual money in their bets but can receive actual prizes for the play money they earn.

Prediction markets like Google's have quickly developed impressive track records, providing better forecasts than deliberating groups.[47] Prediction markets benefit from diverse inputs from people who have financial incentives to use the best information at their disposal to make accurate estimates. If the market moves away from accuracy, others will jump in to bet, and their activity will help correct the market.

Another interesting example is Best Buy's prediction market, Tag-Trade, which allows the retailer's employees to bet on events such as quarterly sales projections, the success of specific products, or whether a new branch would open on time. Best Buy has run hundreds of prediction markets involving thousands of employees. The TagTrade market has outperformed Best Buy's sales team in forecasting quarterly results and construction managers in predicting when stores will open. In doing so it has helped Best Buy outperform its competitors.[48]

Prediction markets are one specific tool that companies can use to enact our recommendation from chapter 4 to ask those whose predictions differ from yours, "Wanna bet?" These sorts of markets can turn disagreement into useful, actionable intelligence by drawing out the disparate information present in your organization and aggregating it to provide a clear forecast on which you can base your decisions. They can also help you implement chapter 4's advice to keep track of probability forecasts—your own and others'—and their accuracy. Employees may be hesitant to tell you that your idea for a new product is unworkable. Their bets against its market success are likely to reveal useful information.

Obviously, structuring an organization-specific prediction market requires some forethought and special technical skills. It's also important to consider whether employee incentives would compete with other work incentives. Companies interested in creating prediction markets may want to hire experts to help set them up. The broader point is that prediction markets further confirm the value of aggregating views across people. When key information is dispersed across people and places, prediction markets may represent one mechanism for aggregating that information.

Prediction markets proved successful in Don's forecasting work with the Good Judgment Project. GJP was one of five teams that competed in a forecasting tournament sponsored by the U.S. intelligence agencies. The teams got forecasting problems such as "Will Syria's President Bashar al-Assad vacate office by 1 April 2013?" Each team then estimated the probability the event would occur by the specified date. In order to experimentally test the best forecasting method, GJP randomly assigned forecasters to different conditions. Individuals in the prediction market condition competed with each other in a market in which prices (and probabilities) were determined by individuals' bets. These markets efficiently aggregated information and made forecasts more accurate than those of the other teams in the competition. GJP won the tournament hands down.[49]

But the accuracy of the prediction markets was matched or exceeded by a simpler approach that also capitalized on the wisdom of crowds. The experiment randomly assigned some forecasters to polls that simply asked them for their probability estimates.[50] Just averaging the best current estimates produced forecasts that were as accurate as those harvested in prediction markets.[51] Organizations seeking to benefit from their employees' collective wisdom do not have to set up prediction markets. They can just ask people what they think, provided those people are comfortable enough with probabilistic thinking to be able to quantify their uncertainty as probabilities and their judgments are independent in the sense that they have not been biased by discussion with others in the organization.

The Wisdom of the Netflix Crowd

Reed Hastings tried to learn from his mistakes after the Qwikster debacle. He confessed on the company blog that he had "slid into arrogance based upon past success," and he resolved to do better.[52] He adjusted decision-making processes at Netflix to elicit the best evidence and stimulate healthy debate, even when that meant encouraging dissent. In fact, the culture at Netflix obligates you to speak up if you disagree with a decision. Withholding your opinion is disloyal because you are choosing not to help the company make a better decision. This culture of open debate and constructive dissent has paid dividends. Netflix now enjoys a market capitalization of $234 billion, up over 5,000 percent since its low following the Qwikster announcement.

Hastings offers the decision to develop children's content as one example of learning from others. He had originally opposed the idea, arguing that no one signs up for a subscription to Netflix so they can watch children's cartoons. Nevertheless, Hastings opened the topic for discussion at a big meeting in 2016 where the top four hundred employees at Netflix sat together in groups of six or seven. They debated whether Netflix should spend more money, less money, or no money on developing content for children. The result was "a tsunami of support for investing in kids' content" and persuaded Hastings to change his mind.[53] Within six months Netflix had hired a vice president for family programming and started producing its own feature films. Within a couple of years Netflix was winning new customers and winning awards for its children's films. Hastings is grateful for the wisdom of the crowd that helped him revise his erroneous beliefs.

All of the above discussions underscore the wisdom of leaders who can learn from those around them. But wise leaders will not stop there. After you have refined your idea with input from others, see if you can get some evidence to road-test your idea. That is the second step in the innovation cycle at Netflix: "For a big idea, test it out." When the stakes are high, see if you can conduct an experiment that will allow you to put your idea to the test.

6

Recruiting the Best Evidence

In late 2007 Brian Chesky and Joe Gebbia decided to rent out four spots on air mattresses in their apartment. For eighty dollars per night Chesky and Gebbia provided their guests with a place to sleep, breakfast, and a tour of the neighborhood. The two roommates had just moved to San Francisco from New York, and they were having trouble paying the rent. They spotted a money-making opportunity when they learned that San Francisco hotels were full, but they could not have known at the time where that opportunity would lead them. The name of the company the two roommates launched a year later paid homage to those air mattresses: *Air Bed and Breakfast*. Airbnb's founding concept was that hosts would provide lodging and an authentic local experience to guests.

Their idea gained traction in 2008 in the lead-up to the Democratic National Convention in Denver. Chesky, Gebbia, and their partner Nathan Blecharczyk developed an online platform where people could offer spare rooms in their homes to convention attendees. It was a success, and Airbnb's rapid growth began. By the time Covid-19 hit the United States in early 2020, Airbnb had over five million listings—three-and-a-half times as many units as Marriott and its related chains—and was facilitating the rental of over two million units each night.

But our focus is on crucial design decisions made in Airbnb's early days, when the founders met with some of the first Airbnb hosts.

Chesky and Gebbia came away convinced that building a friendly and trusting community required that hosts and guests be able to see one another. Consequently, photographs of hosts and guests became a part of Airbnb's online platform. Hosts and guests get to know something about each other in advance of making a match. This contrasts with hotels, which cannot wait to decide whether to accept a reservation until they see what guests look like.

As is the case with many start-ups, the process of creating Airbnb's online platform was rushed, and functionality was key. Decisions needed to be made quickly, including how prices would be set: Should they be fixed? Should they fluctuate in a dynamic supply-and-demand structure like Uber's? Or should a mechanism for negotiation be available for each transaction? Would trust between hosts and guests be built by reputational ratings or through pictures? Hundreds of early decisions such as these would go on to affect millions of decisions made daily by the platform's hosts and guests. In particular, anecdotal feedback the company's leaders received early on from Airbnb hosts heavily influenced the decision to make photos prominent. When asked whether hosts might use photos to discriminate against guests based on their race, Airbnb dismissed concerns.

In 2014 Reed Kennedy, a forty-two-year-old real estate investor, was having trouble booking on Airbnb. The Airbnb website made it appear that the house was available for the dates he wanted it, but when he asked about it, the hosts rejected him. Kennedy, who is Black, wondered whether Airbnb hosts were discriminating against Blacks. He asked a White friend to try. She set up a new account on Airbnb and was able to book the house immediately. When Kennedy inquired with Airbnb the company denied the problem. A member of the company's customer experience team assured Kennedy that "the incidents where you've been declined by hosts has [*sic*] absolutely nothing to do with your race or ethnicity."[1]

Ben Edelman, Mike Luca, and Dan Svirsky—all of them Harvard Business School colleagues of Max at the time—wondered how Airbnb could be so sure its hosts weren't discriminating on race. The three researchers decided to conduct an experiment. They sent inquiries to sixty-four hundred Airbnb hosts in the United States. The inquiries were identical and came from fictitious guests who varied in only one way: half of the requests came from guests with names that are statistically more likely to belong to Caucasians (such as Brett or Todd), while the other half came from guests with names statistically more likely to belong to Blacks (such as Darnell or Jermaine). Researchers use this type of experiment with increasing frequency to find out whether some independent variable(s)—in this case race—affects a dependent variable—in this case, a host's decision to rent to a guest. The results were consistent with a wealth of research in psychology, sociology, and economics: guests with Black-sounding names were approved by Airbnb hosts 42 percent of the time, whereas those with Caucasian names were approved 50 percent of the time.[2] This result was robust across neighborhoods, price categories, type of accommodation being sought (separate apartments to guest rooms), and the number of the host's listings (from single- to multi-unit owners).

One logical, but still troubling, possibility is that hosts were basing their rental decisions on past experiences—that is, they might have had some data that would lead them to the false belief that race is a predictor of guest behavior. But careful analysis by Edelman, Luca, and Svirsky showed that discriminatory decisions by Airbnb hosts were concentrated among hosts who had never had a Black guest. They had no hosting experience on which to base their discrimination.

The publication of this experiment in 2017, combined with frustration from Airbnb customers who had been discriminated against, garnered media attention. The program *Hidden Brain,* on National

Public Radio, featured the research and hosted a Twitter discussion in which hundreds of people, using the hashtag #AirbnbWhileBlack, shared their stories of discrimination by Airbnb.[3] The U.S. Department of Housing and Urban Development, attorneys general in many states, and private attorneys began legal action against Airbnb. The Congressional Black Caucus wrote to the CEO of Airbnb to express their anger. And regulators took notice. The State of California forced Airbnb into an agreement that would allow the state to conduct similar tests, on an ongoing basis, to detect discrimination on the Airbnb platform.

In response to the pressure, Airbnb announced some planned changes. It did not agree to remove names and photos from user profiles right away, but it did commit to increasing the availability of an Instant Booking feature that allowed guests to reserve rooms without prior review by hosts. It also began to provide optional bias training for hosts, gave hosts incentives to use instant bookings, and developed a data science team to study issues that included discrimination by hosts. In 2018, after running its own experiments, Airbnb announced that hosts would no longer be able to see photos of guests before deciding whether to rent to them.

CEO Brian Chesky admitted that Airbnb's founders had not thought about the problem of race discrimination when they designed their platform. He also noted the fact that all three founders were White males. Airbnb had included photos on its listings without systematically thinking through the fact that photos, even more than names, provide information about ethnicity. Despite receiving complaints from guests, Airbnb didn't think to run its own experiments to find out if discrimination was a problem—at least not until after the academic study was published. The researchers' experiment provided a wealth of evidence of what was going on in the hearts and minds of too many Airbnb hosts. The failure of Airbnb's leaders to think about these issues up front meant that they didn't write their own story, but rather ended up playing enablers of discrimination in a story written by Edelman, Luca, and Svirsky.[4] They did not set out to create a discriminatory platform, but they could have done more to prevent one. Thinking about data systemically, in combination with experimentation, could have allowed for more effective leadership.

Today, Airbnb's data science team actively runs experiments to help inform its decisions, and Airbnb has continued to take steps to reduce discrimination on the platform. But for too long progress was slow, secretive, and reactive rather than proactive. Leaders at Airbnb relied too much on their own opinions, informed by intuition. Had they instead sought out information to test their beliefs, they might have been able to avoid a problem for the company and for many of its guests. Leaders who seek out information and test their assumptions by running experiments are better positioned to make informed decisions.

In 2008 the ride-sharing company Uber reached a $10 million settlement on a class-action lawsuit regarding a history of harassment and discrimination within the company. There is ample evidence to suggest that Travis Kalanick, its CEO, created and encouraged a negative work environment, particularly for women and minorities. When the company's new CEO, Dara Khosrowshahi, took over in 2017, he made it clear that diversity and inclusion were core principles of the new Uber. He created a working group on discrimination that had the legal, computer science, and experimental skills needed to build a more ethical firm. Among the members of the working group was Dan Svirsky, one of the authors of the Airbnb study. Today, Uber has come to appreciate that it is better to gather your own data than to wait for others to do it for you.

When leaders have hunches about potential problems in their organization, experiments can prove useful. Experiments also enable leaders to test new ideas and concepts.

A Brief History of Experimentation

In 2002 the Enron Corporation collapsed in what was then the largest bankruptcy in U.S. history. The accounting firm of Arthur Andersen had served as Enron's auditor and had blessed the reporting irregularities that misrepresented Enron's financial condition. At the time, the two of us were working on a paper on conflicts of interest in the auditing industry with the behavioral economist George Loewenstein.[5] Combining our experience consulting and teaching in this industry with our activism aimed at encouraging reform in Washington, we ran experiments testing the hypothesis that when auditors are rewarded for pleasing their clients (by being rehired, providing consulting services, or potentially obtaining jobs with the client) it impairs their ability to provide an independent, or unbiased, audit. We submitted an overview of our work to the *Harvard Business Review* (*HBR*) and ended up with a duo of editors who helped us improve the article. All of the empirical evidence in the paper came from experiments we had run on student research volunteers and on actual auditors.

Like much of the business press, *HBR* had a history of valuing case-based evidence, built around one specific event or organization. It was rare for *HBR* to include experimental evidence in its pages. But our editors were enthusiastic about our arguments and intrigued by the fact that our evidence was based on scientific experiments (fortunately for us, one of them, Gardiner Morse, had worked at the *New England Journal of Medicine,* where experiments had been common for decades). *HBR* now regularly reports the results of experiments, and editors and readers don't find this strange. The leadership community is now interested in what can be learned from experiments.

Earlier in the book we described the influential work of the psychologists Daniel Kahneman and Amos Tversky. While documenting biases in human decision making, they helped connect psychology and economics. They confronted the assumption that humans behaved rationally, a foundational tenet in most economic models. Their work and their collaboration are the subject of Michael Lewis's book *The Undoing Project.* Richard Thaler covers it in his book *Misbehaving,* and you can get it straight from the horse's mouth in Kahneman's *Thinking, Fast and Slow.* In the 1980s economists were in denial about Kahneman's and Tversky's results. Today, behavioral economics is one of the hottest areas of study, and Kahneman has a Nobel Prize in economics. Experiments provided the evidence that persuaded economists to question their assumption of perfect human rationality.

In 2017 Thaler won the second Nobel Prize awarded for behavioral economics. Inspired by Kahneman and Tversky, Thaler conducted experiments cataloguing decision anomalies. His work demonstrated psychological influences on decisions that would not exist if humans were completely rational. These sorts of experiments fundamentally undermined the rationality assumption on which so many economic theories were based.

Through the end of the twentieth century and into the new millennium, Tversky, Kahneman, Thaler, and other early leaders of what today is called behavioral economics reached most of their insights through laboratory experiments. In their book *Nudge,* Thaler and his coauthor Cass Sunstein proposed using our understanding of human decision-making processes to design interventions that would "nudge" people toward better decisions.[6] Thaler and Sunstein don't actually describe many experiments in *Nudge.* Instead, they draw on experimental findings to describe not only the mistakes humans make in everyday life but also how a well-designed decision environment can prompt wiser decisions. Following the book's publication, psychological experiments made their way out of the research laboratory to become a practical tool that influenced millions of real decisions.

Experiments Escape the Laboratory

In 2011 David Halpern and his colleagues convinced British citizens to open their wallets and part with £210 million.[7] The money was put to use paving streets, providing public safety, and doing other good things. It was money that these Britons owed in taxes—money they had failed to pay until Halpern came along. According to Her Majesty's Revenue and Customs, about £34 billion in taxes, or 6.8 percent of all taxes owed (including income and corporate taxes), go unpaid.[8] The British government eventually recovers some of that amount by expending a great deal of time and money pursuing delinquents, but much of the money owed is never paid.

How did Halpern get people to pay up? He sent a letter to a randomly selected subset of tax delinquents informing them that others like them had paid their taxes. He simply added the following lines to the letter for those in the experimental treatment: "We are writing to inform you that we have still not received your tax payment of £___. By now, 9 out of 10 people in your town have paid their taxes. It is imperative that you contact us." The idea drew on research on the psychology of normative social influence, which shows that people tend to fall in line with social norms.[9] If you find out that your neighbors, or people who otherwise have something in common with you, have paid their taxes, you'll be more likely to do so yourself. The results of Halpern's experiment showed the principle's effectiveness with British taxpayers too.

In February 2010, a few months before he became prime minister of Britain, David Cameron laid out a vision for the next age of government, with policies designed to "go with the grain of human nature."[10] Cameron wanted the British government to put the latest scholarly insights to use with the goal of achieving "a real increase in well-being, in happiness, in a stronger society without necessarily having to spend a whole lot more money."

Cameron put Halpern in charge of using the newly emerging field of behavioral economics to fashion tools to help make government run more effectively—including finding ways to get people to pay their taxes. Formerly a psychology professor at Cambridge University, Halpern had left academia to serve in the government. Under Cameron, Halpern founded a small government unit called the Behavioural Insights Team (BIT) and promised he would dissolve the unit if it didn't obtain a tenfold return on costs within two years. The unit's tools built on research from the fields of behavioral decision research (now often called behavioral economics) and social psychology, including ideas inspired by Thaler and Sunstein. BIT was the world leader in using the concepts from *Nudge* to make organizations more effective.

The BIT unit got its start rewriting letters that the government sent to delinquent taxpayers. Drawing on simple psychological insights, BIT was effective at collecting tens of millions of pounds in tax payments. In addition to collecting lots of money, this initial effort served as proof of concept, even for conservative politicians who had been skeptical of the idea of a nudge unit. BIT went on to assess programs in numerous units of the British government, develop better alternatives, and, by using experiments, design and test new interventions.

BIT was such a success that the government's tax collectors created their own nudge unit, leaving BIT to focus on other issues. In the United Kingdom, BIT has worked to increase organ-donation rates, voting rates, employment, diversity, and minority enrollment in universities; to improve energy efficiency, home insulation, road safety, and pension systems; to reduce medical errors; to encourage donations to not-for-profits; and to reduce school dropout rates. Fourteen separate departments of the British government created their own nudge units.[11] And BIT's success motivated governments and other organizations around the world to implement nudges and create nudge units.

Halpern and his colleagues effectively used experiments to test whether seemingly good ideas can actually be viable. As the BIT grew, governments around the globe began replicating it. Canada, Singapore, Denmark, the Netherlands, Peru, and Australia are among many nations that have established offices or agencies staffed by social scientists who help use behavioral insights to improve policy.[12] The U.S. government created its own Social and Behavioral Sciences Team in 2015. The office conducted experiments that, among other things, examined the most effective approaches to disseminating information about government programs, such as income-driven repayment programs for student loans and educational benefits for veterans.

In 2018 the Foundations for Evidence-Based Policymaking Act passed with bipartisan support in Congress during a time when Democrats and Republicans found little else to agree on. The act establishes guidelines for evidence-based decision making at all levels of the U.S. federal government. Federal agencies hire the social scientists in the Office of Evaluation Sciences to help them design and conduct experiments to test the optimal design of systems, communications, and services. Their impressive approach also integrates openness at every stage. They publicly preregister their experimental designs and share the data from their experiments, regardless of how they turn out.[13] They also seek to share their insights with the world by publishing them. This sort of openness allows others to benefit from the insights and outcomes generated by experiments conducted in other parts of government.[14]

The last chapter introduced you to the first step in the innovation cycle at Netflix: take your innovative idea and farm for dissent by collecting critiques and ideas for how to improve it. The second step in that cycle is relevant to this chapter: test it out.[15] That is, figure out how you can run a test that will give you data to inform your decision. Technology firms like Netflix and Amazon have discovered how easy it is for them to experiment with changes to their platforms that would allow them to test how to nudge consumers. They routinely experiment with the layout of web pages, the design of their products, the wording of their advertising, and much else. According to Jeff Bezos, "Our success at Amazon is a function of how many experiments we do per year, per month, per week, per day."[16] Experimentation allows companies to fine-tune their product offerings to maximize their effectiveness and appeal. Today, experiments are ubiquitous in the high-tech world, with Google alone running over ten thousand experiments each year.[17]

Why Experiment?

Leaders confront decisions on a daily, even hourly basis. How can we improve our online platform? Should we screen job applicants without seeing their pictures or names? Should we tell customers the full price of a ticket up front or advertise a lower price and add on extra fees later, when they're about to pay? Should we assess employees one at a time or in comparison with one another?

Leaders might make such decisions based on intuition and experience. They might solicit advice from a specific manager within the firm and defer to their judgment, or they might hire an expert from outside the firm. Leaders regularly ask us for advice. When we give it, we try to base it on the best evidence from published research. In addition, we often recommend that the leader conduct their own experiments to test the new ideas against the status quo using a randomized, controlled sample of employees or customers. This allows the organization to find out if the idea generalizes to their industry and see the magnitude of the effect for themselves. Unfortunately, in our experience many corporate leaders do not yet appreciate the value of experimentation. Oddly, it can be easier to convince a company to roll out a new program worldwide than to conduct a simple experiment that would determine whether the program will work.

Leaders often make the mistake of following their intuition or the assessment of a consultant when they could test the idea instead. This is one more example of the type of leadership overconfidence we discussed in detail in chapter 4, which extends to being overconfident of the advice they get from experts like us. A better strategy is to find the best sources of advice for a problem and to test the advice to verify its effectiveness.

We also suspect that many advisers are reluctant to have their recommendations tested rigorously. These advisers may actually discourage leaders from conducting experiments to evaluate the merits of their proposals. Consulting firms want clients to believe their recommendations are effective. Our discussions with leading consulting firms suggest that many want to appear to be at the forefront of behavioral economics but do not want their clients to be able to measure the value of their advice. Under no circumstances would advisers want to be confronted with a client's request to refund their consulting fees if a proposed change is ineffective. Financial advisers rarely want clients to compare their advice with other investment strategies, such as putting money in index funds. Within companies, project managers often prefer to subjectively assess a project's performance rather than measure it against the clear benchmark that experiments provide. In these cases and many others leaders should demand the use of experiments so that they can find out whether the advice they are considering is effective.

Max led a team working to help an insurance firm that wanted to change the negotiation strategies of thousands of claims adjusters in over one hundred countries, involving tens of billions of dollars per year. We developed a set of proposals that the company enthusiastically implemented in a complex change effort. The intervention included encouraging more honest handling of claims by the insurance company, making fairer first offers, training claims adjusters in dozens of countries, and changing the mindset of what defined an effective claims process. Max repeatedly recommended testing the ideas on a smaller sample of claims adjusters. The organization's leadership was eager to implement the recommendations from Max and his team but was reluctant to test them first. We think that the decision to not experiment was a mistake.

Too many leaders follow their faulty intuitions about what changes in their organizations will be most effective. Wise decision leaders are confident enough to admit what they don't know, design an experiment to test competing alternatives, and identify the best option. When we want to introduce a change, why not do so in a manner that allows us to determine whether the change is actually effective? Failing to experiment wastes organizational resources and impedes learning from the strategies we try.

What a Leader Needs to Know

When the leaders at Penn Medicine and Geisinger Health System wanted to increase vaccination rates, they understood the value of experimenting. They weren't social scientists, so they sought the advice of Angela Duckworth and Katy Milkman—leaders of the Behavior Change for Good project based at the University of Pennsylvania. BCFG connects organizations with ideas from a network of leading scholars, well beyond the University of Pennsylvania.[18] The project identifies lots of ideas from lots of scholars on how to change people's behavior for the better—for example, how to persuade people to get their flu shots—then tests them in dozens of experiments at the same time. Most of the ideas they test have proven effective in other, different contexts.

So why test again? While we know a lot about what might work to some degree in some contexts, we know less about which proven ideas translate to a specific context (such as vaccine uptake), how strong the effect will be, and how long the effect will last—all very important in making a wise leadership decision. When testing ideas, the Behavior Change for Good project implemented a wide variety of interventions—for example, reminding people with text messages, quizzing people about health behavior, putting them in competition with people in other regions—and tracked vaccination rates.

Notice that the leaders of Penn Medicine didn't need to know how to execute an experiment. What they needed to know was that even if they got the best advice possible from leading behavioral scientists, there would still be value in testing. Why? Because there are always questions about the generalizability of findings from one context to another. Many who thought they knew how the experiment would turn out were disappointed. In the end, it proved difficult to increase vaccination above the 42 percent baseline.[19] The most effective treatment only increased vaccination rates to 46 percent with two simple text-message reminders.

More and more of the students coming out of economics, psychology, and professional schools are graduating with the skills to design experiments, and leaders can tap into their expertise. Technology firms are creating platforms that make it easy for their managers to devise and execute experiments even when they don't have sophisticated methodological and statistical skills. What leaders most need is an appreciation of the power of experiments.

What Makes an Experiment?

Experiments have three essential features. First, every experiment has a dependent measure—an outcome of interest. Second, the independent variable creates different experimental conditions. Finally, and most distinctively, experiments assign individuals to conditions at random.

Selecting a dependent measure is essential to specifying the purpose of an experiment. David Halpern wanted to influence payments of delinquent taxes. He knew he could measure and track the tax payments made by British citizens selected to receive his letters.

Halpern predicted that a small wording change in the government's warning letter could encourage delinquents to pay their taxes. The letter's wording was his independent variable. He inserted a single paragraph into the letter and changed nothing else. This simple manipulation is essential to clean causal identification. Halpern might have been tempted to introduce other messages threatening or cajoling the delinquents. If he had, his letter may have been more effective, but the experiment would have been less useful because it would have made it difficult for him to determine which of the many messages affected tax payments.

Random assignment is the sine qua non of an experiment, and it would be difficult to overemphasize its importance. Random assignment is the best way to achieve equivalence between those in the experimental and control groups, making them as similar as possible before the treatment manipulation and allowing for a clean test of the independent variable's effect. For Halpern, random assignment was as easy as randomly selecting some tax delinquents to receive his special letter rather than the standard letter. He also knew that he had a natural control group: the deadbeats who would not get his letter. If you are testing which of two website formats will encourage customers to linger longer, it would be simple to randomly assign visitors to see one of the two formats and measure the duration of their visits.

Sometimes, however, random assignment is difficult or unethical. You cannot randomly assign people to cultures or genders or races. You cannot randomly assign children to families or students to fields of study. If you want to study the effects of something you cannot randomly assign, you may be tempted to control for differences between groups. If you find a difference between genders, say, in how much women and men earn, you might attempt to rule out educational background as an explanation by statistically controlling for years of education or by comparing men and women matched on educational attainment. But because you cannot randomly assign people to condition, it is always possible that the difference is accounted for by a confound—and you can never control for all of them. In the case of gender, the long list of possible confound variables includes differences in physiology, dress, brain structure, hormonal influence, socialization, body size, longevity, and many more. Your inability to account for every possible confound complicates your ability to identify a single independent variable as being uniquely able to explain any difference.

Is It Ethical?

Experiments sometimes conjure up negative associations. Some people think of Nazi doctors who performed horrific surgeries on their prisoners during World War II. In 1947 the Nuremberg Code sought to prevent unethical research. Nevertheless, the outrageous Tuskegee syphilis study, which the U.S. Public Health Service ran for a staggering forty years, from 1932 to 1972, followed four hundred poor Black men with syphilis and withheld treatment. Dozens of study subjects died, and many spread syphilis to their wives and children, just so that the investigators could learn more about the "natural history" of the disease. Governmental and research organizations in most countries have put safeguards into place to prevent such studies.

Experiments are powerful tools that can be used for beneficial or unethical purposes. In 2013, soon after the creation of Harvard's Behavioral Insights Group, Max, the group's co-chair, found himself attending meetings with government officials of the many emerging nudge units around the globe. These officials were interested in working with members of the Harvard group to create experiments that might improve the functioning of their governments. At one particular meeting Max agreed to be part of a small Harvard contingent that met with a behavioral unit of the Singaporean government. When he heard the officials present the initiative and ask for advice on using experiments to test their ideas, he had trouble believing his ears: the Singaporean officials wanted to encourage native Singaporeans to have more babies, without nudging non-native Singaporeans living in Singapore to do the same. To Max, this goal was too close to broad definitions of genocide. Max's objection did not stop the officials from conducting experiments aimed at selective procreation. The problem wasn't the use of experimentation but the program's goal.

To take another example, U.S. Census officials serving under the Obama administration met with members of the Harvard Behavioral Insights Group in December 2016 to seek advice on how to use experiments to improve the accuracy of the census. Many of us decided not to engage with these well-intended public servants because they could not guarantee that the incoming Trump administration wouldn't seek to identify those eligible for deportation using improved data. Indeed, in 2018 the Trump administration, as part of the census in 2020, tried to add a question asking U.S. residents about their citizenship status. The U.S. Supreme Court blocked the move. In July 2020 four states—Iowa, Nebraska, South Carolina, and South Dakota—were sharing driver's license data with the Census Bureau to help the Trump administration determine residents' citizenship status.[20] To many, this effort recalled how Nazis used demographic census information to round up Jews and Roma.

Like arithmetic, statistics, writing, and artificial intelligence, experimentation is a tool that can be used for good or for ill. While some leaders have used experiments to pursue unethical objectives, the experimental method is not inherently unethical. For some, ethical concerns center on the use of random assignment, which they contend treats people like guinea pigs. This concern might lead some to object to a random assigning of people to Treatment A or Treatment B. However, most people find nothing objectionable about trying out a new idea on some customers while maintaining existing practices for others. Rather than a well-reasoned argument, experiment aversion can appear to be an intuitive, System 1 reaction that leaders can solve by how they describe their experiment.[21]

Consider, for example, a hospital seeking to contain the spread of infection by implementing safety procedures. One proposal would put posters around the hospital with reminders of the procedures. Another proposal would list the procedures on the back of employees' hospital-issued ID badges. Which is more effective? The hospital's leadership could guess and pick one option to implement system-wide. However, it is possible they will choose badly. If experimentation provides data that helps leaders select the more effective plan, it could save lives. In this context, as in many others, experimentation can help leaders make decisions that are wiser, more effective, and more ethical.

If the idea of running an experiment makes you squeamish, reflect on your reaction and try to make sense of it. If you are open to the idea that organizations should sometimes try out new ideas, replacing outdated approaches and figuring out how to accomplish their work more effectively, then you should be enthusiastic about using experiments. Experiments provide evidence that helps leaders think systematically about what to try and how, about testing new ideas on small numbers of people, and about looking at trial data systematically to help inform larger decisions. Experimentation is simply a method for trying new ideas in a systematic manner and learning what works.

As a leader, you may be called on to justify your use of experimentation and explain it to a skeptical public. The best reason is that experimentation can help your organization better fulfill its mission. Experimentation can help you serve your customers by providing the information, products, and features they want. Experimentation can help to devise policies and systems that improve the happiness, effectiveness, and productivity of your employees. Experimentation can help you identify the most effective tools, policies, and practices.

Some objections to experiments result from a misunderstanding of their use. After learning about the various experimental conditions, people imagine that assignment to an undesirable condition would feel unfair. Some argue that, instead of running an experiment, leaders should simply implement the best policy. We would agree wholeheartedly if only they knew what it was. Most of the time experimentation can help establish what the best policy actually is. Lacking evidence, leaders would simply be speculating about which policy is best. And as we have already shown, intuition is an imperfect guide. Evidence from experiments can help leaders overcome their weaknesses and make better decisions.

7

Negotiate for One and All

We are routinely amazed by the amount of work that other people are willing to do—procuring and cooking food, bringing the food to us, and cleaning up afterward—in exchange for a shockingly small percentage of our salary. The wonderful institutions that facilitate this trade are restaurants. In turn, restaurants trade with suppliers for the food they serve rather than growing it themselves, and they trade with other people to cook and wait tables. At the same time, one of the cooks might trade with a daycare facility to watch her child while she works at the restaurant. That's just a short list of the most obvious trades that allow us to get our lunch. Trades allow parties to exchange goods or services in return for something of value to them, such as money. Each time we enter such a transaction, we are creating value, which tends to make all parties to the trade better off. These "gains from trade" may represent the most magical source of value creation in economics.

Thanks to the scope of the trades they make, leaders often have the opportunity to create a great deal of value. At a macro level we can see this in the creation of value through trade between countries. Free-trade agreements tend to benefit all countries involved by promoting efficiency.[1] Each country can specialize in what it produces most efficiently, then sell or trade those goods for other goods that would be more expensive for it to produce. Each country gains by focusing production on areas where it has a comparative advantage.

For example, the United States exports more computers than it imports and imports more cars than it exports. In the aggregate, Americans are better off with such trade than they would be without it. Just as we benefit from the profusion of restaurants that provide a variety of lunch options more cheaply than we could prepare them, global trade gives consumers access to a wider selection of goods at lower prices. It can increase competition for companies that might otherwise control domestic monopolies. Free trade also increases the ability of one country to learn from others. Finally, free trade reduces armed conflict because greater commercial exchange increases mutual familiarity, understanding, and interdependence. Countries rarely go to war with their key trading partners.

In 2016, rebounding from the 2008 recession, the United States was experiencing a terrific economic expansion. The development of a series of international free-trade agreements under the Obama administration was central to this expansion, including the Trans-Pacific Partnership. However, the details of any trade agreement and how it is implemented can affect the degree to which each party claims the value that the deal creates. These details require negotiation to apportion the benefits of trade, both between nations and within them. Within any country the benefits of trade are rarely evenly distributed. There will be some individuals, companies, and regions who are worse off as a result of the trade deal, even if they are outnumbered by those who are better off.[2] Those who are hurt are often in industries and markets in which another country produces better or cheaper products. Free trade is costly to less efficient domestic producers who lose business. In the United States the Democratic Party historically has objected to trade agreements opposed by domestic labor unions.

In 2016 Donald Trump inherited a set of United States–China bilateral trade agreements that created net value for both countries. The agreements probably offered more value for China than for the

United States. China, for example, required foreign companies to have a Chinese partner before they could enter Chinese markets. China also often required non-Chinese companies to have their intellectual property "inspected" by the Chinese government, a process many believed led to theft through imitation and piracy. It might have been appropriate to renegotiate the terms of the arrangement. Instead, Trump chose to initiate a trade war that proved more costly for the United States than for China. Trump's strategy reduced trade, destroyed value, and overall made both countries worse off.[3]

All major business schools teach that the ability to both create *and* claim value is the key to negotiation success.[4] While any trade negotiator should care about how much they gain for themselves, wise leaders also focus on how to create the most value to be shared. In his single-minded pursuit of beating the other side, Trump repeatedly failed the United States by foregoing opportunities for value creation. We can reach value-creating agreements in marriage, sales, job negotiations, and trade deals by understanding the other side and making mutually beneficial trades. Leaders also have the opportunity to create value within their organizations by encouraging the pursuit of mutual benefit.

Leading Value Creation within Your Organization

Imagine you are spending a Friday evening with your significant other, who happens to be named Terry. You haven't made any plans but decide that a restaurant followed by a movie is a fine idea. Terry suggests Restaurant A, which you reject and counter with Restaurant C. Both being reasonable people, you compromise on Restaurant B. You agree that the meal is good but not great. Over dinner you discuss movie options. Terry proposes Movie 1, and you counter with Movie 3, which Terry rejects. Again, both of you are reasonable, so you compromise on Movie 2. Like dinner, the movie is good, not great. On the way home it becomes clear that Terry cared more about the restaurant choice, you cared more about the movie choice, and you both would have preferred the combination of Restaurant A and Movie 3 over what you chose, Restaurant B and Movie 2.

In this trivial example of negotiations within the "organization" of your partnership, you failed to make trade-offs across issues. If you had, each party could have gotten what they wanted on the issue most important to them. The value of finding such trade-offs may be the most important lesson from the entire field of negotiation. A well-prepared negotiator should know how important each issue is to their own side and should be thinking about how important each issue is to the other side. Wise agreements make the most of the potential benefits of trade by conceding on relatively unimportant issues in return for more important ones. Identifying what you care about and learning about what the other side cares about allows you to create value based on these differences. If they care about an issue much more than you do, let them have what they want. But don't *give* it away; instead, trade it for something that you care about more. If you actually care about the other side's well-being, you have all the more reason to create value. To be clear, creating value is not just a nice thing to do; it's what negotiators *should* do to increase the size of the pie that the parties have to divide.

Value creation is generally more complex in the negotiations that occur within organizations. In particular, leaders have a responsibility to coordinate value-creating trades between individuals, groups, and divisions in their organization. That essential leadership function—to get troops marching in the same direction—grows complicated when the troops are at odds with one another. Internal conflict is especially likely in conglomerates whose divisions operate autonomously.

General Electric is one of the more successful modern conglomerates. Indeed, it was the world's most valuable company (as measured by market capitalization) in 2000.[5] From its flagship product, the electric lightbulb, GE expanded into markets as diverse as financial services, jet engines, health care, and electric power generation. Such diverse divisions can easily operate at cross-purposes, and this internal warfare can be enormously costly for organizations. Leaders must negotiate the terms of constructive cooperation.

When we teach students about intraorganizational negotiation, we often use negotiation simulations. Max was inspired to write El-Tek by a real conflict within GE.[6] Like GE, the fictional El-Tek is a decentralized organization with various divisions and product groups. Each division operates autonomously. To keep multiple divisions of El-Tek from competing for the same external business, the firm defines each division's markets.

As the simulation describes, El-Tek's Audio Division developed a new magnetic material called Z-25 that was useful in its audio products. It soon became apparent that the magnet had potential beyond audio components. While Audio was interested in the magnet's potential for external sales, it also wanted to use the magnet to improve the sound quality of its audio products and gain an edge on its audio competitors. But El-Tek also had a Magnet Division, which asserted that it should be the obvious producer and seller of the magnet. The Magnet Division insisted it could produce the magnets at a lower cost than Audio could and noted that company policies prohibited the Audio division from selling magnets outside of El-Tek.

In our negotiation classes, we assign our students to represent either Audio or Magnet and invite them to try to negotiate an agreement in pairs. One obvious solution would be for Audio to sell Z-25 to Magnet as an intellectual transfer within the company. But if Magnet sells Z-25 to Audio's competitors, that could undermine Audio's ability to benefit from its innovation. Thus as the two divisions prepared to negotiate, there are two questions at stake. First, how much money (or what royalty rate) will the Magnet Division give to Audio for the technology? Second, for how long will the Magnet Division agree to withhold the product from Audio Division's competitors?

In El-Tek, those representing Audio know the value of keeping the technology away from competitors for various amounts of time. Those representing Magnet know the value of the external market and the cost of losing sales within the audio industry for various amounts of time. If the parties looked at the problem from just their division's perspective, Audio would want a longer restriction, and Magnet would want a shorter restriction. From the perspective of the broader corporation, the parties should try to figure out what would earn the overall corporation the highest profits over the long term. The payoffs specify that Audio would gain more from the first six months of protection than Magnet would lose, but after that Magnet would start losing more than Audio would gain. Thus the best solution from the corporation's perspective would be to restrict the Magnet Division from selling to outside audio companies for six months.

We have used the El-Tek case to teach negotiation to thousands of students around the world, from undergraduates to seasoned executives. Only a minority of our students find the maximum value-creating strategy of restricting the Magnet division for six months. Those who do find the efficient deal usually use one of the following tactics. We present them in descending order, starting with the one that is simplest but requires trust, and ending with the tactic that depends the least on trusting the other side.

Build Trust and Share Information. Many of our students say nice things to their negotiating counterpart to try to set a positive tone in the El-Tek simulation. Often they say they want to do what is best for the overall corporation. Some mean what they are saying; others don't. Among those who do mean it, some know how to implement the idea, others don't. The easiest way for the two parties to maximize value is to fully share information, including the costs and benefits to each of them from various levels of restrictions. This information makes it clear that six months is best for the corporation because it creates the greatest total profit.

Despite its clear benefits, information sharing can be difficult for negotiators, particularly when they fear exploitation. Negotiators often believe that any information they share about their situation or goals could be used against them. If they assume the pie is fixed in size, they see little reason to share information. But there's clearly room for improvement when negotiators in the same company fail to share information that could have helped them.

Ask Questions. If parties weren't worried about claiming value and understood that they could create more value by making trade-offs across issues, sharing information would be an obvious solution. But trust is often lacking, and parties typically care about claiming value as well. As a result, sharing all of your relevant information will not always be wise. What else can you do? One easy answer is to think about what you don't know that the other side may know and then ask some questions.

Too many negotiators, viewing negotiation simply as an opportunity to influence the other party, focus more on talking than listening. When the other side is talking, they focus on what they are going to say next rather than on listening for new, valuable information. In contrast, value creation requires that negotiators focus more on understanding others' interests.

Asking questions increases the likelihood of learning useful information from the other side that will allow you to find wise trades and create value in the process. Here are some useful questions that the Audio division might ask the Magnet division in the El-Tek negotiation:

- What value would you get out of such restrictions?
- How much is six months of restriction worth to you?
- How much is twelve months of restriction worth to you?

Our students too often fail to ask such questions because they are too focused on persuading the other side. Chapter 5 emphasizes the enormous potential benefits of capitalizing on disagreement. Nowhere is this truer than in negotiation, where differences in what parties value create opportunities for mutually beneficial trades. So before you start to negotiate think about information you would like to have, ask the questions necessary to collect this information, and listen carefully to the answers.

You might be thinking, "In the real world, the other side won't always answer my questions." True, but they are more likely to answer if you ask than if you do not!

Give Away Value-Creating Information. If they won't answer your questions, consider giving away some information about the trades you are willing to make. For instance, disclosing that you, the Audio division, want to restrict sales to other audio competitors outside the company will help the Magnet division understand the interests underlying your positions. By initiating information sharing you open the door for both parties to benefit from the social norm of reciprocity. Providing a bit of information also limits your risk: if they *don't* reciprocate, you can stop giving information.

Many negotiators are initially uneasy about giving away information because they equate it to giving away power. But we aren't recommending that you make a concession; rather, we're suggesting that you stay open to learning about differing interests across issues. Strategically disclosing information allows you and the other side to create value. If they are skillful they can use your information to discover mutually beneficial trades. Even if they are less skillful you can get the benefit of reciprocation and jump-start the information-sharing process.

Negotiate Multiple Issues Simultaneously. When going into the negotiations, should you start with the easy issues or the hard issues?

The important issues or the secondary issues? Many negotiators have strong opinions about the order in which issues should be dealt with. We disagree with most answers to these questions, advising you rather to negotiate multiple issues simultaneously. When you reach agreement on one issue at a time, you eliminate the opportunity to make trades across issues. A buyer and seller may be in conflict on each issue, but they are unlikely to be equally passionate about each issue on the table. The relative importance of issues to negotiators becomes apparent when they discuss them simultaneously.

When you negotiate, insist that nothing is settled until everything is settled. It may be necessary to talk about issues and tentative deals one at a time. But when it comes to actually agreeing on issues, we advise you to consider and compare package offers—agreements that cover all the issues in the negotiation. Package offers help the other party trade aspects of your offer that are problematic against counteroffers that show flexibility on some issues while making strong demands on others. For example, if you and Terry had discussed both the dinner and the movie options simultaneously, it would have been easier for you to agree on the superior options for your date.

Our MBA students often ask us for job negotiation advice. Perhaps the most common challenge they confront is when a prospective employer asks them to specify a minimum salary requirement. We advise them to honestly answer that their salary depends on other issues, including bonuses, benefits, the initial job assignment, promotion prospects, job title, location, and more. It would be a mistake to negotiate an agreement on salary without considering these other issues.

Make Multiple Offers Simultaneously. Most negotiators make just one package offer. When the other side says no, you learn little.

Instead, consider making multiple package offers simultaneously—about three packages that are similarly attractive to you. The three package offers will differ on the specific issues, but as a whole you should be indifferent between them.

What if your negotiating counterpart rejects all of them? Follow up by asking, "Which offer do you like the most of the three?" or "If I were to iterate on one of them, which is the best package to start with?" The other party's preference gives you valuable information about where to find the issues they care about most so that you can create more value. When you make multiple package offers simultaneously, you appear more flexible and signal that you are interested in understanding the other party's preferences and needs. So the next time you are preparing to make an offer, consider making three.

Search for Post-Settlement Settlements. Imagine you've just reached a negotiated agreement, but you aren't entirely satisfied with it, and you suspect your counterpart isn't either. Consider asking them whether they would be willing to work with you to find a better agreement, stipulating that they would do no worse than what they just agreed to. Any new agreement you reach must be better for you, better for them, and, if you're in the same organization, better for the organization as well.

The pioneering negotiation scholar Howard Raiffa came up with this idea, which he called a "post-settlement settlement."[7] He suggested that after two negotiators have reached an agreement, they could employ a third party to help them search for a better agreement—one that is better for both parties than the agreement they already reached, or, in the language of economics, one that is Pareto superior. Each party would have the right to veto the new package proposed by the third party and keep the original agreement. Raiffa argued that when negotiators have the assurance of being able to keep their existing agreement, they are likely to be more willing to allow a third party to create a superior agreement, or post-settlement settlement.

This process doesn't necessarily require the help of a third party. Rather, as one of the parties, you might adapt the language proposed by Deepak Malhotra and Max in their book *Negotiation Genius*:

> Congratulations! I think that our hard work has really paid off in a great deal. We're probably both ready to call it a day. I'm wondering, though, whether you might be open to an idea. Though we're both satisfied with the agreement, there are inevitably aspects of the deal that I wish could have been better for me, and you probably feel the same way about other aspects. What if we spent a few more minutes talking about potential improvements to the deal that would make both of us better off? Maybe we've already exhausted those possibilities—but it might be a good idea to see if there are any stones left unturned. Of course, if we can't find ways to make both parties happier, we'll be even more confident that our signed agreement is the right one for everyone. If you're up for it, let's give it a try.[8]

A post-settlement settlement offers a final attempt to create value without either party running the risk of losing value by sharing information. As Raiffa writes: "[W]e must recognize that a lot of disputes are settled by hard-nosed, positional bargaining. Settled, yes. But efficiently settled? Often not . . . they quibble about sharing the pie and often fail to realize that perhaps the pie can be jointly enlarged. . . . [T]here may be another carefully crafted settlement that both [parties] might prefer to the settlement they actually achieved."[9]

These six tactics should help you create value in negotiations. While some of them may appeal to you more than others, we encourage you to be ready to use whichever tactics best fit the situation.

Generally, those presented first will require more trust between negotiators, while the last couple require virtually none.

The Role of Leadership in Value Creation. Many of our students who have participated in El-Tek have significant leadership responsibility yet fail to identify the value-maximizing strategy built into the simulation. Moreover, they are generally surprised to learn after the fact that they could have created value by trading off issues. Somewhat shockingly, they assumed that the pie was fixed in the important negotiations they participated in before attending our class. In most complex negotiations the pie is not fixed, and trade-offs are possible. Debriefing the El-Tek simulation opens the eyes of these experienced, intelligent leaders to the opportunities to expand the pie that they have missed throughout their careers.

Not only have these executives failed to find value-creating trades in their own negotiations, but they have also failed to create environments in which their subordinates and their subordinates' subordinates are likely to find value-creating trades. They may have even destroyed value by encouraging competition within the firm. Although there can be benefits to fostering internal competition that might stimulate innovation, it can also push people to claim rather than create value—making the overall organization worse off. This sort of dysfunctional competition was partially responsible for Kodak's decline in the 2000s. Managers who reigned over Kodak's film businesses stood in the way of developing digital cameras, which threatened to make their products obsolete.[10] Kodak was wealthy and successful in 1975 when one of its engineers invented the world's first digital camera. But entrenched interests blocked the company from taking advantage of the opportunity.

Let's reimagine El-Tek, this time with you atop the organization. The presidents of the Audio and Magnet divisions report to you. How would you like them to negotiate a resolution over the magnetic concept? You and other leaders placed in this role quickly see that they would want the two division heads to put their data together and find the solution that creates the most aggregate value. As CEO, you would want the parties to prioritize sharing information to create value over hiding their information in an attempt to claim value for their own division. How do you do this? In part by creating an internal culture of sharing information to create the most value for the organization. While keeping some information hidden may make sense when personnel are negotiating with an outside organization, the CEO should want to make it unacceptable to risk destroying value by hiding information from a colleague.

A CEO can also provide training in value creation, which is part of the negotiation curricula at all leading business schools (not just Berkeley and Harvard). This training promotes the benefits of sharing information as well as the other value-creating strategies discussed above. Most importantly, having the top leader focus on the benefits of collaboration can go a long way toward creating a value-creating organization.

Creating Value by Lowering the Costs of Resolving Disputes

Making trades across issues typically exemplifies value creation, growing the pie, and allowing each party to get more of what they care most about. But value can also be created by reducing the costs of resolving disputes. Suppose that Amit makes a driving error and gets into a minor accident with Jermaine. If they quickly negotiate for Amit to pay Jermaine's $850 repair bill, they will be better off than if they spend hours arguing about fault, hire lawyers to threaten each other, and eventually resolve the disagreement with Amit paying Jermaine $850 (or $800 or $900, depending on which lawyer "wins"). Speedy resolution avoids the costs of continuing to negotiate. Thus even though only one issue was at stake—the amount Amit would pay Jermaine—an efficient process would be less costly and less unpleasant. When parties spend time and money on resolving a dispute, their final outcomes are worse as a result of these costs.

Consider how insurance works. A policyholder pays an insurer a premium; in return, the insurer pays the cost of a claim to the insurer in the event of an insured event (for example, a car accident). The concept is simple: Premiums are paid in one direction and claims in the other. In mutual insurance companies the policyholders collectively own the company. When a member files a claim, the payment comes from the pool of resources paid by all policyholders; any remaining profits are returned to members as dividends. Historically, members of mutual insurance companies felt like part of a community; as a result, premiums and claims were paid simply and honestly.

Now let's consider a more costly (and often more common) episode of resolving an insurance claim. A policyholder buys a policy to insure their car at the lowest price that they can find through an online search. For the first three and a half years the policyholder pays premiums on time and gives the topic of car insurance little thought. Then the policyholder has an accident and files a claim, one involving damage to the car, medical costs, and pain and suffering from the accident. The cost of repairs and medical bills is clear, but the value placed on the pain and suffering caused by the accident is far less clear. After the insurance company offers an amount that the policyholder believes is too low, the policyholder hires an attorney. As the case gets more complicated, the insurance company hires an external legal firm to represent it as well. After two and a half years of disputing, the parties reach a settlement ten days before going to court. The policyholder has to turn over one-third of the amount that the insurance company eventually pays to their attorney.

Notice that the parties could have reached the same settlement thirty months earlier, saving both sides considerable time and money, lower emotional costs to the policyholder, and greater odds of a continuing customer–provider relationship. All of the costs of an unnecessary dispute reduce value to both parties.

Why do insurance companies spend billions of dollars fighting over the payment of claims? One answer is that some policyholders lie about their claims, either fabricating the claim itself (for example, staging an accident) or exaggerating the magnitude of the loss. Using artificial intelligence, many insurance firms advise insurance companies on how to detect fraud. Meanwhile, policyholders, their lawyers, and insurance activists argue that insurance companies work ruthlessly to minimize what they pay on claims rather than simply pay the fair value of all claims. In his book *Delay, Deny, Defend,* the Rutgers Law School professor Jay Feinman accuses insurers of delaying payments they owe claimants, denying claims they know should be paid, and aggressively defending against legitimate claims.[11] Together, these problems result in a vicious cycle in which each side tries to defend itself against the expected unethical conduct of the other with its own unethical conduct. This dysfunctional pattern increases the costs of resolving even legitimate claims.

In recent years, "insurtech," short for insurance technology, has emerged as a potential remedy to these entrenched patterns in the industry. Insurtech moves much of the business of insurance online. Imagine a world in which a claimant can simply enter the details of their claim online in five minutes or less and find a payment from their insurance provider in their checking account after another five minutes. Not long from now this kind of technology is likely to be widespread. In a simple version of insurtech, consumers compare policies across providers and purchase policies online. More dramatically, some insurtech firms aim to handle the claims process efficiently by using artificial intelligence in place of human interactions to assess the validity of claims.

Some insurance executives fear that policyholders will be more likely to commit fraud if they don't need to even speak to a claims adjuster. Others, like the insurtech company Slice Insurance, believe a digital process is key to reducing fraud and creating a more trusting system.[12] Slice sells short-term insurance policies to people who run home-based businesses, such as renting out their home on Airbnb. Slice is also a technology provider to more traditional insurance companies that see the future of online insurance. Slice creates value in the claims process by reducing the friction of fighting its policyholders. Aware that most people are less likely to lie in a video than in writing, Slice asks claimants to create a short video using their phone's camera to describe the claim. Because ambiguous questions such as "What was it worth?" tend to generate self-serving answers, Slice instead asks claimants to answer specific questions, such as "What did you pay for the lost object?" or "What does it cost to replace it on Amazon.com?" Claimants also report who else knows about the loss, since accountability to others decreases deception. Finally, Slice aims to pay the vast majority of claims in minutes rather than months.

By being honest and inducing honesty, Slice is taking the friction out of the insurance claims process, thereby reducing the value destruction so common in this industry. The founders of Slice saw a business opportunity to capitalize on by being honest and inducing honesty in others. Slice also found a way to create value, even in what appeared to be single-issue, zero-sum negotiations over insurance payouts.

The Trade-off between Cooperation and Competition

On April 20, 2010, an explosion aboard the Deepwater Horizon offshore oil-drilling rig in the Gulf of Mexico killed eleven workers. The explosion ignited an enormous fireball visible from as far as forty miles away, and it burned out of control until the Deepwater Horizon sank two days later. It left an open well at the seabed that gushed 4.9 million barrels of oil into the Gulf of Mexico, making it the largest marine oil spill in history.[13] The result was one of the world's greatest environmental disasters, decimating natural habitats, recreation, fishing, and tourism over a vast area.

Deepwater Horizon was owned by a company called Transocean, which leased the rig to British Petroleum, which in turn contracted with Halliburton. Divided in their authority and pursuing conflicting goals, the companies found themselves at odds over safety. To earn bonuses, BP managers needed to save the company money and beat deadlines. Accordingly, they regularly made decisions that prioritized speed over safety. For example, they omitted a costly, time-consuming test that could have forecasted the disaster that occurred. On the morning of April 20 managers from BP congratulated themselves on their safety record and flew home. Later that day the well blew out, the Deepwater Horizon was engulfed in flames, and eleven crew members lost their lives.

A focus on site-specific performance fostered an atmosphere in which decision makers ignored the cooperative benefits of managing risk, according to an MIT case study of the accident.[14] Because BP compensated managers for performance at their own site, "there was little incentive to share best practices on risk management among the various BP exploration sites."[15] There were "downsides to a system in which a centralized body had little oversight over the setting of performance targets, particularly in an industry where risk management and safety were essential to the long-term success of an oil company."

Innumerable studies have scrutinized the causes of the explosion and spill. Many have noted the power of performance incentives that neglected the larger issues of safety and corporate liability. Formal investigations pinpointed the failure of organizations involved in the disaster to coordinate their efforts: "Federal investigators have been shocked at the apparent lack of cooperation and coordination among the various companies and government agencies involved in the Deepwater Horizon disaster."[16] In the end, the disaster cost BP an estimated $144 billion, not including the toll on the environment and local economies.[17]

Narrow-minded self-interest can be a tragic, unintended consequence of offering incentives for individual performance and ignoring the potential for collective benefit. Organizational life offers innumerable choices between self-interest and the greater good. Should you implement safety checks, or should you meet your own production timetable? Should you speak out against corruption, or should you accept a bribe? Should you take time to teach a coworker what you know, or should you complete your work assignment quickly?

Competition is natural and useful in many contexts but value-destroying in others. Whether people in your organization choose the selfish shortcut or support the team will, to a great extent, be driven by the tone you set at the top and the culture you instill. If, like the managers at BP or those at now-defunct Enron, you provide generous compensation and praise to star performers, employees are likely to get the message that the smart thing to do is pursue their self-interest. If, on the other hand, you emphasize teamwork, collective benefit, and incentives for the group, people are likely to think about their choices differently. When an organization seeks the collective good, the decision to pursue one's self-interest is not smart but selfish and greedy. Indeed, the pursuit of self-interest at others' expense lies at the core of moral transgressions as diverse as lying, cheating, stealing, and exploiting others.

Our industry, academia, seeks to pursue the greater good by creating new knowledge and training the next generation of leaders. Our universities compete with each other and with others for the best students. We also compete to sell executive education programs, hire the best faculty members, and get the top spots in university rankings. At the same time, we cooperate in other areas by routinely and enthusiastically sharing our research with other universities. We are happy to tell our competitors about our pedagogical insights. And we cooperate by training and mentoring PhD students in the hope that our competitors will hire them when they graduate. Such costly cooperation with competitors may seem bizarre, yet it creates value by allowing scholars to discover ideas more effectively, thereby improving the quality of education across universities and producing and disseminating knowledge.

We have both taken part in discussions and disagreements about whether one university should cooperate with another. Should we let our competitor know about our research before it is even published? Should we tell them how excellent our junior faculty colleague is given that they might try to hire them away from us? Should we share our data files, exposing ourselves to the risk that someone could use them to conduct their own research? The tension between cooperating and competing is strong in these situations, yet we strongly endorse cooperation. Cooperation allows you to capitalize on gains from trade, which remains the simplest and most magical method of value creation and mutual gain.

The gains from trading ideas and scientific knowledge are at least as valuable as those to be made from trading food for money in the restaurant industry. Cooperation with others in your industry may increase the chances that others will reciprocate with cooperative moves of their own. They might also seek you out as a partner in the future. Most important, you can take pride in making the world a little better by choosing to cooperate rather than compete.

8

A Higher Purpose

"There is one and only one social responsibility of business—to use its resources and engage in activities designed to increase its profits so long as it stays within the rules of the game," the Nobel Prize–winning economist Milton Friedman wrote in 1970.[1] He argued that companies hire managers to maximize profits (within the bounds of the law) and that focusing on worker happiness, reducing discrimination, improving customer satisfaction, helping the local community, or improving the broader environment should only be a leadership goal if it would lead to improved profitability. In fact, it is unethical for corporate leaders to focus on social responsibility if such concerns would reduce profitability, Friedman believed. That is because, he argued, only people, not corporations, can have responsibilities. Corporations exist to allow shareholders to make money. It is up to shareholders, not to the corporations in which they invest, to decide whether they want to spend their earnings on socially responsible activities.

Friedman's perspective developed as a social movement within economics, and many academics taught their students in business, government, and law schools that leaders have a legal obligation to focus on maximizing profits, not other socially responsible motives. Of course, this was never actually the law; it was Friedman's opinion. His view of managers' moral obligations grew out of economic conceptualizations of rationality and profit maximization: economic models of behavior built on assumptions of simple self-interest. This view also held that organizations would be better off if they maximized corporate profitability. Friedman admitted that some organizations, such as schools or hospitals, might choose values and goals other than profit maximization. But, he argued, unless an organization expressly states its goal to follow some other objective, leaders should assume that profit maximization is its sole objective. Whether the firm causes social good or social harm was not Friedman's concern.

Although his opinion was influential, Friedman was an outlier—a hard-core free-market ideologue. While economists built their theories on assumptions of simple individual rationality, and many market economists accepted profit maximization as the goal of corporations, Friedman made the jump from economic goals to ethics and social responsibility. This leap defied a long history in philosophy that spelled out what constitutes moral behavior. Ethicists have typically defined morality as what is best for the broader community, society, or world. Rooted in the work of Jeremy Bentham, utilitarianism is a moral philosophy developed by John Stuart Mill, Henry Sidgwick, Peter Singer, Joshua Greene, and others. Utilitarianism suggests that ethical behavior is the behavior that maximizes collective value—not just the value of an individual, organization, or group of shareholders. While many philosophical perspectives differ from utilitarianism, most ethical philosophies believe in valuing a broader set of concerns than the family, the clan, or the corporation.

In many ways Friedman's view of the corporation parallels sociobiologists' accounts of how cooperation functions within the family or clan and competition outside the family or clan. Sociobiology, a field that many trace to E. O. Wilson's 1975 book by that name, attempts to explain social behavior with evolutionary principles. The field highlights the evolutionary benefits of cooperating with close kin, even if that means undermining your individual self-interest.[2] People who cooperate with other family or clan members make personal sacrifices for the benefit of the group; as a whole, the tribe is better off as a result of these actions—more likely to survive and reproduce. Our long history of cooperating within family and clan members may explain why our modern behaviors are aimed more at benefiting ourselves, our family, and other members of a relatively well-defined in-group than they are at benefiting broader communities and society at large.

To Friedman, the clan is the corporation, and profit maximization is what ensures the corporation's health and survival. Incentives and structures encourage organizational members to move beyond their self-interest to engage in behaviors that help the overall organization and to refrain from behaviors that benefit broader constituencies at the organization's expense. But when we switch the conversation from profit maximization to ethics, the value we place on broader constituencies changes dramatically.

The philosopher Peter Singer argues that while evolutionary biology may well explain why we focus on the family or clan, it does not justify this focus from an ethical perspective. In fact, other words for valuing your clan above others include tribalism, racism, and nationalism. Similarly, employee incentives and theories like Friedman's that validate a self-interested role for the organization in society help to explain why corporations might act against their social obligations, but it does not make such behavior ethical. In his book *The Expanding Circle* Singer argues that if our goal is ethicality, we shouldn't be limited by sociobiological tendencies shaped more by evolutionary pressures toward reproductive fitness over broader views of morality. If our goal is to act morally, evidence suggests that our System 2 thinking will guide us toward equality for all, toward valuing the utility of all people equally, toward impartiality, and toward justice—many of the ideals that socially responsible leaders seek to achieve. Ethicality requires us to maximize value for a broader and broader circle of people.

Our perspective in this chapter (and this book more generally) is broadly compatible with utilitarianism. But for those who might have disagreements with aspects of utilitarianism (more on those disagreements soon), we simply ask you to consider the collective good as we discuss how leaders can make more ethical decisions and lead others to make more ethical decisions—often without sacrificing the leader's or organization's other goals. Indeed, we seek to empower you and those you lead to make choices consistent with your values. We will consider how easily we contradict our own ideals and offer tools to help do better. These tools use our knowledge of psychology to make it easier for people to make choices that balance their interests, including ethical ones.

Moving beyond Profit Maximization and Reducing Racism

In the midst of the Covid-19 crisis, on May 25, 2020, George Floyd, a Black man, was murdered by a Minneapolis police officer while other officers looked on. Horrified and enraged by Floyd's murder, millions of protesters rose up across the country and the world. Demands to reform policing broadened to seek institutional reform of systems that perpetuate race discrimination. And rather than repeating Friedman's mantra that their only moral obligation is profit, many corporations released statements condemning racism, made donations to the Black Lives Matter cause, and reflected on their existing practices.

Many changed from seeing racism in their organizations as a peripheral concern to directly confronting the issue. One survey found that a large majority of Americans favored CEOs responding to the protests with statements about ending police violence (84 percent), promoting peaceful protest (84 percent), elevating diversity and inclusion in the workplace (78 percent), condemning racial inequity (75 percent), and condemning police killings of unarmed Black people (73 percent).[3] And corporations began to take action. Here is a sample of such responses:

- PepsiCo created a five-year, $400 million initiative to increase Black managerial representation by 30 percent and to double business with Black-owned suppliers.
- Quaker Oats, a subsidiary of PepsiCo, announced it was ending its Aunt Jemima breakfast foods brand, widely viewed as an archaically stereotypical image of a Black woman.
- Adidas committed to hiring at least 30 percent Black or Latinx workers for new positions.
- PayPal committed to bolstering its internal diversity, equity, and inclusion (DEI) practices and invested $530 million in supporting Black-owned and minority-owned businesses in the United States.
- Comcast committed $100 million toward DEI efforts and partnerships with civil rights organizations.
- Multiple technology firms turned down profitable opportunities connected to racial profiling. IBM stopped investing in facial recognition software. Microsoft and Amazon stopped sharing their software with police.
- Ben and Jerry's ice cream, a company that historically has shown concern for DEI, further committed itself to go beyond profit maximization and to fight against systemic racism. Its actions include advocating for a bill investigating slavery reparations and a bipartisan task force on police reform.
- NASCAR banned the Confederate flag from its races.[4]

Some corporations had already pursued racial justice well before George Floyd's murder, but the burst of action prompted by Floyd's death was unprecedented. Many leaders had been complacent, allowing immediate profit imperatives to crowd out other considerations. In the summer of 2020 many of them became aware for the first time that they and many other nice people within their organization unknowingly engaged in so-called ordinary prejudice; even in the absence of intentional bias their organizations had been part of a system whose structures effectively discriminated in ways that were unintentional.[5]

Many people behave in racist and sexist ways without having bad intentions, and leaders need to manage these unintentional discriminatory behaviors. Research on ordinary prejudice starkly documents the harms created by implicit cognition. The psychologists Mahzarin Banaji and Anthony Greenwald have shown how easily we all tend to favor our groups over others without being aware of our preferences; that is, our preferences are implicit in our behavior rather than following explicit declarations of intent.[6] Research on ordinary prejudice highlights that we have attitudes and associations about men versus women, Whites versus Blacks, and often "our" group versus "their" group. Banaji's and Greenwald's use of the term "ordinary" clarifies that the regular thought processes we use to categorize, perceive, and judge information lead to systematic preferences for our group. Banaji and Greenwald have developed, along with the psychologist Brian Nosek, an online test, the Implicit Associations Test, or IAT (www .implicit.harvard.edu), which offers to assess our implicit attitudes, including those that we may even explicitly deny.

The IAT cannot tell you whether you are racist or sexist; instead, it measures the strength of an implicit association between two pairs of categories, such as Male/Female and Science/Arts. We generally think of our attitudes as being within the scope of our conscious awareness and control. But research on implicit attitudes documents that when we meet someone our minds automatically activate stereotypes of the person's race, sex, and age.[7] Even people with strong egalitarian values can't help relying on stereotypes. People of European ancestry are often less comfortable interacting with people of African ancestry than with other White people.[8] Most White people have no conscious ill will toward Black people, but they are less comfortable around people who seem different from themselves.

Closely related to ordinary prejudice is a vast literature on in-group favoritism, or tribalism. Tribalism is an enormous challenge confronting leaders, including leaders in our industry. In 2019 Harvard successfully defended its admissions policies in federal court against charges that the university discriminated against Asian applicants. The lawsuit was the most recent chapter in a long-standing argument that Harvard imposes quotas limiting the number of Asian Americans accepted for admission. The case was complicated, and we agreed with the judge that Harvard was not guilty of the allegations (of course, Max may be guilty of being affected by conflict of interest on this assessment). Nonetheless, the case forced Harvard to reveal many embarrassing details of its admissions policies.

To begin with, tangential to the subject of the lawsuit, Harvard admitted to providing legacy preferences in the admissions process.[9] Legacy admission refers to the tradition of admitting the unqualified or marginally qualified children of alumni, donors, and other well-connected individuals. In our view, legacy admissions, which may constitute 10–15 percent of freshman classes at most Ivy League schools, are among the most shameful practices of elite universities. The typical Harvard University legacy student is significantly less qualified than the average nonlegacy student in every relevant area but sports.[10]

In court Harvard argued that legacy consideration "helps to cement strong bonds between the university and its alumni."[11] The university also argued that donations from parents of legacy admits allow

Harvard to provide financial support for its neediest students. But legacy preferences have the perverse effect of favoring the demographic category most well represented among the alumni population: wealthy Whites. Evan Mandery, a 1989 Harvard graduate and a professor at the John Jay College of Criminal Justice in New York, argues that "there's no plausible moral claim that accidents of birth that advantage you—like being a man, or being a white man, or being a rich, white man—should give you a *further* advantage."[12] Other critics of legacy admission practices argue that it is unethical for organizations with such a public purpose to discriminate against people who aren't part of the tribe in order to keep the tribe happy.[13]

By contrast, the University of California does not consider legacy when making admissions decisions. This more ethical policy may help to explain why the University of California system has so effectively opened opportunities for talented children of poor families. A quarter of undergraduates at UC Berkeley (where Don teaches) are the first person from their families to attend college, and 38 percent grew up speaking a language other than English at home.[14]

Legacy admissions policies may sound like a niche example of in-group favoritism that isn't relevant to your own work. But we ask you to take a moment to recall the last time you did a favor for a friend, a relative, a friend of a friend, or some other acquaintance. Perhaps you helped someone find an apartment, get a job, connect with a potential mentor, or work around some institutional obstacle. Most of us are not only happy to provide such help, but also view it positively. Lending a helping hand is a good thing, right? But consider that we are typically asked for favors from people like ourselves—people from our church, our alma mater, our family, or colleagues. Such people are likely to have things in common with us. In particular, they are likely to share our race, gender, and social class. In truth, it is easier for us to identify with people who are like us than with people who are different from us. As a result, White people end up opening doors for other White people. When those in the majority allocate scarce resources (such as jobs, college admissions, and mortgages) to those similar to them, they privilege their in-group.

Research repeatedly shows that banks are less likely to approve mortgages for African Americans than for Caucasians, even after controlling for a variety of factors, including house location, applicant's income, and creditworthiness.[15] One reading of this finding is that banks and their employees are hostile to African Americans. Sometimes that may be true. A more insidious possibility is that White loan officers may be too lenient toward unqualified White applicants, doing them favors by approving their mortgages. If mortgage funding is limited, less remains available for nonwhite applicants.

Research documents a shift over the past few decades from so-called old-fashioned racism to modern racism.[16] Old-fashioned racism manifested itself as explicit hostility toward Blacks and members of other minority groups. Modern racism is more subtle and may be more common in organizations. All of us need to be aware that racial attitudes can affect our judgment without our conscious awareness and in ways that are at odds with our intentions and values. Implicit prejudice and modern racism highlight a compelling and important domain in which moving from System 1 to System 2 can empower us to behave in ways that are more consistent with the values we profess.

Confronting Ethical Challenges More Deliberatively

When leaders read about egregious cases of corporate wrongdoing in the media they often infer that such ethical breaches are not a concern for them or their organization. After all, they view themselves and their employees as good people. This belief is quite consistent with journalists' focus on identifying and describing the bad apples accountable for tragic events. The bad apples account helps clarify why the so-called nice people ignored implicit racism in their organizations: since the nice people weren't malicious or overtly racist they didn't see a need to address racism in their organizations—at least, not until after George Floyd's murder. Shining a spotlight on bad apples obscures the blame that the rest of us deserve for contributing to racism and other forms of unethical behavior. In fact, the vast majority of unethical behavior occurs without anyone's conscious intention to behave badly.

Cognitive biases allow nice people to engage in unethical behavior without realizing that they are doing so. This lack of awareness constrains willful control over our ethical decisions, leading to *bounded ethicality*.[17] The term nods at bounded rationality—the human limitations that impede us from being perfectly rational in pursuing our goals.[18] Similarly, bounded ethicality encompasses psychological processes that lead people to engage in ethically questionable behaviors that fall short of their own values, including ordinary prejudice and in-group favoritism. It applies more broadly to decisions that not only harm others but also are inconsistent with our conscious beliefs and preferences. System 1 thinking fosters the biases created by bounded ethicality and in turn leads to decisions that deviate from our personal moral standards.

Deliberation generally leads to more rational decisions than intuition or gut feelings. Deliberation can also lead to more ethical decisions—ones that create more collective value. Consider the footbridge dilemma, a variation of the more famous trolley problem in philosophy. In the footbridge dilemma, a runaway trolley is barreling toward five people standing on a track. You are standing on a bridge over the track next to a railway worker who is wearing a large backpack. You have the option of saving the five people by pushing the man (and his heavy backpack) off the bridge and onto the track below. If you push him, he will die an instant and painless death, and his body will

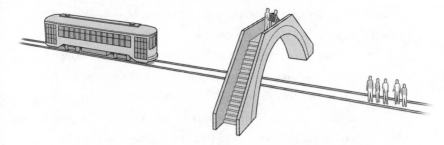

Figure 8.1. The footbridge dilemma (Illustration by Robert Shonk)

stop the trolley to save the five people on the tracks.[19] If you do nothing, the five people will die. By the way, in Trolleyland you face no legal concerns for pushing or not pushing the man. Would you push him?

Confronted with this choice, most people say they would not push. Their reasons are typically at odds with utilitarianism, which would save five lives at the cost of one. In explaining why they wouldn't push, people typically say that others have rights, that pushing would be murder, and that the ends don't justify the means.[20] But these moral intuitions are fragile and vulnerable to trivial contextual variations. Change the scenario slightly, and people's feelings shift. Suppose that instead of standing on a bridge the man is on a side track to which you can divert the trolley with the flip of a switch. In this scenario, most people are more comfortable sacrificing one life to save five.

Because even utilitarians bring real-world baggage to their decision making, some might hesitate to push the man off the bridge. After all, the norms that govern our societies create second-order value. That is, if it is okay to push people off a bridge, people will no longer be free to walk where they choose; our society would become more fearful. Thus utilitarians value rights, freedoms, and autonomy because these concerns have long-term value. Other philosophers reject this second-order logic as a basis for valuing rights, freedoms, and autonomy, arguing that they have intrinsic worth. Deontologists, for example, require that we value justice as an end in itself and that we base moral action on whether an action is right or wrong, independent of the consequences. Deontologists argue that no one has the right to push the guy off the bridge. Meanwhile, libertarians believe that individuals have personal freedoms and autonomy that outweigh utilitarian concerns; they too would be against giving the guy a push.

Deontologists and libertarians, have argued with utilitarians for decades. While we find these arguments fascinating, we have no expectation of resolving them. Our goal is simply to guide you to do as much good as possible while making the adjustments you deem to be appropriate vis-à-vis your concerns about rights, freedom, and autonomy in specific situations. Regardless of the value you place on justice, rights, and whether the ends justify the means, we think we can provide you with pathways for doing more collective good. As it turns out, the decisions recommended by utilitarianism align with other philosophies most of the time, since they share the goal of doing more good and less harm. Utilitarianism is not focused simply on saving lives; it is more broadly focused on maximizing pleasure and minimizing pain (creating value) across all sentient beings.

During the Covid-19 pandemic, leaders in politics and health care sought guidance for ethical dilemmas. To take an extreme example, imagine that a hospital has limited medical equipment to save either a ninety-eight-year-old person with cancer or a healthy young person of fifteen. Because some people have more pleasure left to enjoy in life than others, saving their lives will create more value than saving the lives of those with less upside potential (to state it crassly). Many factors affect a person's future expected value in life, but age is an obvious one. Most people faced with this painful choice would reluctantly favor saving the fifteen-year-old. Utilitarians view such dilemmas through the lens of quality-adjusted life years, or QALYs. Philosophers in the effective altruism movement aim to save as many life years as possible, adjusting for the expected enjoyment those years will create.[21] Without knowing anything else about the fifteen-year-old and the ninety-eight-year-old, most decision makers would estimate that they would save more QALYs by saving the fifteen-year-old.

Unfortunately, such definitions aren't just theoretical, existing only in Trolleyland. As the Covid-19 pandemic reached the United States in 2020, Max and his colleagues conducted an experiment aimed at giving hospital physicians and other medical decision makers guidance on how to identify the fairest way to allocate limited medical supplies.[22] We asked one group of participants to imagine a physician who must decide whether to give the last available ventilator in the hospital to the sixty-five-year-old coronavirus patient who arrived first or to the twenty-five-year-old coronavirus patient who arrived moments later. They were told to assume that the patient who gets the ventilator will live to age eighty, that the one without the ventilator will die from their illness, and that the ventilator was equally capable of saving either patient. We then asked them, "To what extent is it morally acceptable for the doctor to give the last ventilator to the younger patient?"

About half of the participants said it would be moral to give the ventilator to the younger person, and their answers were strongly associated with their age. In accordance with self-serving biases, while 66 percent of people eighteen to thirty found it moral to give the ventilator to the younger person, only 33 percent of people sixty or older agreed.

We asked another group of participants the same question but first invited them to put themselves into the equation. To encourage more deliberative thinking, we adapted the philosopher John Rawls's "veil of ignorance." Rawls argued that we can make more ethical decisions when we stand behind a veil of ignorance—that is, when we don't know our role in the situation—whether we are rich or poor;

Asian, African American, or Caucasian, etc. Following Rawls, we asked this group of participants to imagine they had a 50 percent chance of being the older patient, with fifteen years left to live if they are saved, and a 50 percent chance of being the younger patient, with fifty-five years to live if saved. We first asked them what they would prefer the decision rule to be under this veil. Not surprisingly, about three-quarters said they would want the doctor to follow the utilitarian principle, giving the ventilator to the younger patient with more years to live. Once they had thought through what they would want under the veil, we then asked whether they thought it would be moral to give the ventilator to the younger person. Now a higher percentage (62 percent) found the utilitarian course of action to be more ethical. And consistent with the veil-of-ignorance technique it was the older participants who changed their views the most, now focusing on saving as many QALYs as possible. In fact, with the veil added, age no longer predicted who found it acceptable to give the ventilator to the younger person.

Table 8.1 tells us something about fairness principles. "First come, first served" may be a fair, valid principle, but so is the idea of saving the most QALYs. Which rule is fairer? When participants consider the situation from the perspective of both claimants for the ventilator under a veil of ignorance, the majority, even among older participants, indicated that saving more life-years is fairer—it would be their choice if they didn't already know who they are. The implication for your leadership is clear: Where there is disagreement over the right principle, invite others to consider the problem from a variety of perspectives. How would they feel about it if they were a customer rather than a salesperson?

In chapter 2 we discussed the superior ability of System 2 (deliberative thought) to generate more rational decisions than our intuitive System 1 thinking. Adapting this dual-processing logic to the realm of

Table 8.1. Percentage of Participants Favoring the 25-Year-Old
by Age and Condition

	Control Condition	Veil of Ignorance Condition
Age 18–30	66%	62%
Age 31–59	47%	61%

moral reasoning, the philosopher Joshua Greene finds ample evidence that System 2 thinking is less prone to bias and leads to better and more moral decisions than System 1. The veil of ignorance is one empirically documented tool for moving people toward System 2 thinking and improving the ethicality of their decisions. But it's not the only tool we have.

We also know that humans make better, more ethical decisions comparatively rather than individually. As noted in chapter 2, Max and his colleagues Iris Bohnet and Alexandra van Geen found that when people are evaluating employees one at a time they favor men for mathematical tasks. In the absence of a clear comparison standard people are more likely to rely on intuitions biased by gender stereotypes. But when they compared two applicants people focused more on job-relevant criteria, were more ethical (less sexist), and hired better candidates. More broadly, thinking about the multiple options (such as who should get the ventilator) will lead to greater ethicality than intuitive assessments will. As a leader, you can help others make choices that are more consistent with their own values by inviting them to consider multiple options.

In the midst of the Covid-19 pandemic Roger Severino, the director of the Office for Civil Rights at the U.S. Department of Health and Human Services, exemplified the hazards of considering one option rather than thinking comparatively when making critical decisions. He wrote in a March 28 news release, "Our civil rights laws protect the equal dignity of every human life from ruthless utilitarianism. . . . I want to make sure in this time of crisis, we don't forget the foundational principles that are part of what makes America so special. . . . That we do care for everybody, that every person in America deserves equal dignity and respect."[23] Severino announced that his office was opening a series of civil rights investigations of those who pursue utilitarian policies. Severino declined to provide any help for those facing dilemmas regarding the allocation of scarce treatments. Leaving such decisions to frontline physicians increases their stress and inevitably results in inconsistent decision making among doctors, thereby exacerbating fairness concerns. Moreover, shifting from careful consideration of difficult trade-offs to ad hoc decision making by individual physicians for each patient is likely to result in less deliberative choices.

Finally, given that our intuitions lead us to make less moral decisions, another tool for promoting System 2 thought is to precommit to the goals that you seek to achieve before you have a specific decision in front of you. In his research with his fellow researchers Linda Chang, Mina Cikara, and Iris Bohnet, Max found that when employers first think through the criteria that define a good employee before considering a specific candidate, they make less sexist decisions and hire better employees.[24]

If we want to be more ethical and create more value for the broader world, we need to empower our wiser and more ethical decision-making processes. These are likely to come more from deliberation than from intuition, from precommitment rather than impulsive choices, and from choices made between options rather than options considered one at a time. They also depend on having the courage and foresight to consider both the intended and potential unintended consequences of our goal-directed actions. As a leader, you have a special obligation to consider how others may respond to your directives.

Auditing Your Leadership and Your Organization

Without realizing it, many leaders create environments that unintentionally encourage unethical behavior. There are a number of areas in which leaders can audit their organizations to identify opportunities to encourage greater ethicality.

Do whatever it takes. Leaders may unwittingly encourage unethical behavior when they demand results at any cost. Do not fool yourself into thinking you are empowering your people to act independently when you tell them to do whatever it takes. After all, there may be many ways to achieve a goal, some of which have unacceptable costs or side effects. Autocrats and crime bosses may obfuscate their culpability by delegating their dirty work. Engineers can make systems appear more efficient by dumping untreated toxic waste. Purchasing can reduce costs by outsourcing production to sweatshops in other countries. Law enforcement personnel can quell uprisings by beating, tear-gassing, or shooting peaceful protesters.

Leaders will be tempted to disavow their culpability for unethical actions taken by subordinates. In June 2020 reporters asked U.S. Attorney General William Barr about his role in an incident in which law enforcement tear-gassed a crowd of peaceful protesters near the White House so that President Trump could walk across the street to be photographed in front of a church while holding a Bible. "I'm not involved in giving tactical commands like that," Barr said, defending himself in an interview. "My attitude was get it done, but I didn't say, 'Go do it.' "[25] Like Barr, leaders sometimes deny responsibility for unethical actions by blaming intermediaries who do their bidding.

In 2011 Professor Lucas Coffman of Boston College reported the results of an economic game called the Intermediation Game that shed light on the psychology of delegation.[26] At its heart, the Intermediation Game is simply a dictator game. In the classic dictator game, a "dictator" has complete autocratic control over how to divide some

amount of money between herself and a "receiver." Hundreds of studies have reported the results of dictator games played by thousands of
study participants. The most notable feature of these results is that
dictators take less than 100 percent of the money and share some of
their money with powerless recipients. Dictators who take most or all
of the money for themselves appear greedy, and observers will punish
them when possible.

The Intermediation Game inserts an intermediary between the
dictator and the recipient. The dictator has the opportunity to sell the
dictatorial profits to the intermediary. When they do so, the dictator
is able to charge the intermediary handsomely for the right to exploit
the recipient. The dictator's profits increase, and recipients receive
less. Most notably, dictators are judged less harshly for delegating
their dirty work to an intermediary than when they do the dirty work
themselves, even though it is obvious that the dictator was benefiting
as if they had chosen to take the money.

What is the leadership lesson here? It can be tempting to delegate
the distasteful details to those lower in the hierarchy, but wise leaders
will anticipate potentially unethical consequences of goal pursuit.
Leaders who want to empower others to make wise choices must be
cognizant of the methods they use to achieve their aims and aware of
their influence on others. You cannot assume that if someone has
moral qualms about carrying out an order that they will object. Empowering others to act ethically is easier when they have the permis-
sion, confidence, and power needed to voice their own ethical
concerns without fear of retribution or censure.

Conflicts of interest. Real estate agents make money from transactions. They earn nothing by warning you to consider your ability to
afford a big mortgage payment. Merger-and-acquisition professionals
also make money when the acquisition closes, not when they give
good advice that prevents bad deals. Too many financial advisers earn

fees based on transactions rather than on giving their clients good advice. Surgeons typically earn more when they operate than when they don't. Physicians get paid for recommending patients for clinical trials. And attorneys who get paid by the hour earn more when their clients' legal battles persist. All these conflicts of interest occur when a professional is torn between receiving personal benefits and doing what is best for their clients, their patients, or society at large.

In most cases these conflicted professionals are nice people who do not want to believe they are corrupt. Nevertheless, evidence suggests few of us are truly immune. We ourselves have probably been guilty of favoring job candidates whose research affirms our own work. We want to think of ourselves as being honest and objective, even though we are quite familiar with (and have contributed to) the literature that questions the objectivity of our judgment.

We all also tend to extend this false belief in our objectivity to the advice we obtain from professionals whom we trust. Although we worry about the degree to which corporate lobbying may corrupt other politicians, we reelect our own representatives. Although we may worry about the degree to which pharmaceutical salespeople can influence other physicians, we trust our doctors. And although we worry about how incentives may bias the behavior of real estate agents, when our agents urge us to increase our offer on a house we are likely to comply. In truth, even if our elected representatives, doctors, and real estate agents are well-intentioned, ethical people they may find it difficult to provide truly objective advice when it would cost them personally.[27]

When important industries end up the focus of government oversight for possible conflicts of interest, the industries typically concede by offering to provide public disclosures of their potential conflicts. Disclosure of donations to politicians and political parties is at the center of most campaign-finance legislation. Disclosure of auditors' conflicts of interest is also a main focus of the Sarbanes-Oxley Act of 2002, which was created in the aftermath of Enron and other corporate scandals. Disclosure is an easy compromise since it does little to disrupt the existing system: those with a conflict of interest simply need to report the conflict, and they often do so in places that few people read (for example, in small print in the endnotes of a report). The Society for Professional Journalists, the American Medical Association, and the New York Stock Exchange all have codes of ethics requiring disclosure of potential conflicts of interest. All of this disclosure is interesting and reassuring to many. Unfortunately, it is not very effective.

In fact, Don's work with his colleagues Daylian Cain and George Loewenstein provides evidence that disclosure can actually *increase* professionals' bias.[28] We paired up experimental participants, assigning one to the role of estimator and the other to the role of adviser. All participants first estimated the amount of money held in each of six jars filled with coins. Each adviser inspected the jars closely, while the estimators could see the jars only briefly and from a distance; thus the advisers had better information on which to base their estimates. Advisers then advised their clients (the estimators) about the amount of money in the jars. Estimators were rewarded based on the accuracy of their estimates. Advisers, however, had a conflict of interest: the more their estimator overestimated the amount of money in the jar, the more they earned. Thus advisers had an incentive to mislead the estimators into guessing high. In addition, half of the estimators learned about the advisers' pay arrangement; the other half did not. Advisers whose conflicts of interest were disclosed provided more biased (higher) estimates than advisers whose motives were not disclosed. And disclosure did not motivate estimators to discount their advisers' advice sufficiently. In sum, disclosure led advisers to make more money and estimators to make less than would have been the case without disclosure. This research suggests that professionals forced to disclose conflicts of interest might be more self-serving than those who do not make such disclosures.

If disclosure isn't the answer, then what can be done to address conflicts of interest? Most important, leaders can encourage the professionals in their organization to get advice from people who don't have an incentive for the organization to make a specific decision. For example, get a second opinion on the advisability of the corporate acquisition you are planning from a banker who would not stand to benefit from the deal. Second, recognize that disclosure does not solve conflicts of interest, since even the most honest people are biased. Consider divesting decision makers from the investments, commitments, relationships, or interests that could potentially bias them. When divestment is not possible, consider recusing those with conflicts of interest from key decision-making roles. Third, accept that no one is immune from the pernicious effects of conflicts of interest—including yourself and your advisers. Be ready to admit you might be biased and recuse yourself.

Overclaiming credit. "No sort of scientific teaching, no kind of common interest, will ever teach men to share property and privileges with equal consideration for all," wrote Fyodor Dostoevsky in 1880.[29] "Every one will think his share too small and they will be always complaining and attacking one another."

Ninety-nine years later, in 1979, the psychologists Michael Ross and Fiore Sicoly, working at the University of Waterloo in Canada, confirmed Dostoevsky's dim view of people's ability to share equally—specifically, to share credit—in a study that asked married couples to each estimate their contribution to household activities. On average, the marital partners each thought they contributed more than they actually did in reality.[30] Since this original result, overclaiming of credit for work performed has been demonstrated in many contexts, including academia, athletics, and fundraising.[31] Coauthors of academic papers with four authors, on average, think they each did 35 percent of the work—for a total of 140 percent, far above the accurate 100 percent. In May 2020, at the height of the Covid-19 pandemic, the *New York Times* reported that 45 percent of fathers believed they led the majority of the homeschooling, while 80 percent of mothers credited themselves.[32] Consistently, people tend to honestly believe they contributed more to an enterprise than they actually did.

Greater clarity regarding contributions can reduce egocentric biases. Part of the reason it is so common for partners in a collaborative project—whether that is homeschooling or a joint venture—to believe that they did the majority of the work is that they focus on their contributions. Getting more explicit about exactly which efforts matter can help bring interpretations into alignment. For example, couples will find it easier to agree on what percentage of the vacuuming each one does than what percentage of the housework each one does. Housework is a broad category with ample opportunities for interpretation. Leaving the category vague allows the spouse who washes the clothes to focus on that, whereas the one who always makes the bed will naturally think of that more easily.[33] You can help reduce conflict and improve coordination in groups you lead by inviting team members to consider others' perspectives, and maybe even ask them to guess what percentage of the work others think they are doing on specific tasks.

Why do joint ventures so often end in disappointment? Partners may be skeptical that the other side will do its share.[34] As a result, they contribute mediocre talent to the enterprise rather than their firms' best talent, which they save for projects in which the firm is fully invested. Adding in the tendency of each side to overclaim credit for its contributions, it becomes apparent that each side will feel entitled to contribute less than half of the effort and resources needed. Each side then views the other side's behavior as unfair and justifies their own behavior, souring the relationship.

There are ways for leaders to manage this overclaiming challenge. When Max and his colleagues asked Harvard MBA students to estimate how much of the work they did in their study groups, the average group's estimates added up to 139 percent of the 100 percent of work completed. When we instead first asked each participant to think about the contribution of each member, including themselves, the average total of the claimed work done by the group fell to 121 percent.[35] Unpacking individual contributions didn't eliminate overclaiming, but it did reduce the magnitude of the bias. As our study shows, leading group members to take the perspective of each other member can reduce overclaiming and improve group performance. Recognizing the widespread tendency to overclaim has important implications for a group's viability. When a colleague makes a claim that you find unbelievable, before arguing consider that you might also be guilty of overclaiming credit—and that it is more likely that your colleague is biased rather than dishonest. Your information is selective and colored by your perspective. Consider what others know that you don't and how their own egocentric perspectives, like yours, may have influenced their perceptions.

Conclusion

In 2019, the Business Roundtable, an association of American corporate interests, issued a statement on the purpose of a corporation that looked beyond Milton Friedman's narrow ideology.[36] The statement declared, "While each of our individual companies serves its own corporate purpose, we share a fundamental commitment to all of our stakeholders." These stakeholders include not just a company's shareholders, but also its employees, customers, suppliers, and the communities in which they operate. The statement takes an expansive view of the moral obligations of businesses and those who lead them.

We endorse this expansive view and add that leaders are responsible not just for their own moral decisions, but also for the moral decisions of those they lead. This means you need to do more than simply aim to behave with integrity and tell others to do likewise. Ethical leadership requires an understanding of the psychological processes that keep us from acting as ethically as we intend. Leaders can create structures and incentives that promote value creation for the collective good. Resist the temptation to delegate your dirty work; you may be encouraging others to cut corners by doing whatever it takes to achieve ambitious goals. Moreover, you can broaden your focus from your team or organization to all those affected by your actions, and harness talent to make the world a better place.

Colin Kaepernick's kneeling was not profit-maximizing for himself or his team; Milton Friedman would not have approved. But his decision to kneel was an act of leadership that set the stage for a change in the decisions and actions of millions of others. At first, many passionately endorsed Kaepernick and others criticized him; the *New York Times* called him "the most polarizing figure in American sports."[37] But Kaepernick primed society for change. When George Floyd died under a White police officer's knee, many came to understand the brutality that led Kaepernick to sacrifice his own football career in the pursuit of justice. Leaders make intentional choices with the goal of changing and improving the decisions of others. Ethical decisions create greater good for all.

9

Nudging Toward Better Leadership

During the Covid-19 pandemic of 2020 we got used to standing on painted lines and stickers to create distance between us and other store customers. Following the advice of posters in bathrooms, we sang "Happy Birthday" twice when we washed our hands, and we pumped hand sanitizer as soon as we got home. Basketball rims and nets were removed from courts, and seats were blocked off in waiting rooms.

Each of these changes is a nudge—a tweak to the environment designed to steer us toward making decisions, both for ourselves and for those around us. Nudges are often based on psychological and economic principles. Richard Thaler and Cass Sunstein presented the idea in *Nudge*, which offered a structure for designing more efficient and beneficial organizational and societal systems.[1]

Long before Covid-19, and even before the term "nudge" was popularized, Max, along with his colleagues Jonathan Baron and Katherine Shonk, asked readers of their book *You Can't Enlarge the Pie* (2001) to consider two alternatives:

(a) If you die in an accident, your heart will be used to save another person's life. In addition, if you ever need a heart transplant, there will be a 90 percent chance that you will get one.

(b) If you die in an accident, you will be buried with your heart in your body. In addition, if you ever need a heart transplant, there will be a 45 percent chance that you will get one.[2]

Most people prefer Option (a) so strongly that you might wonder why we would bother to ask the question. The answer is that the U.S. government has maintained an organ donation policy that resembles Option (b), despite the availability of Option (a).

As of 2020 over 110,000 people in the United States were on waiting lists for organs, and more than one thousand were dying each month due to the lack of an available organ.[3] Yet the answer to increasing organ donations is no great mystery. We could easily copy laws passed in Austria, Belgium, France, and Sweden which presume that residents consent to donate their organs upon death. By contrast, in many U.S. states residents must explicitly opt in to organ donation while alive rather than having their consent presumed after death. The federal government could simply change the default. The researchers Eric Johnson of Columbia University and Dan Goldstein of Microsoft Research found that European countries with *out-by-default* programs similar to the existing U.S. system had organ donations rates between 4 and 28 percent, while European countries with *in-by-default* programs had rates between 86 and 100 percent.[4]

The organ donation example highlights just one of the many enormous and costly inefficiencies that affect health, wealth, and education across society—and the ability of nudges to prompt better decisions. But perhaps the domain where nudges have had their greatest success is in the area of retirement savings. Before Thaler published *Nudge* with Sunstein, he worked with his former doctoral student Shlomo Benartzi (now on the faculty at UCLA) on the question of how to get employees to enroll in retirement plans that can provide substantial benefit. They created a program, Save More Tomorrow, that nudged employees to commit to save more by applying a portion of future raises to retirement savings.[5] Save More Tomorrow drew on multiple psychological biases that prevent people from enrolling in retirement programs, including impatience, procrastination, and loss aversion. Our impatience impedes long-term benefits (more money in the future) that require short-term sacrifice (giving up a little money in the present). By failing to save enough for retirement, people act as if they undervalue the future benefits of saving and investing. Save More Tomorrow encourages commitment because people are more likely to choose what they know they *should* do when considering the future rather than the present.[6] The program also eases the psychological burden of a present loss by increasing the savings rate in tandem with the size of one's paycheck. As a result, employees never see their take-home pay decline. The extra retirement savings come from foregoing gains (from pay increases) rather than from a decrease in current disposable income.

Another important feature was making enrollment automatic— giving employees the option to opt out, as in the organ-donation policies in many European countries.[7] Moreover, enrollment need only happen once. (By comparison, long-term improvements in diet, exercise, and study habits tend to require repeated virtuous choice.) In Thaler's and Benartzi's initial study, Save More Tomorrow tripled savings rates in just over two years. TIAA-CREF, Fidelity, Vanguard, T. Rowe Price, and Hewitt Associates have all implemented plans based on Save More Tomorrow. Over 60 percent of large employers in the United States have now adopted automatic retirement-contribution escalation plans.[8] Automatic enrollment in retirement plans and thoughtful program designs that account for psychological barriers to enrollment are now common in national-level retirement systems in the United Kingdom, New Zealand, and Turkey.

From a Story to a System for Improving Decisions

The organ-donation findings and Save More Tomorrow existed before Thaler and Sunstein wrote their groundbreaking book. *Nudge* took a huge leap forward by presenting a structure for designing systems that could lead thousands, even millions, of people to make better decisions.[9] In *Nudge* Thaler and Sunstein argued that decision-making research (reviewed throughout this book) can be used to anticipate the mistakes people will make; and leaders can act as "choice architects" to create the environment to correct for these mistakes and nudge people toward better, more ethical decisions. The authors of *Nudge* emphasize that their approach is libertarian in that it leaves people in control of their decisions—but also paternalistic in that system architects guide people toward wiser decisions.[10]

As we discussed in chapter 2, improving intuition turns out to be difficult. This book has instead advised overriding flawed intuitions with deliberative analysis. We advocate policies robust to human imperfections. A well-designed nudge guides the choices of lazy or biased System 1 thinkers, while also allowing freedom for System 2 deliberation. The nudge concept shows how to create environments in which intuition won't lead people too far astray; as a result, organizations are allowed to take on some of the burden of debiasing from the individual decision maker. *Nudge* provided a simple, powerful framework that fundamentally changed the field of behavioral economics.

Nudge moved from being a book to a social-science movement. The idea enabled governments and other organizations to take a systemic approach to creating positive change on a mass scale. Chapter 6 highlighted the importance of experiments in the UK's Behavioural Insight Team. The ideas for what to test came from social psychology and behavioral economics—from Kahneman, Tversky, Cialdini, Thaler, and others.

By 2014 the BIT unit, along with Singapore's nudge unit, the government of the Australian province of New South Wales, and Harvard's Behavioral Insights Group, organized an annual conference that attracted eight hundred participants. BIT also became a central

Figure 9.1. Nudge units around the world (Behavioural Insights Team [2018])

organizing force that enabled other emerging behavioral insights units to learn what nudges were working across contexts. Governments increasingly saw nudging as a cost-effective alternative to traditional tools such as mandates, bans, economic incentives, subsidies, taxes, and fines. By 2018 the map of active nudge units focused on public policy covered the world (Figure 9.1).

Nudges automatically enroll people in programs designed to reduce poverty, simplify paperwork, and streamline the process of applying for financial aid for college.[11] Cities, states, and countries continue to develop nudge units, and consulting firms now treat them as a new area of practice. Along the way, the UK's BIT team transitioned from being a unit of government to being a profitable consulting firm partially owned by the government.

While numerous corporations, including Merck and Swiss Re, have created nudge units, tech firms have been at the forefront of adopting nudges and carrying out experimental testing. As we described in chapter 6, they found that they could compare the effectiveness of various ideas by crafting and running simple experiments. Even if they lacked sophisticated psychological predictions, they had hundreds of thousands of users. They didn't need to understand the psychology behind people's preferences; they just wanted to know what worked best. Tech firms found themselves working on problems that few could have imagined at the beginning of the millennium.

The result has been systems that are easier to understand and use. This has many benefits, but too many of them go to the companies and too few to their users. YouTube, for instance, discovered the power of defaults when it implemented its autoplay feature. Autoplay makes continued watching automatic. The next video starts playing a few seconds after the last finished unless you take swift action to stop it. When YouTube implemented autoplay in 2015, the duration of users' visits to the site leapt up. Videos and advertisements will keep playing, one after another for up to four hours, unless the viewer takes action to stop them. The change also increased the importance of YouTube's recommendation algorithm that selected the next video based on what was likely to hold the viewer's eyeballs.

Are Nudges the Best Way to Affect the Decisions of Others?

While there are many success stories in which nudges improve decisions, some have questioned whether nudges are the most cost-effective solution to important policy issues.[12] To find out, nudges should be compared against other tools that could have been used to achieve the same change in behavior. For some results, like Save More Tomorrow, the magnitude of the changes and improvements was obvious. For many nudges the absolute change in behavior was far more modest. How can leaders judge the effectiveness of such nudges?

A team of researchers, led by Shlomo Benartzi, John Beshears, and Katy Milkman, set off to find a way to think about the value of nudges in comparison to other available tools.[13] Reviewing the 2015 summary reports of the U.S. and U.K. nudge units, they pinpointed four commonly studied domains: retirement savings, college enrollment, public health, and energy consumption. For each area, they identified a metric to measure the effectiveness of interventions. For example, for energy consumption they looked at household energy use. They then reviewed every paper in top academic journals that measured those metrics from 2000 to 2015 and noted whether the intervention studied was a nudge, a tax incentive, a reward, or an educational program.

The comparison showed that nudges weren't always the most effective ways to change behavior *if money was no object*. Noting the power of monetary incentives, John Beshears once observed, "It's no surprise that if you pay someone thousands of dollars to do something, they will do it."[14] By comparison, nudges are often quite inexpensive.

Consider the problem of getting students to enroll in college. State and federal governments have invested in grants and tax breaks to decrease the cost of college. Colleges also offer financial aid, but to be eligible families have to apply. A 2012 study led by Professor Eric Bettinger of Stanford showed what happens when H&R Block tax preparers prefill the FAFSA—the required federal financial aid form—while preparing the taxes of parents of potential college applicants.[15] They found that every thousand dollars invested in this effort increased enrollment by 1.53 students. In contrast, the *most* effective traditional effort, providing monthly stipends to enrolled students, added only 0.0351 students per one thousand dollars. The difference in effectiveness per dollar differs by a factor of more than forty to one.

The effects of nudges in other domains were also surprisingly strong, although a bit less dramatic. For example, analysis of the comparative effectiveness of different strategies to induce energy conservation found that providing information on how your energy use compares to that of your neighbors reduced energy consumption by about double what could be obtained through traditional education and incentives. For retirement savings, the most effective nudge was more than six times better than other interventions. Nudges reduced the cost of increasing flu vaccination rates by two-thirds. Overall, nudges are a cost-effective way of changing behavior. Clearly, leaders who neglect them may be missing an opportunity.

Are Nudges Overhyped?

Two other researchers, Stefano DellaVigna and Elizabeth Linos (both faculty at UC Berkeley), examined whether the published papers on nudging are creating outsized perceptions of their effectiveness. Their analysis of twenty-six studies published in academic journals—all reporting rigorous experiments with random assignment, a control group, no financial incentives, and a binary dependent variable—provides a more tempered view of the effectiveness of nudging.[16] On average, they observe, these studies show that nudges change behavior in the desired direction by 8.7 percent. But they also noted that nudge units were simultaneously running lots of studies that were not making it to publication. In all likelihood, they speculated, experiments that made it through the publication process might have larger effects—maybe even much larger. This would imply that 8.7 percent was an inflated estimate of the power of nudges as tested more broadly. And because the press promotes the most impressive results of nudges, it is easy to exaggerate their effectiveness.

DellaVigna and Linos next gained the cooperation of two of the largest organizations running nudges in the United States, the UK Behavioural Insights Team's North American office (which was working with U.S. cities) and the White House's Social and Behavioral

Science Team. They identified 126 field experiments that tested nudges on more than 23 million people. Like the studies DellaVigna and Linos examined in the published literature, all the experiments had random assignment, a control group, and no financial incentives. But fewer than 10 percent of these experiments had been documented in a publicly available working paper or academic publication.

In comparison to the 8.7 percent average change in the core outcome documented in the academic research, the average effect found in the 126 nudge unit studies was only 1.4 percent. These results were nevertheless statistically significant, but the nudges were about one-sixth the size of those documented in the published literature. Of the possible causes described above, DellaVigna and Linos conclude that publication bias explains much of the difference in the size of the effects observed. Publication bias results from academic journals' interest in publishing the largest, most surprising, and most impressive results.

Interestingly, DellaVigna and Linos asked relevant professionals to predict the degree to which nudges would affect the dependent variables in studies. Most forecasters, the majority of whom were academic researchers and graduate students, overestimated the impact that the nudges would have on outcomes. Nudge practitioners, by contrast, made more accurate estimates. DellaVigna and Linos concluded that because the academic forecasters were familiar with the published studies, they may have extrapolated the findings in the literature to the broader use of nudging, leading them to overly optimistic expectations.

We believe that Benartzi's, Beshears's, and Milkman's comparison of the cost-effectiveness of nudges as documented within the academic literature remains on solid ground. DellaVigna and Linos highlight the need to be cautious when predicting what future nudges can achieve. Their work also stresses the need to tap the right expertise to identify the right nudge for the right situation. Leaders need to be able to identify what the existing literature suggests about which nudges to test and to understand that institutional constraints may limit the value of nudging. More and more consulting services are offering expertise in behavioral insights and nudging. As leaders purchase this expertise, they should carefully examine the background, rigor, and track records of those designing the interventions.

We also note that just because they are cost effective does not mean nudges can solve every problem. Consider, for instance, reducing carbon emissions. Nudges can be effective, as when informing people of their neighbors' energy usage prompts them to use less themselves.[17] However, they cannot compare with the impact of a substantial carbon tax, the policy many economists endorse to reduce carbon emissions.[18] In principle, there is no reason we could not both nudge and tax. In practice, however, there is a risk that policy makers treat cost-effective nudges as substitutes for more powerful incentives.[19] Especially when carbon taxes are politically unpopular, politicians may prefer the easy solution to the effective one.

The Ethics of Nudging

When Kahneman and Tversky conducted their landmark experiments on judgment and decision-making biases they focused on individual decision makers. With *Nudge*, Thaler and Sunstein shifted the focus toward the decisions of others. Some nudges help people satisfy their own self-interest but others focus on improving societal outcomes. Most nudges have externalities—side effects on parties other than the target of the nudge. For example, when a person saves more for retirement as a result of a default in her organization, later in life she is less likely to need help from family members or to depend on public services. Thus many people benefit when someone saves more for retirement. Similarly, your decisions to live a healthier lifestyle or pursue college education affect loved ones.

Filing truthful tax returns and agreeing to donate your organs upon death are behaviors that are good for society but of questionable benefit to you. Just to be clear, we are in favor of you paying your taxes honestly and donating your organs. But there's a difference between nudging you to do what is in your best interest versus nudging you to do what's best for society. Nudges that focus primarily on helping (1) the target of the nudge, (2) society, and (3) for-profit companies are related, yet conceptually distinct. Here, we review some of the ethical concerns about nudging aimed at each of these three goals.

The ethics of nudging to help people help themselves. It is easiest to justify nudges to get employees, customers, stakeholders, and citizens to do what is in their self-interest. Yet even within this domain there has been backlash against nudging. The most common critiques against nudges, even when they're aimed at helping people, are variations of the "harm principle" and the "epistemic principle."

In his book *On Liberty* (1859) the philosopher John Stuart Mill, a famous utilitarian, argued that people should have the freedom to make whatever decisions they like, as long as they are not harming others. Mill's harm principle is based on his assumption that we can better increase human happiness by letting people decide for themselves what is in their best interest than by letting other people "take the liberty" of deciding for them. He viewed the harm principle as a means toward the utilitarian goal of maximizing collective good (as we discussed in chapter 8) based on what he knew at the time.

Since Mill's day we've learned from social science research that in many contexts it is possible to systematically predict how people can be made better off than if left to their own devices. Thus based on what we know today the harm principle can be at odds with utilitarianism, since people systematically make choices that harm themselves. At times, mild nudges can help people without restricting their freedom to choose. For example, automatically enrolling employees in a retirement plan improves their saving for a pleasant retirement without taking away their ability to opt out. We believe that if Mill were alive today he would approve of nudges like this because they help people without restricting their freedom.

Nevertheless, the paternalistic concerns that flow from the harm principle continue to this day. "The libertarian streak that runs through much of the U.S. recoils at any efforts at manipulation, especially by government," argues the noted psychologist Barry Schwartz. "It is disrespectful. The intentions of government can't be trusted. Neither can its own assessment of what is in the best interests of citizens."[20] Yet Schwartz convincingly argues that libertarians exaggerate the risk that experiments and nudges will lead to greater government control. Nudging can respect dignity and autonomy while also helping people become wiser, healthier, and wealthier.

The epistemic principle, firmly rooted in traditional neoclassical economics, argues that no one knows what is best for them better than the person themselves. Advocates of this principle believe that no government entity, organization, or leader can know more about what a person wants than that person does. As we have documented throughout this book, this principle is simply wrong. Benevolent leaders can identify nudges that make people better off than they would be if left to their own devices.[21]

The ethics of experiments focused on helping society. In many cases behavioral scientists and government officials are trying to figure out how to improve society by changing individuals' behavior. Such realms include organ donation, increasing honest reporting (on tax returns, insurance forms, and so on), making donations to charity, and a variety of other prosocial behaviors. Using nudges to get people to make decisions that make the world better is a tougher ethical challenge than getting them to make decisions that help themselves. In this section, we'll use the example of nudging to increase organ donations upon death—to benefit others rather than the donor. Based on utilitarianism and a philosophical concept called the veil of ignorance, we come down strongly in favor of using effective nudges to encourage organ donation.

Utilitarianism encourages decisions that improve society. So if we believe government leaders have a responsibility to guide people's behavior toward greater overall benefit for society, most of us would agree that utilitarianism is a pretty good standard. Most of us would also agree that the benefit of organ donation to the recipient (prolonged life) outweighs the loss incurred by the (dead) donor. Certainly some people object to organ donation based on their religious beliefs, yet we can assume that these objections focus on the donor's loss rather than on the recipient's gain—which leads to our second guiding principle.

As we discussed in chapter 8, the practice of trying to adopt a veil of ignorance can help government leaders think through whether a specific nudge would truly be in the collective good—that is, whether it is ethical. Naturally, government leaders should strive to maintain the dignity, autonomy, and free will of citizens, but we believe these concerns should be balanced against the utilitarian goal of maximizing societal welfare. The veil of ignorance is a fine tool for thinking through what would be best for society. Hence leaders choosing between an out-by-default or in-by-default organ donation system might imagine that at some point in the future they will either be (1) deceased, and their organs can be used to save other human beings, or (2) in need of an organ that could be obtained from a recently deceased human being. Given equal odds of being an organ provider or recipient, would you prefer an in-by-default or an out-by-default system? We believe most people, after examining the problem through the veil of ignorance, would choose the in-by-default system. The veil of ignorance can thus be a useful guide to nudging for the greatest good.

The ethics of nudging people to buy your stuff. Richard Thaler typically signs copies of *Nudge* "Nudge for good." This simple plea reveals Thaler's concern that nudges, like many useful tools, may be used for ill. This can be especially true when for-profit companies nudge people to buy their products, watch their videos, or share their data. Thaler and Sunstein call exploitative nudges "sludge."[22]

When you use sludge to increase your company's profits, ethical concerns become more complex. We aren't lawyers, so we'll focus on what is ethical, not on what is legal. Nor will we make recommendations (at least not here!) for what we think should be illegal. We also add that we do not believe that nudges aimed at selling products and services are ethically problematic, per se. In fact, if your goal is to get the word out about a reasonably priced service that you believe will benefit customers, we hope you will use the most effective tools at your disposal.

At other times for-profit firms use nudges to try to get consumers to make decisions that would be against their self-interest but profitable for the firm. Often the harm inflicted on the consumer is greater than the benefit to the corporation. One such example is subscription services for which it is easy to sign up but difficult to exit. Clearly, utilitarians object to such behavior and would discourage you, as a leader, from engaging in such practices. And we would agree that nudging that creates net harm to the consumer raises important ethical concerns.

In his ethical analysis of nudging and manipulation, Sunstein argues that when nudges are aimed at keeping customers or employees from engaging their more deliberative thought processes, this should raise ethical red flags. Thus it is ethically problematic for a company to nudge consumers away from System 2 thought to persuade them to make a purchase or keep watching videos online. And just as we believe that it is appropriate for corporations to decline unethical profit opportunities, even when they are legal, we also believe corporations should decline profitable opportunities to exploit their customers, their communities, or their countries by using the power of nudges.

A Power Tool for Leaders

In most of this book we've offered tools to help leaders make better decisions and create an environment that helps others to make better decisions as well. In this chapter we broaden the discussion to suggest how leaders might improve the decisions of *many* other people, including people they may never meet. Even accounting for their limitations, nudges remain important tools for leaders seeking to design organizations that prompt better decisions. Such design requires insights into human behavior and decision making, insights we have attempted to provide. Finally, while acknowledging the key ethical pitfalls of nudging, we conclude that, in many contexts, nudges can help you, as a leader, achieve the ethical goal of doing as much good as you can.

The great thing about nudges is that they can be simple and subtle. They are often inexpensive to implement, which can make them easy and politically expedient. But leaders who implement them must not allow them to become a substitute for more substantive interventions. Effective leadership depends on knowing when a simple nudge provides the best approach and when change requires more substantive interventions.

10

Designing a Better Decision Factory

Idealized conceptualizations of leadership lionize heroic figures who inspire followers to achieve the impossible. We hope this book moves you to imagine leadership differently. A leader's capacity to design the organizational context, set defaults, and establish expectations may be more powerful than any motivational speech. The decision context shapes the way people think, the choices that seem most natural, and the behavior most likely to prevail. We have identified essential tools that belong on the utility belt of every leader. By instituting routines that establish wise defaults and asking well-timed questions you can increase the probability that others will choose wisely. These tools can help orient decisions toward the collective good and contribute to the welfare of many.

We think of organizations as decision factories. More than anything else, the quality of your decisions determines the outcomes you achieve. And your ability to facilitate good decisions by those around you amplifies your leverage to improve your organization's effectiveness. Future successes depend on you selecting the course of action with the highest expected value. How profitable you are next year depends on the products and initiatives in which you choose to invest now. Your vulnerability to future lawsuits depends on the legality of current decisions.

This short concluding chapter offers recommendations that grow directly out of the lessons you've learned. Some of them would qualify as "choice architecture," but they extend beyond traditional nudges. Some simple, actionable recommendations include artful reminders, invitations to think again, or new conceptions of familiar problems. They are small adjustments to common day-to-day issues that can have large potential consequences because they leverage your influence over others and the systems in which they operate. They serve the goal of making it easy for those around you to choose better.

Chapter 1 set the stage by offering a new vision of leadership. A leader need not be the one who changes others' hearts and minds with motivational visions of herculean efforts and grand achievements. The reality of leadership is more prosaic than this heroic archetype. We argued that leaders should think of their work as enabling and empowering others to do their best by providing them with useful tools, helpful guidance, and relevant information. Rather than building the road and leading a march down it, a leader can often be more effective by posting useful signage that helps others figure out the most efficient way to get where it is they want to go. We are not against road building, but we try to be realistic about the effort it requires; we offer more efficient approaches that can produce more effective good because leaders can implement them more easily.

- Use the opportunities created by your role as a leader to design the organizational, social, and decision-making environment.
- Design the decision environment to help others choose wisely, consistent with their interests and the greater good.

Chapter 2 noted how the siren song of intuition lures us to accept gut instincts that feel right but can easily misdirect us. The alternative to intuition is a deliberative decision process that systematically considers your interests, explores the alternatives, and makes the choice with the highest expected value. Wise leaders notice when others are inclined to rely on flawed intuition and open their eyes by asking about the key considerations that might inform a more deliberative decision: What is the full menu of possible alternatives? What would success look like? What are the probabilities of various likely outcomes? Which alternative has the highest expected value? Simply asking these questions can help prompt a deliberative frame of mind that puts intuitive impulses in their place.

Because intuition is vulnerable to the persuasive power of a good story, those who weave compelling narratives can be more influential than they deserve to be. As a leader, you can defuse this dynamic by reminding people of the big picture. Yes, Anu might be the job candidate whom everyone finds more charismatic, but is charisma the top trait you sought? What traits or abilities are likely to make someone successful at the job, and did your interview process allow you to assess it? As leader, you are well positioned to help reduce the impact of the confirmation bias in others' judgments. Seek ways to help others consider the possibility that they might be wrong. Simply ask, "How might you be wrong?" or "What happens if we're wrong about that?" At other times, it may be worth asking, "What information are we missing?" or "What information would we like to have to make a fully informed decision?"

- Counteract the persuasive power of a good story by refocusing on facts and expected value.
- Ask what information you would like to have to make a fully informed decision.

Noticing what information is missing is at the heart of the lessons in chapter 3. Noticing the missing information is not an easy assignment. For one thing, thanks to the confirmation bias, the human mind is much better at identifying the presence of something than its absence. For another thing, the set of missing information is potentially infinite. If you are choosing between two job candidates, you probably lack information on their blood types, their shoe sizes, their sleep habits, and a long list of irrelevant factors. But there may be some relevant information that you have to seek out. What do those who have worked with the candidate say about their behavior toward subordinates? Do they treat those below them in the status hierarchy with respect? You can help others notice essential information they lack by simply posing the question, "What would you like to know in order to help you make this decision?"

- Ask yourself what information is missing and seek it out.
- Draw others' attention to missing information by asking, "What information would you like to have?"

Appreciating how much you don't know may help temper your decision confidence. This is a good thing, as chapter 4 explains. Too many leaders, seeing greater confidence as a virtue, attempt to talk themselves and others into being overconfident. They strive to portray certainty in their decisions, even when they know the probability of success is less than 100 percent. It is then easy for them to get carried away setting confident goals, as if greater ambition always produced greater achievement. One way leaders do this is by setting big, hairy, audacious goals and then delegating with the instruction to do whatever it takes. Doing whatever it takes can come at the cost of safety or ethics.

Wise leaders instill as much confidence as is appropriate, and no more. This may indeed require them to elevate others' ambitions and expand their vision of what is possible. Often you will see potential in others that they themselves do not appreciate yet. You can encourage them to pursue goals they had not dared to consider. But smart goal setting acknowledges that success is rarely guaranteed. Setting a goal comes with a distribution of likely outcomes. Sometimes it will be worth betting on the long shot if the prize is big enough. However, placing smart bets requires getting better at thinking in expected values, weighing both payoffs and probabilities. Help others get better at forecasting probabilities by keeping track of predictions and keeping score of their accuracy.

Instead of rewarding people for attaining good outcomes, which confound talent with luck, it is better to reward good decisions even when they get unlucky. Smart poker players, for instance, will bet heavily on four of a kind, even though it will sometimes lose to a straight flush. Amazon is one company that tries to reward good decision processes by basing decisions on well-justified forecasts with high expected values, and it demands that big decisions be documented ahead of time in their famous six-page memos. The company rewards good decision processes, even when these decisions do not ultimately succeed. Research shows that this sort of process accountability leads to wiser, more deliberative, and less biased decisions.[1]

- Set goals with positive expected values that balance reward with realism.
- Help others get better at forecasting by eliciting their predictions and keeping score of their accuracy later.
- Reward good decision processes rather than good decision outcomes.

Chapter 5 encouraged you to exploit the wisdom of the crowd. Rather than thinking that, as leader, you need to have all the answers, you can use the wisdom around you by structuring decisions to allow for diverse inputs and encouraging constructive debate. Sometimes it may require you to promote respectful disagreement, as when Reed

Hastings "farms for dissent" at Netflix by actively soliciting criticisms. Sometimes this may require you to silence your own voice or to hold back, so as to encourage others to speak up and share their unique perspectives.

We ought to note the democratizing implication of our advice. If you, as a leader, open yourself to feedback from others and to learning from them, you will relinquish some control even as you gain in wisdom. While it may not gratify your ego, it can correct your errors before they become disasters. This corrective influence only grows more important as you advance in your career and rise in the hierarchy. The more important you become, the higher the stakes attached to your decisions, but the more reluctant others will be to criticize you; consequently, you stand to benefit more from soliciting that critical feedback.

One useful practice is formally convening meetings whose agenda is to anticipate failure. Premortems imagine that the decision has turned out badly.[2] Why? Can you do anything to improve the prospects of success? Sometimes you may need to appoint a trusted ally to serve as devil's advocate, whose job it is to make the con case by pointing out weaknesses and problems. Other times you as leader may be in a position to serve as your own devil's advocate, questioning your assumptions and considering the possibility that you might be wrong. "Red teaming" constitutes a team with the assignment to test defenses, disrupt plans, and otherwise burst the organization's bubble of enthusiasm and confidence.[3]

- Capitalize on the wisdom of the crowd by seeking diverse inputs on important decisions.
- Gather votes or ratings ahead of important decisions. These may inform a discussion of the decision or even replace the need to meet.

- Appoint a devil's advocate or a red team whose explicit assignment it is to find weaknesses and identify failures.

Chapter 6 suggested experimentation as a tool for gathering information to help make decisions. Rather than pretending to know all the answers, honest leaders will admit that there are important questions whose answers they do not yet know. When those questions are important enough and time allows it, it may be worth conducting an experiment that can test the effectiveness of alternative courses of action. Chapter 6 offers ideas for how you can conduct experiments in your own company to test your ideas for effective product features, promotional campaigns, and advertisements. There are many useful resources available to those who want to learn more about conducting experiments.[4]

It is also possible for you to benefit from experiments that others have already conducted. People around the world sign up to get vaccinated against Covid-19 because they know the results of randomized, placebo-controlled experimental trials show that the vaccines are effective at reducing infection and sickness as much as 95 percent of the time.[5] Studies of vaccine effectiveness, organizational defaults, and decision nudges are printed in academic journals. Those journals aspire to share research results with the world. They may have useful answers to the questions you are asking, or they may inspire ideas for potential experimental designs you could conduct.

- When you need data to help inform an important decision, consider conducting an experiment.
- Consult the published research literature.[6]
- Use data to help you monitor progress toward your goals and assess the effectiveness of your decisions; when possible, preserve a control group against which you can compare your actions.

Chapter 7 invited you to think about facilitating mutually beneficial trades. Too many leaders attempt to stimulate competition between people who seek rewards in the organization. While some rivalry can be healthy, organizations are not perfectly competitive markets where the invisible hand of competition produces the optimally efficient allocation of resources. Self-interest often comes at the expense of colleagues and the organization. Workers motivated to win in competitions with colleagues can do so by sabotaging their rivals or cheating. It doesn't take many such competitors to impair or even destroy a company. We know from our own classrooms that pitting students against each other in competition for grades can undermine their willingness to help each other and sabotage collaborative learning.

Companies that provide outsize rewards to rising stars run the risk of motivating individual achievement at the expense of collaboration. Google learned the hard way that lavish individual rewards do not necessarily produce the most committed employees or the most constructive effort. The company changed its Founders Awards to instead provide experiences for high-performing teams. Instead of rewarding an individual with a cash award, the company would instead send the entire team on a vacation together to Hawaii or Disneyland.[7] These team experiences did more to build camaraderie, increase happiness, and strengthen commitment.

When you think about allocating limited resources within your organization, whether awards or job assignments, think about doing so in a way that can integrate the interests of the parties involved to enjoy gains from trade. The key to this is to avoid the simple impulse to compromise to resolve a disagreement. Instead, try to understand the underlying interests of the parties and try to think broadly about the potential issues involved. Then see if you can help craft agreements that give the parties more of what they want on the issue(s) they care about the most. When you do, you will be making all the parties, collectively, better off, generating more stable agreements and more of a bond with the organization.

- Create value by negotiating mutually beneficial trades between people, both within your organization and with people outside it.
- Think about trading off across issues, such that disagreements get resolved not by compromise but by seeing that people get what they care most about.

Chapter 8 asked you to think about the ethical implications of your work. It reminded all of us how easy it is to ignore the ethical implications of our professional decisions by failing to think about how our work affects others. We may be perpetuating systemic inequities without intending to do so. For example, imagine you are selecting talented and ambitious young people for an unpaid internship that offers useful training, connections, and letters of recommendation that can be stepping-stones to a rewarding career. Such internships can be useful screening devices that help you identify truly committed candidates. But they can also effectively weed out talented candidates from poor families unable to support them while they are doing unpaid work.

More important, chapter 8 invited you to help others think about the ethical implications of their work. One simple way to do so is to invite them to consider how others might view the ethics of their decisions. It can be enlightening for people to consider how their actions might appear when splashed across the front page of the local newspaper. How might rivals, enemies, or competitors interpret their behavior? Encourage people to get out of their own personal perspective and consider the broader ethical landscape; it can have profound implications. Consider how the world would look if everyone chose as you do. Would you choose such a system, even if there were a chance you could wind up on the unlucky end of inequalities?

Audit your leadership by considering the ways in which you may be unintentionally encouraging or perpetuating unethical behavior.

- Think about how ethical choices might appear to critical audiences.
- Empower others to choose consistent with their own values.

Chapter 9 explicitly considered the potential for decision architecture to facilitate wise choices. Building on the insights into human foibles, biases, and limitations provided by the first eight chapters, chapter 9 asked how you, as a leader, can build systems resilient to human limitations. It turns out that there are clever ways to set up retirement plans that take into account human impatience and myopia. When people focus on the present and neglect future consequences, they will save too little and spend too much. But they also tend to believe that they will be more virtuous in the future, so they will willingly commit to saving income from future raises. Enrolling people in these sorts of smart savings plans represents a good default choice.

Wise leaders can establish defaults without restricting people's freedom to choose. For instance, providing default options for health care, life insurance, and investments can improve outcomes. When it comes to choosing investments, it is too common for people, overwhelmed by the options, to leave their money parked in a savings or money market account earning paltry interest rates. Most people would be better off if their savings were invested for them, by default, in a low-cost stock index fund. But beware the temptation to select exploitative defaults. For instance, making automatic subscription renewal the default and forcing customers through an arduous process to cancel their subscriptions is bad choice architecture. Knowing the power of defaults obligates you to use that power responsibly, not exploitatively.

- Select good defaults so that the failure to make an active choice still yields pretty good results for most people.
- When possible, make it easy for people to actively select something other than the default.

When your decision factory runs smoothly, its systems, processes, and people will churn out good decisions. Sometimes well-designed defaults can lead to pretty good decisions most of the time without much effort. Other times, you will do more good by encouraging people to reconsider their intuitive impulses and invest in thoughtful reflection. Sometimes a well-running decision factory operates harmoniously, supported by ethical policies that prioritize justice and integrative negotiations that seek to maximize collective benefit. Other times respectful disagreement and honest criticism will disrupt the status quo and question your assumptions.

Good decisions do not guarantee success, but they do allow you to place smart bets with high expected values. In reality, that's the best you can do. Consultants and purveyors of snake oil who guarantee success are trying harder to get your money than to convey honest information. Even a small improvement in the number of games you win can make all the difference between glory and obscurity. The world's best tennis players aspire to win 52 percent of their games.[8] The world's best poker players play only a minority of hands dealt them; and they win only the minority of hands they play.[9] Our greatest hope is that you learn to make the choice with the highest expected value as often as you possibly can. If this book helps you do so, it will have been well worth its price and the value of the time you spent reading it.

We have offered tools to put these basic principles to use in your work and in your life. In writing this book, we hope to open up new ways of thinking about leadership, both the ways in which you already act as decision architect, but also the opportunities all around you to be more intentional in how you do so. We hope we have helped you identify a few more of these opportunities to exert a positive influence on others' decisions. Even small changes can have big consequences because the impact of leaders' actions is multiplied by the number of people they influence.

Appendix: Decision Biases

The human mind, for all its miraculous powers, is not perfect. We do impressively well navigating a complex world but nevertheless fall short of the rational ideal. This is no surprise—perfect rationality assumes we have infinite cognitive processing capacity and complete preferences. Lacking these, we adapt by using shortcuts or simplifying heuristics to manage challenges that threaten to exceed our cognitive limitations. These heuristics serve us well much of the time, but they can lead to some predictable errors.[1]

We group these errors into four types, based on the heuristics that give rise to them. The first is the availability heuristic, which serves as an efficient way of dealing with our lack of omniscience. Since no one knows everything, we rely instead on the information that is available to us. The second is the confirmation heuristic, which simplifies the process by which we gather new information. The third is the representativeness heuristic, which stands in for full understanding of cause and effect relationships. We make assumptions about what causes what, relying on the similarity between effects and their putative causes. Finally, framing helps us establish preferences, deciding how good or bad something is by comparing it to alternatives.

Availability

Lacking omniscience, we must rely on the information we possess. This leads to predictable problems when our information is biased. Consider, for example, the problem of forecasting the

APPENDIX

Table A.1: Decision-Making Heuristics, Along with the Cognitive Limitations that Necessitate Them and the Biases that Result from Them.

Limitation on	Heuristic	Resulting biases
Knowledge	Availability	Ease of recall
		Retrievability
		Anchoring
Gathering information	Confirmation	Hindsight bias
		Curse of knowledge
		Overconfidence (overprecision in judgment)
		Conjunction fallacy
Understanding cause and effect	Representativeness	Insensitivity to sample size
		Misconceptions of chance
		Neglect of regression to the mean
		Power of reference points
Preference completeness	Framing	Power of interpersonal comparisons
		Loss aversion
		Endowment effect

probabilities of future events. Chapter 2 encouraged you to maximize expected value, but doing so depends on estimating the probabilities of outcomes such as returns on investment, career success, or happiness in marriage. Forecasting often necessitates the costly collection of data to help establish base rates.[2] The data, in turn, can inform a Bayesian calculation of likely probabilities. For instance, before deciding whether to eat the truffles or the oysters, you should collect data on others who have been delighted or sickened after eating each of these delicacies. Needless to say, this is not how most of us estimate probability. Instead, we rely heavily on ease of recall.

How risky is it to eat raw oysters? Well, how many people do you know who got sick after eating oysters? Few of us collect data on the percentage of all oyster meals that resulted in food poisoning. Instead, we rely on the information readily available to us. The more people you know sickened by oysters, the less likely you are to order them. To pick another example, how likely is my house to be burglarized? Is it worth buying a security system? Faced with this decision, we are at risk of having our decisions biased by a sales pitch from a salesperson who encourages us to vividly imagine being burglarized, thereby increasing its perceived likelihood.

Reliance on the availability heuristic gives recent and memorable events outsize influence in your likelihood judgments. After experiencing a dramatic event such as a burglary, a wildfire, a hurricane, or an earthquake, your interest in purchasing insurance to protect yourself from that risk is likely to go up. That may be justifiable if the experience represents credible evidence that the risk is higher than you thought it was before, such as if a burglary signals burglars on the loose in your area or if wildfires are the consequence of climate change that increases the risks of future fires. However, those who experience earthquakes then want to purchase more earthquake insurance, even though the probability of another big quake actually goes down following an earthquake.[3] Moreover, evidence suggests that personally experiencing something (like vomiting all night after consuming oysters) has an outsize influence on our estimates of future likelihood even relative to directly observing someone else just like you experiencing the same event.[4] Personal experience is simply more vivid and salient than statistics.

The availability heuristic leads us to exaggerate vivid, dramatic, or memorable risks—those we can easily retrieve from memory. For instance, Americans are excessively fearful of terrorist attacks, interpersonal violence, and police brutality. While these risks are real, their probability is also very low relative to the risk of cancer, heart disease, and auto accident. The availability heuristic is not only about estimating risks. It can also bias the way we think about opportunities. If you don't know anyone who has attended college, invested in the stock market, or started a company, it is easy to assume that these activities are unadvisable or unrealistic for you too. One tragic consequence is that many talented young people from poor families fail to apply to selective colleges and universities because they assume they cannot afford the pricey tuition. But in truth, admissions committees care about cultural, geographic, and socioeconomic diversity; they can offer financial aid to make college affordable even for families of modest means.

The availability heuristic biases all of us toward overreliance on what we know or the data we have on hand. Sometimes information is easier to recall because it is emotionally vivid, but other information is privileged simply due to the quirks of human memory. One study asked people to think of as many words as they could of the form _ _ _ _ **i n g**.[5] They thought of more than twice as many as did those who tried to think of words of the form _ _ _ _ _ **n** _, although the latter is a subset of the former.

However, you can reduce your vulnerability to the availability bias by asking yourself what information you would like to have in order to make a fully informed decision—and then go seek it out. Don't rely just on what you can think of spontaneously: actually go collect data. Especially when the stakes are high, this extra effort is likely to be worth it. You can also help others avoid falling victim to the availability bias by encouraging them to think about the information they need to make fully informed decisions.

As a leader, you can reduce the biasing effect of availability by encouraging others to ask what information they would like to have to make a fully informed decision. The information that comes to mind most readily is not necessarily the most informative. They can avoid overreliance on readily available information by seeking out the information they need. Vivid, emotional, or recent instances are particularly likely to hold sway when people estimate likelihood by relying on intuition. Instead, encourage others to gather evidence on actual rates of occurrence, actual risk, and actual base rates.

Confirmation

One of the challenges that impedes us in seeking out the most useful evidence to inform our decisions is that confirmation is so much more natural than disconfirmation. There are innumerable ways in which your social networks, your friends, your brain, and the world will feed you confirming information that affirms what you already believe.

Facebook's filtering algorithms seek to give us more of what we like, or at least more of what will keep us on Facebook.[6] That does not include exposing us to the perspectives of those who disagree with us and getting us to question our beliefs. Instead, what keeps us coming back for more is when we feel ourselves affirmed and supported by others who share our views.[7] So that is what we get. You believe the earth is flat? YouTube can help connect you to a group of like-minded others. You fear that powerful corporations are trying to control you via vaccines or chemtrails from planes? Reddit helps you find others who share your fears. Even your Google searches are more likely to affirm than question your assumptions. Searches like "Moon landing fake" turn up more evidence of a giant conspiracy to fake the moon landing than searches for "Moon landing real" do.

It's not just big tech. The people around you are also in on it. The people who work for you, the people who want to sell you things, even your friends—mostly they say nice things to you. This is especially true when you are in the role of the leader who has some power over them. If they value having a positive relationship with you, they will be more likely to voice praise and appreciation than complaints and criticisms. This means—especially as your career and your status advance—you become increasingly insulated from disconfirming information that tells you you are wrong, misguided, or confused.

Even our own brains are better at confirmation than disconfirmation. We are, as a rule, better at identifying the presence than the absence of something. Identifying who is missing from a group is more difficult than determining who is present. That has the dangerous consequence of making it easier to find evidence for whatever we're looking for. No doubt you have had the experience of learning a word and then hearing it used all around you. Or maybe you research a particular model of car and suddenly start seeing it on the roads everywhere. Simply the wording of a question can recruit different information. For instance, my students generate more complaints about a reading assignment when I ask, "Was that article boring?" than when I ask, "Was that article interesting?"

Anchoring bias is one consequence of our talent for coming to conclusions consistent with our initial hypothesis. The classic anchoring effect is assimilation: the conclusion people land on is too close to the place they started. In one demonstration researchers asked research volunteers in their study to think of the last three digits of their phone number.[8] Then volunteers estimated the date on which Attila the Hun was defeated in Europe. Their estimates were correlated with their phone numbers, despite the phone numbers' obvious irrelevance. Their phone number gave them a starting place, and they didn't move far enough from it. Other examples are commonplace. List prices on houses and cars represent anchors that influence the way we think of them, even when we know those prices were set arbitrarily or even with the intention of manipulating us.[9]

As these sorts of anchoring effects illustrate, confirmation can bias our thought processes even when we are motivated to be accurate. It is even more powerful when it serves a motivation to believe that we are good or virtuous or right. Virtue and sanctimony can align when we defend our group and its belief systems. The motivation to believe that our friends, leaders, and teachers are right can make it difficult to hear evidence that questions them. Instead, confirmation of our belief systems affirms us as virtuous and good. Confirming those beliefs and being able to say "I told you so" is so deeply satisfying that we tell it to ourselves.

Our talent for recalling confirmatory evidence contributes to the hindsight bias.[10] "I knew that was going to happen!" can offer comforting affirmation. As soon as we learn some surprising result, such as the outcome of the 2016 U.S. presidential election, our brains get to work trying to understand that result by recruiting explanations, facts, and theories that can help explain it. The result is that we wind up seeing the past as having been more predictable than it actually was.[11] If you want to get better at understanding the limits of your knowledge, improve the calibration of your forecasts, and make more accurate probability estimates, our advice is simple: you should track your predictions so that you are less likely to fall victim to the hindsight bias. When you make an investment, commit to a production schedule, or set a goal write down your prediction for what will happen. How much will the investment's value actually go up? How likely are you to meet the planned milestones on the production schedule?

But the human mind is not hopelessly destined to affirm what it already believes regardless of the truth. There are, in fact, important circumstances in which discrepant facts are particularly memorable. For example, the one negative comment in an otherwise glowing performance appraisal is often the one that sticks with us.[12] Those criticisms can provide useful information. Try to understand them. What can you learn from that unhappy customer, mistake, or accident? If you care about improving, or even just getting an accurate self-appraisal, you need to be able to hear both the compliments and the complaints.

The automatic tendency to think first of information that confirms your expectations will make it easy for you to jump to conclusions. It will make it easy for you to become overconfident, too sure that the evidence supports your beliefs. You will, for instance, find it easier to agree with your political allies and support your in-group.[13] But if you want to make better decisions, remind yourself to ask what your critics or opponents would say about that same issue. Chapter 4 encouraged you to use the scout mindset. You can help the people who work with you to make better decisions by encouraging them to think more like a scout than like a soldier, think more like a judge weighing the evidence than like an attorney defending a client. You can, for instance, explicitly ask them, "What if you're wrong?" or "What evidence contradicts your argument?"

Representativeness

Chapter 2 opened with a hiring decision between Mina and Anu. Anu is more likable and charismatic; you can imagine enjoying working with her or just engaging in friendly small talk. It is easy to tell a story in which Anu's better fit with the company's culture would predict better work performance, longer tenure, and greater career potential. Because getting to know a job candidate helps put together such a story and assess the candidate's likability, unstructured face-to-face job interviews have always been by far the most popular way to select employees. The problem is that these interviews are terrible at predicting future job performance.[14] Likability and perceived fit simply aren't as important as our intuitions tell us they are. There are alternatives to the interview that are cheaper, better, and less biased—like a simple intelligence test.[15] However, the popularity of interviews persists because they are so intuitively appealing; they allow us to feel that we have identified that special je ne sais quoi in a candidate and to imagine that this might predict their performance on the job, even while the evidence suggests that these feelings are mostly misleading.

Our reliance on our intuitive sense of the fit between cause and effect can even lead us to violate obvious mathematical laws. Consider the conjunction fallacy, illustrated by the Linda problem from Tversky and Kahneman.[16] The problem begins with a short profile of Linda, who is "31 years old, single, outspoken, and very smart. She majored in philosophy. As a student, she was deeply concerned with issues of discrimination and social justice, and she participated in antinuclear demonstrations." Armed with this profile, the challenge is to rank a series of descriptions with regard to their likelihood. They include the following:

Linda works in a bookstore and takes yoga classes.
Linda is a bank teller.
Linda is a bank teller who is active in the feminist movement.

Most people think Linda sounds like a feminist and so rank the likelihood that she is a feminist bank teller higher than the probability that she is a bank teller. But this is wrong. The set of feminist bank tellers must be smaller than the set of all bank tellers. Because Linda's feminism seems so intuitively obvious, it is easy to let intuition lead us astray.

You will be tempted to rely on intuition to judge cause and effect, and the representativeness heuristic will incline you to favor beliefs consistent with common sense. For instance, human understanding of the causes of disease often relies more on misleading intuition than on epidemiological science. Many continue to believe in treatments and cures for which there is scant evidence, from hydroxychloroquine as a treatment for Covid-19 to homeopathy as a treatment for, well, everything.[17] Often these putative cures hold some intuitive appeal, such as the homeopathic principle that "like cures like."[18] So, for instance, to treat the symptoms of a common cold, a homeopath may prescribe allium cepa. The pill would include diluted essence of onion. The idea is that since onions make your nose run, they can be used to treat the runny nose that comes with a cold.

By contrast, few found the germ theory of disease persuasive when the Persian physician Ibn Sina proposed it in 1025.[19] The idea that invisibly small viruses could produce such large consequences felt counterintuitive. More popular was the idea that disease was caused by evil spirits or toxic miasmas.[20] It took hundreds of years and mountains of scientific evidence to persuade the public that they should wash their hands and disinfect wounds to reduce the risk of infection. Countless lives were lost in unsanitary hospitals before the medical establishment accepted that they were killing their patients by transporting germs on their hands from the sick to the healthy. Even during the Covid-19 pandemic many still doubted the effectiveness of masks to prevent disease transmission via respiratory droplets, despite the evidence for their effectiveness.[21]

The power of representativeness can blind us to foundational statistical principles. For instance, we often expect the past to be representative of the future, neglecting the power of regression to the mean. We are therefore surprised again and again when last season's star athlete or employee fails to repeat their stupendous performance. In fact, last year's performance was the combination of both skill and luck. The skill is likely to persist, but the luck will be different. As a result, the very best performers are likely to decline in the future and the very worst are likely to improve. If this fact is at odds with your intuition, you're in good company. But just imagine that you're tracking rolls of a die rather than job performance. It's all luck and no skill. A high roll of six is likely to be followed by a lower one; a roll of one is likely to be followed by a higher one.

Following intuitive guidance and representative evidence makes us vulnerable to numerous biases. The alternative is to bring a critical mind to the relevant evidence. The gold standard of evidence for cause and effect is an experiment with random assignment to condition.[22] But many circumstances require only simple statistical or mathematical logic. For instance, realizing that the probability that Linda is a feminist bank teller must be smaller than the probability that she is a bank teller is a simple matter of logic. We can avoid falling victim to the biases caused by the representativeness heuristic by thinking critically about cause and effect, avoiding assuming causal relationships without evidence, and assuming that every measure includes noise, chance, and error.

Framing

The rational ideal assumes we have complete preferences. Complete preferences require us to know how much we like, well, everything. It would require you to know how sour you like your kimchi, the thread count of your sheets, and how much you would be willing to pay for a ride on SpaceX's Dragon space craft. Our preferences should be constant and coherent. We shouldn't prefer A to B sometimes but switch to preferring B over A with superficial and irrelevant changes in context.

In chapter 2 you encountered the classic framing problem describing a car manufacturer that employs six hundred people but has fallen on hard times. The corporate plan people prefer depends on whether the question's frame implies that the relevant reference point is either losing all the jobs or saving all the jobs. The typical person leans toward risk aversion when contemplating gains and risk seeking when contemplating losses. When they are trying to avoid a loss, they are more willing to accept risks than when they are pursuing a gain. This is one reason, for instance, why investors are more willing to sell investments that have appreciated in value than ones that have declined.[23] The important consideration ought to be the investment's prospects of future returns, not the price at which you happened to acquire it. By selling their winners, investors avoid risk by locking in their gains. By holding on to their winners, investors accept the risk of future price fluctuations in the hope that the price could come back up and they could avoid realizing the loss.

In reality, context frames our preferences in important ways. Frames drive our choices in ways that rational theory would not predict. We routinely behave as if we are risk averse when we consider choices about gains but flip to being risk seeking when we think about the same prospect as a loss. This reversal of risk preferences owes itself to the fact that we think about gains and losses relative to a reference point—usually the status quo or, in the case of investments, the purchase price.

The rational ideal also assumes that you have infinitely sensitive utility. That is, in a life filled with joys, luxuries, delights, and indulgences, adding a 22nd bedroom to your mansion gives you as much pleasure as the first did. At the other end of the spectrum, in a life filled with misfortune, discrimination, abuse, and privation, the one-hundredth insult from a passerby to your homeless encampment is as painful as the first. In fact, we exhibit declining marginal utility, reacting less and less to each addition increment of gain or loss from the status quo. The 184th billion added to Jeff Bezos's net worth did not affect him as much as the first did.

Declining marginal utilities threaten to make us indifferent to changes in life circumstance. But in fact we aren't. Jeff Bezos continued to work even after his net worth made him the richest person alive. Even the wealthiest seek more, and even the most destitute avoid loss. A simple reason is that we habituate to our life's circumstances and react instead to changes in the status quo, gratified by gains and outraged by losses. This is why framing influences our preferences. We think about prospects as gains or losses from a reference point, usually the status quo.

How does framing simplify? It doesn't.[24] It adds a normatively irrelevant consideration: the reference point. Rational agents with complete preferences and full information can employ a cardinal scale for which the reference point is irrelevant. For example, when buying a music dictionary, the fully informed buyer would know whether twenty thousand dictionary entries were sufficient. But in the absence of a useful reference point, ordinary people find it harder to evaluate and so turn up their noses at a music dictionary with twenty thousand entries and a torn cover.[25] That is, until they learn that the alternative music dictionary with an intact cover only has ten thousand entries. But framing can help clarify relative standing when absolute assessments are difficult. Finding out that your coworkers get paid more than you can suddenly make your salary seem inadequate. Finding out that other runners cover your usual route in half the time it takes you can suddenly make your performance disappointing.

That reference point has profound consequences for our preferences. One is the so-called endowment effect, our attachment to the stuff we happen to have—our current endowment.[26] Let's imagine, just to pick one example, that you happen to have a profusion of bicycles in your garage. Your car cannot fit into the garage because there are so many bikes. Would you want to get rid of that cute old Schwinn with the banana seat? What? And miss out on the chance that your niece would want to ride it someday? On the other hand, what if you happened to find an old bike like that on the street, free for the taking; would you want to find room for it in your garage? Certainly not! Losing what you have is more painful than a similar gain, and so you resist change.

The endowment effect can contribute to the status quo bias, which leads us to be irrationally attached to the existing endowment of possessions, privileges, and practices. The status quo bias may be at work when a colleague dismisses your brilliant innovation with, "That's just not the way we do things around here." The status quo bias contributes to the power of defaults, as we described in chapter 9, and, as with other framing effects, enables persuasion strategies that manipulate perceptions of the status quo.

If there were a neutral frame of reference, that could eliminate framing biases—but there rarely is one. You can think of every prospect, outcome, or payday as either a gain or a loss, depending on your reference point. Chapter 3 tells the sad story of the French financier René-Thierry Magon de la Villehuchet, who focused on what he had lost to Bernie Madoff's Ponzi scheme. But it was equally true that he remained one of the world's wealthiest and most fortunate people. What is the right frame? Was de la Villehuchet a winner or a loser? There is no right frame. Instead, the best advice we can give you is to think about each outcome from a variety of different frames. How do different framings affect your feelings? Do any of those framings help you think more clearly about the choice available to you? If you have already made your choice, are there any frames that make you feel better about the outcome? Use the power of framing to your advantage.

One organizational practice that helps reduce the power of the status quo is so-called zero-based budgeting. When planning budgets, most companies start with last year's budget and consider increases or decreases from there. Zero-based budgeting, by contrast, starts with a blank slate and asks how much each department needs. Similarly, some investment managers and hedge funds try to avoid the framing power of the status quo by asking, "If we didn't own any investments, which stocks would we want in our portfolio?"

As a leader, you can reduce the dysfunctional framing effects on others' choices by helping them think about the problem from a variety of perspectives. If there is a neutral frame, you should use that.

More often, there are multiple viable reference points, some of which feel like losses and some of which feel like gains. Many restaurateurs' plans for surviving the Covid-19 pandemic in 2020 felt like a painful loss in comparison to the prior year. On the other hand, it was also easy for many of them to focus on the fact that mere survival represented a gain relative to so many other restaurants.

Perfectly Imperfect

If you were going to design an agent to make the most of its limited abilities, you would have to build in coping mechanisms that would allow it to implement shortcuts and decision heuristics that would be good enough for it to get by. That's a useful way to think about human cognitive abilities. We're not perfect, but we have coping mechanisms that help us muddle through. There is also value in understanding those coping mechanisms because they can get you into trouble. Mindless reliance on intuitive decision heuristics can feel natural but is also vulnerable to bias.

If you want to learn more about your all-too-human biases, there are a number of excellent books you might consider. Perhaps the most memorable presentation was *Thinking, Fast and Slow* by the Nobel Prize–winner Daniel Kahneman.[27] Michael Lewis tells the story of Kahneman's collaboration with Amos Tversky in his book *The Undoing Project*.[28] In their work together, Kahneman and Tversky catalogued some of the most important heuristics people use and the biases to which those heuristics make us vulnerable. Richard Thaler, who won a Nobel Prize for his work in behavioral economics, offers a personal history of the movement in *Misbehaving*.[29] Other books have also considered biases in human judgment and the errors in decision making that they produce.[30] For those seeking a textbook on judgment and decision making, we humbly recommend our own, *Judgment in Managerial Decision Making*, but ours is not the only text worthy of note.[31] Despite the existence of these other resources, we wanted to include this appendix for those who needed a reminder. This reminder highlights the value of decision leadership—helping others to overcome their limitations better and make wiser decisions. The ten chapters in this book show how to work with other people, capitalizing on their strengths and working with their limitations in order to help them make the best decisions they can.

Acknowledgments

We met in 1995. Don was working at an industrial supply company where he was on the fast track to a managerial position he did not want. Instead, he had discovered his passion to understand how people at companies like his made decisions. So he went door to door at the Kellogg Graduate School of Management at Northwestern looking for an escape—a research assistant position, paid or unpaid. Max, who was a professor at Kellogg at the time, saw potential, and the two of us have been working together ever since. Along the way, we have jointly and separately benefited from lots of other collaborators, too numerous to list. But some are simply central to the work you are currently reading.

Quite simply, this book would not have been possible without the support, love, and guidance of the colleagues, coauthors, and collaborators who inspired us and from whom we learned so much. We want to specifically thank Modupe Akinola, Cameron Anderson, Mahzarin Banaji, Dan Benjamin, John Beshears, Iris Bohnet, Severin Borenstein, Eugene Caruso, Dolly Chugh, Clayton Critcher, Stefano DellaVigna, Amelia Dev, Tina Diekmann, Ellen Evers, Francesca Gino, Joshua Greene, George Loewenstein, Jenn Logg, Mike Luca, Ulrike Malmendier, Kathleen McGinn, Doug Medin, David Messick, Ted Miguel, Katy Milkman, Leif Nelson, Mike Norton, Mike O'Donnell, Hannah Perfecto, Matthew Rabin, Todd Rogers, Andy Rose, Juliana Schroeder, Steve Tadelis, Ann Tenbrunsel, Liz Tenney, Chia Tsay, and

Ting Zhang. We owe a special debt of thanks to those in this group who read early drafts of this book and generously shared their ideas, feedback, and suggestions for how to make it better: Sandy Campbell, Ariella Kristal, Nate Meikle, and Barry Schwartz.

We should sound a note of appreciation for the decision leaders with whom we have the privilege of working, including Ann Harrison (Dean of the Haas School at UC Berkeley), Carol Christ (UC Berkeley Chancellor), Srikant Datar (Dean, Harvard Business School), and Kathleen McGinn (Senior Associate Dean, Harvard Business School). Special thanks go to Katie Shonk, our personal editor; to our literary agent, the inimitable Margo Fleming; and our editor at Yale University Press, Seth Ditchik.

Notes

Chapter 1. Leading the Decisions of Others

1. Sam Farmer, "The Ex-Green Beret Who Inspired Colin Kaepernick to Kneel Instead of Sit during the Anthem Would Like to Clear a Few Things Up," *Los Angeles Times*, September 17, 2018, sec. Sports, https://www.latimes.com/sports/nfl/la-sp-kaepernick-kneel-boyer-20180916-story.html.

2. Nick Wagoner, "Transcript of Colin Kaepernick's Comments after Preseason Finale," ESPN.com, September 2, 2016, https://www.espn.com/blog/san-francisco-49ers/post/_/id/19126/transcript-of-colin-kaepernicks-comments-after-preseason-finale.

3. "Trump to Anthem Protesters: 'Get That Son of a B——off the Field,' " NBC Sports, September 22, 2017, https://www.nbcsports.com/bayarea/49ers/trump-anthem-protesters-get-son-b-field.

4. BBC News, "NFL and Nike: Are Protests Hurting the Game's Ratings?," *BBC News*, September 10, 2018, sec. Newsbeat, https://www.bbc.com/news/newsbeat-45471429.

5. Ben Pickman, "Drew Brees: 'I Will Never Agree with Anybody Disrespecting the Flag,' " Sports Illustrated, accessed November 11, 2020, https://www.si.com/nfl/2020/06/03/saints-drew-brees-comments-kneeling-flag.

6. "Brees Apologizes: I 'Completely Missed the Mark,' " ESPN.com, June 4, 2020, https://www.espn.com/nfl/story/_/id/29265750/drew-brees-completely-missed-mark-comments-flag.

7. Nick Selbe, "Roger Goodell Offers Apology to Colin Kaepernick: 'I Wish We Had Listened Earlier,' " Sports Illustrated, August 23, 2020, https://www.si.com/nfl/2020/08/24/roger-goodell-apologizes-colin-kaepernick-national-anthem-protest.

8. Michael Rosenberg, "What Do You Think of Colin Kaepernick Now?," Sports Illustrated, accessed April 19, 2021, https://www.si.com/nfl/2020/06/01/colin-kaepernick-and-george-floyd-protests.

9. Thomas Carlyle, *On Heroes, Hero-Worship and the Heroic in History* (Chapman and Hall, 1840).

10. Julie S. Downs, George Loewenstein, and Jessica Wisdom, "Strategies for Promoting Healthier Food Choices," *American Economic Review* 99, no. 2 (April 2009): 159–64, https://doi.org/10.1257/aer.99.2.159.

11. Jessica Wisdom, Julie S. Downs, and George Loewenstein, "Promoting Healthy Choices: Information versus Convenience," *American Economic Journal: Applied Economics* 2, no. 2 (April 2010): 164–78, https://doi.org/10.1257/app.2.2.164.

12. Laszlo Bock, *Work Rules!* (New York: Hachette, 2015).

13. Teresa Wiltz, "Pelting the Pelts," *Washington Post*, February 11, 2000, https://www.washingtonpost.com/archive/lifestyle/2000/02/11/pelting-the-pelts/515beb9b-c355-4101-8a33-b11c8c254468/.

14. Saulius Šimčikas, "Is the Percentage of Vegetarians and Vegans in the U.S. Increasing?" (Animal Charity Evaluators, August 16, 2018), https://animalcharityevalu ators.org/blog/is-the-percentage-of-vegetarians-and-vegans-in-the-u-s-increasing/.

15. Tom Levitt, "Covid and Farm Animals: Nine Pandemics That Changed the World," *The Guardian*, September 15, 2020, https://www.theguardian.com/environ ment/ng-interactive/2020/sep/15/covid-farm-animals-and-pandemics-diseases-that-changed-the-world.

16. Cass R. Sunstein and Martha C. Nussbaum, *Animal Rights: Current Debates and New Directions* (Oxford: Oxford University Press, 2004).

17. Matthew Madia, "Chambliss Placing Hold on Sunstein Nomination," Center for Effective Government, June 30, 2009, https://www.foreffectivegov.org /node/10163.

18. Eric A. Posner and Cass R. Sunstein, *Law and Happiness* (Chicago: University of Chicago Press, 2010).

19. Cass R. Sunstein, *The World According to Star Wars*, 1st ed. (New York: Dey Street Books, 2016).

20. Richard H. Thaler and Cass R. Sunstein, *Nudge: Improving Decisions about Health, Wealth, and Happiness* (New Haven: Yale University Press, 2008).

21. Cass Sunstein, *Simpler: The Future of Government* (New York: Simon and Schuster, 2013).

22. William Fleeson, "Toward a Structure-and Process-Integrated View of Personality: Traits as Density Distributions of States," *Journal of Personality and Social Psychology* 80, no. 6 (2001): 1011.

23. Lee Ross and Richard E. Nisbett, *The Person and the Situation: Perspectives of Social Psychology* (New York: McGraw-Hill, 1991).

24. William Fleeson, "Moving Personality Beyond the Person–Situation Debate: The Challenge and the Opportunity of Within-Person Variability." *Current Directions in Psychological Science* 13, no. 2 (April 1, 2004): 83–87, https://doi.org/10.1111/j.0963–7214.2004.00280.x.

25. Alissa Fishbane, Aurelie Ouss, and Anuj K. Shah, "Behavioral Nudges Reduce Failure to Appear for Court," *Science*, October 8, 2020, https://doi.org/10.1126/science.abb6591.

26. Cass R. Sunstein, *Sludge: What Stops Us from Getting Things Done and What to Do about It* (Cambridge: MIT Press, 2021).

27. Jack Welch et al., *Winning*, vol. 84. (New York: HarperCollins, 2005).

28. Jack Welch, "When to Go With Your Gut," LinkedIn, November 12, 2013, https://www.linkedin.com/pulse/20131112125301–86541065-when-to-go-with-your-gut/.

29. Douglas W. Hubbard, *How to Measure Anything: Finding the Value of Intangibles in Business* (New York: John Wiley and Sons, 2010).

30. Ryan B. Scott and Zoltán Dienes, "The Conscious, the Unconscious, and Familiarity," *Journal of Experimental Psychology: Learning, Memory, and Cognition* 34, no. 5 (2008): 1264–88, https://doi.org/10.1037/a0012943.

31. Richard E. Nisbett and Lee Ross, *Human Inference: Strategies and Shortcomings of Social Judgment* (Englewood Cliffs, NJ: Prentice Hall, 1980).

Chapter 2. Guts vs. Brains

1. Daniel K. Walco and Jane L. Risen, "The Empirical Case for Acquiescing to Intuition," *Psychological Science* 28, no. 12 (December 1, 2017): 1807–20, https://doi.org/10.1177/0956797617723377.

2. Marla Tabaka, "Iconic Entrepreneurs Use Their Intuition to Succeed: What You Need to Know About Following Your Gut," Inc.com, September 30, 2019, https://www.inc.com/marla-tabaka/iconic-entrepreneurs-use-their-intuition-to-succeed-what-you-need-to-know-about-following-your-gut.html.

3. Daniel J. Simons and Christopher F. Chabris, "The Trouble with Intuition," *Chronicle of Higher Education*, May 30, 2010, https://www.chronicle.com/article/the-trouble-with-intuition/.

4. Richard A. Posner, "Blinkered," *The New Republic*, January 24, 2005, https://www.law.uchicago.edu/news/posner-reviews-blink.

5. Daniel Kahneman, Rose interviews Kahneman, interview by Charlie Rose, March 15, 2012, https://web.archive.org/web/20120315141302/http:/www.charlierose.com/view/interview/12185.

6. Max H. Bazerman and Don A. Moore, *Judgment in Managerial Decision Making*, 8th ed. (New York: Wiley, 2013).

7. Others have written eloquently about identifying the right problem to solve. We especially recommend Chip Heath and Dan Heath, *Decisive: How to Make Better Choices in Life and Work* (New York: Random House, 2013).

8. Keith E. Stanovich and Richard F. West, "Individual Differences in Reasoning: Implications for the Rationality Debate," *Behavioral & Brain Sciences* 23 (2000): 645–65.

9. Dolly Chugh, "Societal and Managerial Implications of Implicit Social Cognition: Why Milliseconds Matter," *Social Justice Research* 17, no. 2 (2004).

10. Edward Luce, "Ikea's Grown-up Plan to Tackle Child Labour," Financial Times, September 14, 2004, https://www.ft.com/content/b08b6b0e-066e-11d9-b95e-00000e2511c8.

11. Christopher A. Bartlett, Vincent Dessain, and Anders Sjoman, "IKEA's Global Sourcing Challenge: Indian Rugs and Child Labor" (Harvard Business Publishing, 2006), https://hbsp.harvard.edu/product/906414-PDF-ENG.

12. Robyn M. Dawes, "A Case Study of Graduate Admissions: Application of Three Principles of Human Decision Making," *American Psychologist* 26, no. 2 (1971): 180–88; Jennifer M. Logg, Julia A. Minson, and Don A. Moore, "Algorithm Appreciation: People Prefer Algorithmic to Human Judgment," *Organizational Behavior and Human Decision Processes* 151 (2019): 90–103.

13. "Standard Deviation," in *Wikipedia*, May 8, 2021, https://en.wikipedia.org/w/index.php?title=Standard_deviation&oldid=1022056251.

14. Samuel A. Swift et al., "Inflated Applicants: Attribution Errors in Performance Evaluation by Professionals," *PLoS ONE* 8, no. 7 (2013): e69258, https://doi.org/10.1371/journal.pone.0069258.

15. Daniel Kahneman and Dan Lovallo, "Timid Choices and Bold Forecasts: A Cognitive Perspective on Risk and Risk Taking," *Management Science* 39 (1993): 17–31.

16. Gerd Gigerenzer, Ulrich Hoffrage, and Heinz Kleinbölting, "Probabilistic Mental Models: A Brunswikian Theory of Confidence," *Psychological Review* 98, no. 4 (1991): 506–28; Kahneman and Lovallo, "Timid Choices and Bold Forecasts: A Cognitive Perspective on Risk and Risk Taking"; Arnold C. Cooper, Carolyn Y. Woo, and William C. Dunkelberg, "Entrepreneurs' Perceived Chances for Success," *Journal of Business Venturing* 3, no. 2 (1988): 97–109.

17. Alex Rees-Jones, "Quantifying Loss-Averse Tax Manipulation," *Review of Economic Studies* 85, no. 2 (2018): 1251–78.

18. Much of this section is based on the writing of Matthew Rabin (2000), including Rabin and Bazerman (2019), which applied Rabin's original work to leadership decision making. Matthew Rabin, "Risk Aversion and Expected-Utility Theory: A Calibration Theorem," *Econometrica* 68, no. 5 (2000): 1281–92.

19. Matthew Rabin and Max Bazerman, "Fretting about Modest Risks Is a Mistake," *California Management Review* 61, no. 3 (2019): 34–48.

20. Max H. Bazerman, "Negotiator Judgment: A Critical Look at the Rationality Assumption," *American Behavioral Scientist* 27, no. 2 (1983): 211–28.

21. Daniel Kahneman and Amos Tversky, "Prospect Theory: An Analysis of Decision under Risk," *Econometrica* 47, no. 2 (1979): 263–91.

22. Rabin, "Risk Aversion and Expected-Utility Theory: A Calibration Theorem."

23. Daniel Kahneman and Amos Tversky, "The Framing of Decisions and the Psychology of Choice," *Science* 211, no. 4481 (1981): 453–58.

24. Michael Ghaffary, "A Lawyer's Risk Aversion Begins in Law School: Systematic Risk Aversion in Law Students Compared to MBA Counterparts," May 2006.

25. Rabin and Bazerman, "Fretting about Modest Risks Is a Mistake," 34–48.

26. Rabin and Bazerman, "Fretting about Modest Risks Is a Mistake.

27. Ovul Sezer et al., "Overcoming the Outcome Bias: Making Intentions Matter," *Organizational Behavior and Human Decision Processes* 137 (2016): 13–26.

28. Paul C. Nutt, "Expanding the Search for Alternatives during Strategic Decision-Making," *Academy of Management Perspectives* 18, no. 4 (November 1, 2004): 13–28, https://doi.org/10.5465/ame.2004.15268668.

29. Iris Bohnet, Alexandra van Geen, and Max H. Bazerman, "When Performance Trumps Gender Bias: Joint vs. Separate Evaluation," *Management Science* 62, no. 5 (2016): 1225–34.

30. Max H. Bazerman et al., "The Inconsistent Role of Comparison Others and Procedural Justice in Reactions to Hypothetical Job Descriptions: Implications for Job Acceptance Decisions," *Organizational Behavior and Human Decision Processes* 60, no. 3 (1994): 326–52.

31. Ilana Ritov and Daniel Kahneman, "How People Value the Environment: Attitudes versus Economic Values," in *Environment, Ethics, and Behavior: The Psychology of Environmental Valuation and Degradation. The New Lexington Press Management Series and the New Lexington Press Social and Behavioral Science Series*, ed. Max H. Bazerman and David M. Messick (San Francisco: New Lexington Press/Jossey-Bass Inc., Publishers, 1997), 33–51.

32. Edward H. Chang et al., "The Isolated Choice Effect and Its Implications for Gender Diversity in Organizations," *Management Science* (2020).

33. Brian J. Lucas et al., "A Longer Shortlist Increases the Consideration of Female Candidates in Male-Dominant Domains," *Nature Human Behaviour* (2021): 1–7.

Chapter 3. Be Investigator-in-Chief

1. Robert Maxwell, "A Restaurant Ruined My Life," *Toronto Life*, October 30, 2017, https://torontolife.com/food/restaurant-ruined-life/.

2. Ibid.

3. Ibid.

4. Ibid.

5. Colin F. Camerer and Dan Lovallo, "Overconfidence and Excess Entry: An Experimental Approach," *American Economic Review* 89, no. 1 (1999): 306–18.

6. Don A. Moore, J. M. Oesch, and C. Zietsma, "What Competition? Myopic Self-Focus in Market-Entry Decisions," *Organization Science* 18, no. 3 (2007), https://doi.org/10.1287/orsc.1060.0243.

7. Don A. Moore and Daylian M. Cain, "Overconfidence and Underconfidence: When and Why People Underestimate (and Overestimate) the Competition," *Organizational Behavior & Human Decision Processes* 103 (2007): 197–213.

8. Phil Rosenzweig, *The Halo Effect* (New York: Free Press, 2007).

9. Diana B. Henriques, *The Wizard of Lies: Bernie Madoff and the Death of Trust* (New York: Times Books/Henry Holt, 2011).

10. Alex Berenson and Matthew Saltmarsh, "Madoff Investor's Suicide Leaves Questions," *New York Times*, January 1, 2009, sec. Business Day, https://www.nytimes.com/2009/01/02/business/02madoff.html.

11. Lauren Feiner, "SoftBank Values WeWork at $2.9 Billion, down from $47 Billion a Year Ago," CNBC, May 18, 2020, https://www.cnbc.com/2020/05/18/softbank-ceo-calls-wework-investment-foolish-valuation-falls-to-2point9-billion.html.

12. Peter Eavis and Michael J. de la Merced, "WeWork I.P.O. Is Withdrawn as Investors Grow Wary," *New York Times*, September 30, 2019, sec. Business, https://www.nytimes.com/2019/09/30/business/wework-ipo.html.

13. Eliot Brown, "How Adam Neumann's Over-the-Top Style Built WeWork: 'This Is Not the Way Everybody Behaves,' " *Wall Street Journal*, September 18, 2019, sec. Business, https://www.wsj.com/articles/this-is-not-the-way-everybody-behaves-how-adam-neumanns-over-the-top-style-built-wework-11568823827.

14. Reeves Wiedeman, *Billion Dollar Loser: The Epic Rise and Spectacular Fall of Adam Neumann and WeWork* (Boston: Little, Brown, 2020).

15. Jack Kelly, "The Wild Story of WeWork: The Once-Heralded Unicorn Now Under the Microscope," *Forbes*, September 23, 2019, https://www.forbes.com/sites/

jackkelly/2019/09/23/the-wild-over-the-top-story-of-wework-the-once-heralded-unicorn-is-now-under-the-microscope/.

16. Lizzie Widdicombe, "The Rise and Fall of WeWork," *New Yorker*, November 6, 2019, https://www.newyorker.com/culture/culture-desk/the-rise-and-fall-of-wework.

17. Feiner, "SoftBank Values WeWork at $2.9 Billion, down from $47 Billion a Year Ago."

18. Julie Bort, "How WeWork Paid Adam Neumann $5.9 Million to Use the Name 'We,' " Business Insider, accessed November 19, 2020, https://www.businessinsider.com/how-wework-paid-adam-neumann-59-million-to-use-the-name-we-2019-8.

19. Widdicombe, "The Rise and Fall of WeWork."

20. Gabriel Sherman, " 'You Don't Bring Bad News to the Cult Leader': Inside the Fall of WeWork," Vanity Fair, November 21, 2019, https://www.vanityfair.com/news/2019/11/inside-the-fall-of-wework.

21. Ibid.

22. Sam Nussey, "SoftBank's Son Sticks with Gut-Led Investing in Chat with Alibaba's Ma," Reuters, December 6, 2019, https://www.reuters.com/article/us-softbank-group-alibaba-idUSKBN1YA0HB.

23. Max H. Bazerman, *The Power of Noticing: What the Best Leaders See* (New York: Simon and Schuster, 2014).

24. Max H. Bazerman, George Loewenstein, and Don A. Moore, "Why Good Accountants Do Bad Audits," *Harvard Business Review* 80, no. 11 (2002).

25. Francesca Gino and Max H. Bazerman, "When Misconduct Goes Unnoticed: The Acceptability of Gradual Erosion in Others' Unethical Behavior," *Journal of Experimental Social Psychology* 45 (2009): 708–19.

26. David T. Welsh et al., "The Slippery Slope: How Small Ethical Transgressions Pave the Way for Larger Future Transgressions," *Journal of Applied Psychology* 100, no. 1 (2015): 114–27.

27. Warren G. Bennis and Robert J. Thomas, *Geeks and Geezers: How Era, Values, and Defining Moments Shape Leaders—How Tough Times Shape Good Leaders* (Boston: Harvard Business School Press, 2002).

28. Nisbett and Ross, *Human Inference: Strategies and Shortcomings of Social Judgment*.

29. Michael Lewis, *Moneyball: The Art of Winning an Unfair Game* (New York: W. W. Norton, 2003).

Chapter 4. Calibrate Your Confidence

1. Mike Baker, "When Did the Coronavirus Arrive in the U.S.? Here's a Review of the Evidence," *New York Times*, May 15, 2020, sec. U.S., https://www.nytimes.com/2020/05/15/us/coronavirus-first-case-snohomish-antibodies.html.

2. Aaron Blake and JM Rieger, "Timeline: The More than 50 Times Trump Has Downplayed the Coronavirus Threat," *Washington Post*, May 7, 2020, https://www.washingtonpost.com/politics/2020/03/12/trump-coronavirus-timeline/.

3. Ibid.

4. Christopher Sherman, "Mexico: More Social Spending, No Business Bailout for Virus | World News | US News," *U.S. News and World Report*, April 5, 2020, https://www.usnews.com/news/world/articles/2020-04-05/mexico-more-social-spending-no-big-business-bailout.

5. Ernesto Londoño, Manuela Andreoni, and Letícia Casado, "Bolsonaro, Isolated and Defiant, Dismisses Coronavirus Threat to Brazil," *New York Times*, April 1, 2020, sec. World, https://www.nytimes.com/2020/04/01/world/americas/brazil-bolsonaro-coronavirus.html.

6. Boris Johnson, "Prime Minister's Statement on Coronavirus (COVID-19): 19 March 2020," GOV.UK, March 19, 2020, https://www.gov.uk/government/speeches/pm-statement-on-coronavirus-19-march-2020.

7. 이치동, "Moon Declares 'War' against Virus, Puts Gov't on 24-Hour Alert," Yonhap News Agency, March 3, 2020, sec. Politics, https://en.yna.co.kr/view/AEN20200303004700315.

8. Larry Buchanan, K. K. Rebecca Lai, and Allison McCann, "U.S. Lags in Coronavirus Testing After Slow Response to Outbreak," *New York Times*, March 17, 2020, sec. U.S., https://www.nytimes.com/interactive/2020/03/17/us/coronavirus-testing-data.html.

9. Susan Strongman, "Covid-19 Pandemic Timeline," 2020, http://shorthand.radionz.co.nz/coronavirus-timeline/index.html.

10. Blake and Rieger, "Analysis | Timeline."

11. Alana Wise, "Trump Falsely Claimed 'Total' Authority Over States—Now He's Backpedaling," NPR.org, accessed July 23, 2020, https://www.npr.org/2020/04/14/834641661/trump-falsely-claimed-total-authority-over-states-now-he-s-backpedaling.

12. Agencies, "South Korea Mers Outbreak Is 'Large and Complex,' Says WHO, as 14th Victim Dies," *The Guardian,* June 13, 2015, http://www.theguardian.com/world/2015/jun/13/south-korea-mers-outbreak-is-large-and-complex-says-who-as-14th-victim-dies.

13. Agencies.

14. Beth Cameron, "I Ran the White House Pandemic Office. Trump Closed It," *Washington Post*, March 13, 2020, https://www.washingtonpost.com/outlook/nsc-pandemic-office-trump-closed/2020/03/13/a70de09c-6491–11ea-acca-80c22bbee96f_story.html.

15. "COVID Live Update: 159,068,260 Cases and 3,308,747 Deaths from the Coronavirus—Worldometer," accessed May 10, 2021, https://www.worldometers.info/coronavirus/?utm_campaign=homeAdvegas1?%22%20%5Cl%20%22countries.

16. Isaac Sebenius and James K. Sebenius, "How Many Needless Covid-19 Deaths Were Caused by Delays in Responding? Most of Them," *STAT* (blog), June 19, 2020, https://www.statnews.com/2020/06/19/faster-response-prevented-most-us-covid-19-deaths/.

17. As of this writing, more than half a million have lost their lives.

18. Sen Pei, Sasikiran Kandula, and Jeffrey Shaman, "Differential Effects of Intervention Timing on COVID-19 Spread in the United States," *Science Advances* 6, no. 49 (December 1, 2020): eabd6370, https://doi.org/10.1126/sciadv.abd6370.

19. Robert Iger, "The Ride of a Lifetime: Lessons Learned from 15 Years as CEO of the Walt Disney Company," 2019.

20. Randy Komisar and Jantoon Reigersman, *Straight Talk for Startups: 100 Insider Rules for Beating the Odds—From Mastering the Fundamentals to Selecting Investors, Fundraising, Managing Boards, and Achieving Liquidity* (New York: HarperCollins, 2018).

21. Rebecca Knight, "How to Handle the Pressure of Being a Manager Right Now," *Harvard Business Review*, April 30, 2020, https://hbr.org/2020/04/how-to-handle-the-pressure-of-being-a-manager-right-now.

22. Walter Isaacson, *Steve Jobs* (New York: Simon and Schuster, 2011).

23. Tom Lutey, "Trump: 'We're Going to Win So Much, You're Going to Be So Sick and Tired of Winning,'" *Billings Gazette*, May 26, 2016, https://billingsgazette.com/news/government-and-politics/trump-we-re-going-to-win-so-much-you-re-going-to-be-so-sick/article_2f346f38–37e7–5711-ae07-d1fd000f4c38.html.

24. Cameron Anderson et al., "A Status-Enhancement Account of Overconfidence," *Journal of Personality and Social Psychology* 103, no. 4 (2012): 718–35, https://doi.org/10.1037/a0029395.

25. Celia Gaertig and Joseph P. Simmons, "Do People Inherently Dislike Uncertain Advice?," *Psychological Science* 29, no. 4 (2018): 504–20.

26. Celia Gaertig and Joseph Simmons, "Should Advisors Provide Confidence Intervals around Their Estimates?" (Society for Judgment and Decision Making,

Cyberspace, December 12, 2020), https://www.youtube.com/watch?v=SZuxy25qwsg&feature=youtu.be.

27. Suze Wilson, "Three Reasons Why Jacinda Ardern's Coronavirus Response Has Been a Masterclass in Crisis Leadership," The Conversation, accessed March 18, 2021, http://theconversation.com/three-reasons-why-jacinda-arderns-coronavirus-response-has-been-a-masterclass-in-crisis-leadership-135541.

28. Steve Kerr, Kerr at the Haas Culture Conference, Conference keynote interview, January 17, 2020.

29. Brad Stone, *The Everything Store: Jeff Bezos and the Age of Amazon* (Boston: Little, Brown, 2013).

30. Donald Trump and Tony Schwartz, *Trump: The Art of the Deal*, 1st ed. (New York: Random House, 1987).

31. Don A. Moore, *Perfectly Confident* (New York: Harper Collins, 2020).

32. Julia Galef, *The Scout Mindset* (New York: Portfolio, 2021).

33. The European Union: Austria, Belgium, Bulgaria, Croatia, Cyprus, Czechia, Denmark, Estonia, Finland, France, Germany, Greece, Hungary, Ireland, Italy, Latvia, Lithuania, Luxembourg, Malta, Netherlands, Poland, Portugal, Romania, Slovakia, Slovenia, Spain, Sweden (https://europa.eu/european-union/about-eu/countries_en).

34. Ray Dalio, *Principles: Life and Work* (New York: Simon and Schuster, 2017).

35. David Gelles et al., "Boeing Was 'Go, Go, Go' to Beat Airbus With the 737 Max," *New York Times*, March 23, 2019, sec. Business, https://www.nytimes.com/2019/03/23/business/boeing-737-max-crash.html.

36. Sim B. Sitkin et al., "The Paradox of Stretch Goals: Organizations in Pursuit of the Seemingly Impossible," *Academy of Management Review* 36, no. 3 (2011): 544–66.

37. Edwin A. Locke and Gary P. Latham, *A Theory of Goal-Setting and Task Performance* (Englewood Cliffs, NJ: Prentice Hall, 1990).

38. Jim Collins and Jerry I. Porras, *Built to Last: Successful Habits of Visionary Companies* (New York: Harper Collins, 1994).

39. Ibid.

40. Niraj Chokshi, "U.S. Watchdog's Report Faults Boeing's Disclosures on 737 Max Software," *New York Times*, July 1, 2020, sec. Business, https://www.nytimes.com/2020/07/01/business/boeing-faa-737-max.html.

41. Annie Duke, *Thinking in Bets* (New York: Penguin, 2018), https://books.google.com/books?id=hOZFDwAAQBAJ.

42. Mo Nuwwarah, "World Vegetarian Day: Poker's Crossover With Plant-Based Diets," October 1, 2018, https://www.pokernews.com/news/2018/10/world-vegetarian-day-poker-crossover-32242.htm.

43. Max H. Bazerman and William F. Samuelson, "I Won the Auction but Don't Want the Prize," *Journal of Conflict Resolution* 27, no. 4 (1983): 618–34.

44. Nathan Heller, "Is Venture Capital Worth the Risk?," *New Yorker*, January 20, 2020, https://www.newyorker.com/magazine/2020/01/27/is-venture-capital-worth-the-risk.

45. Elizabeth R. Tenney, Jennifer M. Logg, and Don A. Moore, "(Too) Optimistic about Optimism: The Belief That Optimism Improves Performance," *Journal of Personality and Social Psychology* 108, no. 3 (2015): 377–99, https://doi.org/10.1037/pspa0000018.

46. Robert Trivers, *The Folly of Fools: The Logic of Deceit and Self-Deception in Human Life* (New York: Basic Books, 2011).

47. Londoño, Andreoni, and Casado, "Bolsonaro, Isolated and Defiant, Dismisses Coronavirus Threat to Brazil."

48. Caleb P. Skipper et al., "Hydroxychloroquine in Nonhospitalized Adults with Early COVID-19," *Annals of Internal Medicine*, July 16, 2020, https://doi.org/10.7326/M20-4207.

49. Lee Brown, "Belarus President Believes Vodka and Saunas Will Cure Coronavirus," *New York Post*, March 30, 2020, https://nypost.com/2020/03/30/belarus-president-believes-vodka-and-saunas-will-cure-coronavirus/.

50. Katie Rogers et al., "Trump's Suggestion That Disinfectants Could Be Used to Treat Coronavirus Prompts Aggressive Pushback," *New York Times*, April 24, 2020, sec. U.S., https://www.nytimes.com/2020/04/24/us/politics/trump-inject-disinfectant-bleach-coronavirus.html.

51. Sophia Ankel, "Tulsa Rally: Trump Said He Ordered Slowdown in Coronavirus Testing—Business Insider," *Business Insider*, June 21, 2020, https://www.businessinsider.com/tulsa-rally-trump-said-ordered-to-slow-down-coronavirus-testing-2020-6.

52. Robert H. Frank, *Success and Luck: Good Fortune and the Myth of Meritocracy* (Princeton: Princeton University Press, 2016).

53. John T. Jost, *A Theory of System Justification* (Cambridge: Harvard University Press, 2020).

54. Daniel Kahneman, *Thinking Fast and Slow* (New York: Farrar, Straus and Giroux, 2011).

55. Bryce G. Hoffman, *Red Teaming: How Your Business Can Conquer the Competition by Challenging Everything* (New York: Crown Business, 2017).

Chapter 5. Advice, Persuasion, and Collaboration

1. Reed Hastings and Erin Meyer, *No Rules Rules: Netflix and the Culture of Reinvention* (New York: Penguin, 2020).

2. Netflix, *Netflix CEO Reed Hastings Apologizes for Mishandling the Change to Qwikster*, 2011, https://www.youtube.com/watch?v=7tWKotW1fig.

3. Saturday Night Live, "Netflix Apology," *Saturday Night Live*, 2013, https://www.youtube.com/watch?v=0eAXW-zkGlM.

4. Jason Gilbert, "Qwikster Goes Qwikly: A Look Back at a Netflix Mistake," *HuffPost*, October 10, 2011, https://www.huffpost.com/entry/qwikster-netflix-mistake_n_1003367.

5. Hastings and Meyer, *No Rules Rules*.

6. Ibid.

7. Ted Sorensen, *Kennedy* (New York: Harper and Row, 1965), 306.

8. Irving L. Janis, *Groupthink: Psychological Studies of Policy Decisions and Fiascoes*, 2nd ed. (Boston: Houghton Mifflin, 1982).

9. Dale T. Miller and Cathy McFarland, "Pluralistic Ignorance: When Similarity Is Interpreted as Dissimilarity," *Journal of Personality and Social Psychology* 53, no. 2 (1987): 298–305.

10. Dalio, *Principles: Life and Work*.

11. Taylor Soper, " 'Failure and Innovation Are Inseparable Twins': Amazon Founder Jeff Bezos Offers 7 Leadership Principles," GeekWire, 2016, https://www.geekwire.com/2016/amazon-founder-jeff-bezos-offers-6-leadership-principles-change-mind-lot-embrace-failure-ditch-powerpoints/.

12. Janet A. Sniezek and Timothy Buckley, "Cueing and Cognitive Conflict in Judge-Advisor Decision Making," *Organizational Behavior and Human Decision Processes* 62, no. 2 (1995): 159–74; Ilan Yaniv and Eli Kleinberger, "Advice Taking in Decision Making: Egocentric Discounting and Reputation Formation," *Organizational Behavior and Human Decision Processes* 84, no. 2 (2000): 260–81; Richard P. Larrick, Katherine A. Burson, and Jack B. Soll, "Social Comparison and Confidence: When Thinking You're Better than Average Predicts Overconfidence (and When It Does Not)," *Organizational Behavior and Human Decision Processes* 102, no. 1 (2007): 76–94.

13. Albert E. Mannes, Richard P. Larrick, and Jack B. Soll, "The Social Psychology of the Wisdom of Crowds," in *Frontiers of Social Psychology: Social Judgment and Decision Making*, ed. Joachim I. Krueger (New York: Psychology Press, 2012), 227–42.

14. Jack B. Soll and Richard P. Larrick, "Strategies for Revising Judgment: How (and How Well) People Use Others' Opinions," *Journal of Experimental Psychology: Learning, Memory, and Cognition* 35, no. 3 (2009): 780–805.

15. Richard P. Larrick and Jack B. Soll, "Intuitions about Combining Opinions: Misappreciation of the Averaging Principle," *Management Science* 52, no. 1 (2006): 111–27.

16. Don A. Moore, *Perfectly Confident* (New York: HarperCollins, 2020).

17. F. Gino and Don A. Moore, "Effects of Task Difficulty on Use of Advice," *Journal of Behavioral Decision Making* 20, no. 1 (2007): 21–35, https://doi.org/10.1002/bdm.539.

18. Mannes, Larrick, and Soll, "The Social Psychology of the Wisdom of Crowds."

19. D. Kahneman, O. Sibony, and C. Sunstein, *Noise* (Boston: Little, Brown Spark, 2021).

20. Plato, *Essential Dialogs of Plato*, trans. B. Jowett (Boston: Little, Brown, 2005).

21. James Surowiecki, *The Wisdom of Crowds* (New York: Random House, 2005).

22. Francis Galton, "Vox Populi (The Wisdom of Crowds)," *Nature* 75, no. 7 (1907): 450–51.

23. Mannes, Larrick, and Soll, "The Social Psychology of the Wisdom of Crowds."

24. Albert E. Mannes, Jack B. Soll, and Richard P. Larrick, "The Wisdom of Small Crowds," *Journal of Personality and Social Psychology* 107, no. 2 (2014): 276–99.

25. Norbert L. Kerr and R. Scott Tindale, "Group Performance and Decision Making," *Annual Review of Psychology* 55 (2004): 623–55.

26. Norman Dalkey and Olaf Helmer, "An Experimental Application of the Delphi Method to the Use of Experts," *Management Science* 9, no. 3 (1963): 458–67.

27. Michael Diehl and Wolfgang Stroebe, "Productivity Loss in Brainstorming Groups: Toward the Solution of a Riddle," *Journal of Personality and Social Psychology* 53, no. 3 (1987): 497–509.

28. John Gapper, "The Curse of the Consultants Is Spreading Fast," Financial Times, May 10, 2017, https://www.ft.com/content/ecfcaf46–34bc-11e7–99bd-13beb0903fa3.

29. Ibid.

30. Duff McDonald, *The Firm: The Story of McKinsey and Its Secret Influence on American Business* (New York: Simon and Schuster, 2014).

31. "McKinsey & Company," Forbes, accessed April 21, 2021, https://www.forbes.com/companies/mckinsey-company/.

32. "McKinsey Pricing Sheet Email—DocumentCloud," accessed March 23, 2021, https://www.documentcloud.org/documents/6988833-McKinsey-Pricing-Sheet-Email.html#document/p1/a571760.

33. Martin Birchall, "Consultancy Pioneer Is Still Setting the Pace," *Sunday Times*, June 8, 2006.

34. "Rethinking McKinsey," The Economist, November 21, 2019, https://www.economist.com/business/2019/11/21/rethinking-mckinsey.

35. Justin Peters, "How McKinsey Helps Companies Avoid Responsibility," Slate, June 24, 2020, https://slate.com/business/2020/06/mckinsey-companies-avoid-responsibility-management-consulting.html.

36. "The Firm That Built the House of Enron," The Guardian, March 23, 2002, https://www.theguardian.com/business/2002/mar/24/enron.theobserver.

37. Ben Chu, "McKinsey: How Does It Always Get Away with It?," The Independent, February 7, 2014, https://www.independent.co.uk/news/business/analysis-and-features/mckinsey-how-does-it-always-get-away-it-9113484.html.

38. Duff McDonald, "Galleon Scandal's Executive Conundrum," CNN, October 23, 2009, https://money.cnn.com/2009/10/22/news/companies/galleon_scandal_rules.fortune/index.htm.

39. Stephen Gandel and Reuters, "What Caused Valeant's Epic 90% Plunge," Fortune, March 20, 2016, http://fortune.com/2016/03/20/valeant-timeline-scandal/.

40. John Gapper, "McKinsey's Fingerprints Are All over Valeant," Financial Times, March 23, 2016, https://www.ft.com/content/0bb37fd2-ef63–11e5-aff5–19b4e253664a.

41. Michael Forsythe and Walt Bogdanich, "McKinsey Advised Purdue Pharma How to 'Turbocharge' Opioid Sales, Lawsuit Says," New York Times, February 1, 2019, https://www.nytimes.com/2019/02/01/business/purdue-pharma-mckinsey-oxycontin-opiods.html.

42. Maya Salam, "The Opioid Epidemic: A Crisis Years in the Making," New York Times, October 26, 2017, sec. U.S., https://www.nytimes.com/2017/10/26/us/opioid-crisis-public-health-emergency.html.

43. Andrew Edgecliffe-Johnson, "McKinsey Reaches $45m Opioid Settlement with Nevada," Financial Times, March 22, 2021, https://www.ft.com/content/f54a515e-6cfe-4d0d-90fd-fdbff5c34e00.

44. Walt Bogdanich and Michael Forsythe, "How McKinsey Has Helped Raise the Stature of Authoritarian Governments," New York Times, December 15, 2018, https://www.nytimes.com/2018/12/15/world/asia/mckinsey-china-russia.html.

45. Cass R. Sunstein and Reid Hastie, Wiser: Getting beyond Groupthink to Make Groups Smarter (Cambridge: Harvard Business Press, 2015).

46. Justin Wolfers and Eric Zitzewitz, "Prediction Markets," Journal of Economic Perspectives 18, no. 2 (2004): 107–26.

47. Bo Cowgill and Eric Zitzewitz, "Corporate Prediction Markets: Evidence from Google, Ford, and Firm X," Review of Economic Studies 82, no. 4 (293) (2015): 1309–41.

48. Phred Dvorak, "Best Buy Taps 'Prediction Market,' " *Wall Street Journal*, September 16, 2008, https://www.wsj.com/articles/SB122152452811139909.

49. Philip E. Tetlock and Dan Gardner, *Superforecasting: The Art and Science of Prediction* (New York: Signal, 2015).

50. Jason Dana et al., "Are Markets More Accurate than Polls? The Surprising Informational Value of 'Just Asking,' " *Judgment and Decision Making* 14, no. 2 (2019): 135–47.

51. A couple of caveats are in order here. One advantage of markets is continuously updated prices. Updating a poll requires that people update their forecasts. The group's current consensus should discount stale forecasts. Markets also provide incentives, and rewarding poll forecasts requires incentive-compatible scoring rules such as the Brier score. See Kenneth C. Lichtendahl, and Robert L. Winkler, "Probability Elicitation, Scoring Rules, and Competition among Forecasters." *Management Science* 53 (2007): 1745–55.

52. Edward Moyer, "Netflix CEO: 'I Slid into Arrogance,' " CNET, accessed March 16, 2021, https://www.cnet.com/news/netflix-ceo-i-slid-into-arrogance/.

53. Hastings and Meyer, *No Rules Rules*.

Chapter 6. Recruiting the Best Evidence

1. Chitra Ramaswamy, " 'Prejudices Play Out in the Ratings We Give'—the Myth of Digital Equality," *The Guardian*, February 20, 2017, sec. Technology, http://www.theguardian.com/technology/2017/feb/20/airbnb-uber-sharing-apps-digital-equality.

2. Benjamin Edelman, Michael Luca, and Dan Svirsky, "Racial Discrimination in the Sharing Economy: Evidence from a Field Experiment," *American Economic Journal: Applied Economics* 9, no. 2 (April 2017): 1–22, https://doi.org/10.1257/app.20160213.

3. Shankar Vedantam, *#AirbnbWhileBlack: How Hidden Bias Shapes the Sharing Economy*, Podcast, *Hidden Brain*, accessed March 2, 2021, https://www.npr.org/2016/04/26/475623339/-airbnbwhileblack-how-hidden-bias-shapes-the-sharing-economy.

4. Michael Luca and Max H. Bazerman, *The Power of Experiments: Decision Making in a Data-Driven World* (Cambridge: MIT Press, 2020).

5. Bazerman, Loewenstein, and Moore, "Why Good Accountants Do Bad Audits."

6. Thaler and Sunstein, *Nudge: Improving Decisions about Health, Wealth, and Happiness*.

7. Katrin Bennhold, "Britain's Ministry of Nudges," *New York Times*, December 7, 2013, sec. Business, https://www.nytimes.com/2013/12/08/business/international/britains-ministry-of-nudges.html.

8. Matt Chorley, "Tax Gap Widens to Reveal £34billion Owed to HMRC Went Unpaid Last Year," Mail Online, October 16, 2014, https://www.dailymail.co.uk/news/article-2795758/osborne-warned-mega-problem-tax-gap-widens-reveal-34billion-owed-hmrc-went-unpaid-year.html.

9. Robert B. Cialdini, *Influence: Science and Practice* (Boston: Allyn and Bacon, 2009).

10. David Cameron, *The Next Age of Government*, accessed December 31, 2019, https://www.ted.com/talks/david_cameron_the_next_age_of_government.

11. David Halpern, *Inside the Nudge Unit: How Small Changes Can Make a Big Difference* (New York: Random House, 2015).

12. Apolitical, "These 10 Governments Are Leading the World in Behavioural Science," March 1, 2019, https://apolitical.co/en/solution_article/these-10-governments-are-leading-the-world-in-behavioural-science.

13. Kelly Bidwell, Personal communication, Telephone interview, August 7, 2020.

14. Stefano DellaVigna and Elizabeth Linos, "RCTs to Scale: Comprehensive Evidence from Two Nudge Units," Working paper, NBER, 2020, https://www.nber.org/papers/w27594.

15. Hastings and Meyer, *No Rules Rules*.

16. Ben Clarke, "Why These Tech Companies Keep Running Thousands of Failed Experiments," Fast Company, September 21, 2016, https://www.fastcompany.com/3063846/why-these-tech-companies-keep-running-thousands-of-failed.

17. Luca and Bazerman, *The Power of Experiments*.

18. Both Max and Don are part of the Behavioral Change for Good network.

19. Katherine L. Milkman et al., "A Megastudy of Text-Based Nudges Encouraging Patients to Get Vaccinated at an Upcoming Doctor's Appointment," *Proceedings of the National Academy of Sciences* 118, no. 20 (May 18, 2021), https://doi.org/10.1073/pnas.2101165118.

20. Iowa joins three other states sharing citizenship data with U.S. Census, July 17, 2020, KCCI Des Moines. https://www.kcci.com/article/iowa-joins-3-other-states-sharing-citizenship-data-with-us-census/33349980.

21. Michelle N. Meyer et al., "Objecting to Experiments That Compare Two Unobjectionable Policies or Treatments," *Proceedings of the National Academy of Sciences*, May 9, 2019, 201820701, https://doi.org/10.1073/pnas.1820701116.

Chapter 7. Negotiate for One and All

1. Tejvan Pettinger, "Benefits of Free Trade," Economics Help, July 28, 2019, https://www.economicshelp.org/trade2/benefits_free_trade/.

2. As a nation, we could do better distributing the benefits of free trade to compensate those most negatively affected by it. We ought to strengthen the social safety net under those whose jobs are jeopardized by foreign competition and provide them with employment alternatives.

3. Jim Tankersley and Keith Bradsher, "Trump Hits China with Tariffs on $200 Billion in Goods, Escalating Trade War," *New York Times*, September 17, 2018.

4. Deepak Malhotra and Max H. Bazerman, *Negotiation Genius* (New York: Bantam, 2007).

5. Rainer Zitelmann, "Why CEOs Need to Be Able to Deal With Conflict: Learning from Jack Welch," *Forbes*, November 18, 2019, https://www.forbes.com/sites/rainerzitelmann/2019/11/18/why-ceos-need-to-be-able-to-deal-with-conflict-learning-from-jack-welch/#474d4973121c.

6. Max H. Bazerman and Jeanne M. Brett, "El-Tek Simulation" (Dispute Resolution Research Center, Northwestern University, 1991).

7. Howard Raiffa, "Post-Settlement Settlements," *Negotiation Journal* 1 (1985): 9–12.

8. Malhotra and Bazerman, *Negotiation Genius*.

9. Raiffa, "Post-Settlement Settlements," 9.

10. Chunka Mui, "How Kodak Failed," *Forbes*, January 18, 2012, https://www.forbes.com/sites/chunkamui/2012/01/18/how-kodak-failed/.

11. Jay M. Feinman, *Delay, Deny, Defend: Why Insurance Companies Don't Pay Claims and What You Can Do About It* (New York: Portfolio, 2010).

12. Max has consulted for Slice.

13. Office of the Maritime Administrator, "Deepwater Horizon Marine Casualty Investigation Report," August 17, 2011, https://www.register-iri.com/wp-content/uploads/Republic_of_the_Marshall_Islands_DEEPWATER_HORIZON_Marine_Casualty_Investigation_Report-Low_Resolution.pdf.

14. Christina Ingersoll, Richard M. Locke, and Cate Reavis, "BP and the Deepwater Horizon Disaster of 2010," *MIT Sloan School of Management, Case Study*, 2012.

15. Ibid

16. Saadi Afraz, "THE CASE OF BRITISH PETROLEUM," August 9, 2020, https://www.academia.edu/3775991/THE_CASE_OF_BRITISH_PETROLEUM_THE_EVENT.

17. Yong Gyo Lee, Xavier Garza-Gomez, and Rose M. Lee, "Ultimate Costs of the Disaster: Seven Years after the Deepwater Horizon Oil Spill," *Journal of Corporate Accounting and Finance* 29, no. 1 (2018): 69–79, https://doi.org/10.1002/jcaf.22306.

Chapter 8. A Higher Purpose

1. Milton Friedman, "A Friedman Doctrine—The Social Responsibility of Business Is to Increase Its Profits," *New York Times*, September 13, 1970, sec. Archives, https://www.nytimes.com/1970/09/13/archives/a-friedman-doctrine-the-social-responsibility-of-business-is-to.html.

2. E. O. Wilson, *Sociobiology: The New Synthesis* (Cambridge: Harvard University Press, 1975); Peter Singer, *The Expanding Circle: Ethics and Sociobiology* (Princeton: Princeton University Press, 1981).

3. Richard Feloni and Yusuf George, "These Are Notable Corporate Responses to George Floyd Protests," *JUST Capital* (blog), June 30, 2020, https://justcapital.com/news/notable-corporate-responses-to-the-george-floyd-protests/.

4. Ibid.

5. Mahzarin R. Banaji and Anthony G. Greenwald, *Blind Spot: Hidden Biases of Good People* (New York: Random House, 2013).

6. Ibid.

7. C. Neil Macrae and Galen V. Bodenhausen, "Social Cognition: Categorical Person Perception," *British Journal of Psychology* 92, no. 1 (2001): 239–55.

8. Jennifer A. Richeson and J. Nicole Shelton, "When Prejudice Does Not Pay: Effects of Interracial Contact on Executive Function," *Psychological Science* 14 (2003): 287–90; J. Nicole Shelton, Jennifer A Richeson, and Jacquie D. Vorauer, "Threatened Identities and Interethnic Interactions," *European Review of Social Psychology* 17 (2006): 321–58.

9. Max Larkin, "Lawsuit Alleging Racial 'Balancing' at Harvard Reveals Another Preference—For Children of Alumni," WBUR, November 5, 2018, https://www.wbur.org/edify/2018/10/12/harvard-admissions-legacy-preference.

10. The Economist, "The Curse of Nepotism," *The Economist*, January 8, 2004.

11. Larkin, "Lawsuit Alleging Racial 'Balancing' at Harvard Reveals Another Preference—For Children of Alumni."

12. Max Larkin and Mayowa Aina, "Legacy Admissions Offer an Advantage—And Not Just at Schools Like Harvard," NPR.Org, November 4, 2018, https://www.npr.org/2018/11/04/663629750/legacy-admissions-offer-an-advantage-and-not-just-at-schools-like-harvard.

13. Larkin, "Lawsuit Alleging Racial 'Balancing' at Harvard Reveals Another Preference—For Children of Alumni."

14. Janet Gilmore, "In a Competitive Year, Berkeley Admits 13,321 Prospective Freshmen," *Berkeley News*, July 2, 2015, https://news.berkeley.edu/2015/07/02/berkeley-admits-more-than-13000-prospective-freshmen/.

15. David M. Messick and Max H. Bazerman, "Ethical Leadership and the Psychology of Decision Making," *Sloan Management Review* 37, no. 2 (1996): 9–22.

16. Arthur P. Brief et al., "Just Doing Business: Modern Racism and Obedience to Authority as Explanations for Employment Discrimination," *Organizational Behavior and Human Decision Processes* 81, no. 1 (2000): 72–97; Chugh, "Societal and Managerial Implications of Implicit Social Cognition: Why Milliseconds Matter."

17. Dolly Chugh, Max H. Bazerman, and Mahzarin R. Banaji, "Bounded Ethicality as a Psychological Barrier to Recognizing Conflicts of Interest," in *Conflicts of Interest*, ed. Don A. Moore et al. (Cambridge: Cambridge University Press, 2005), 74–95.

18. Herbert A. Simon, *Models of Bounded Rationality*, vol. 3 (Cambridge: MIT Press, 1997).

19. Adapted from Philippa Foot, "The Problem of Abortion and the Doctrine of the Double Effect," in *Virtues and Vices* (Oxford: Basil Blackwell, 1978); Judith Jarvis Thomson, "Killing, Letting Die, and the Trolley Problem," *The Monist* 59 (2011): 204–17; Joshua Greene, *The Moral Self* (New York: Penguin Group, 2011).

20. Greene, *The Moral Self*.

21. William MacAskill, *Doing Good Better: Effective Altruism and a Radical New Way to Make a Difference* (London: Guardian Faber, 2015).

22. Karen Huang et al., "Veil-of-Ignorance Reasoning Mitigates Self-Serving Bias in Resource Allocation during the COVID-19 Crisis," *Judgment and Decision Making* 16, no. 1 (2021).

23. Sheri Fink, "U.S. Civil Rights Office Rejects Rationing Medical Care Based on Disability, Age," *New York Times*, March 28, 2020, sec. U.S., https://www.nytimes.com/2020/03/28/us/coronavirus-disabilities-rationing-ventilators-triage.html.

24. Linda W. Chang et al., "Pre-Commitment to Evaluation Criteria Improves Decision-Making," Working paper, 2020.

25. Matt Zapotosky, "Barr Seeks to Dissociate Himself from Move on Demonstrators Outside Lafayette Square," *Washington Post*, June 5, 2020, https://www.washingtonpost.com/national-security/barr-seeks-to-dissociate-himself-from-move-on-demonstrators-outside-lafayette-park/2020/06/05/47cb96b6-a78e-11ea-bb20-ebf0921f3bbd_story.html.

26. Lucas C. Coffman, "Intermediation Reduces Punishment (and Reward)," *American Economic Journal: Microeconomics* 3, no. 4 (2011): 77–106.

27. Don A. Moore et al., *Conflicts of Interest: Challenges and Solutions in Business, Law, Medicine, and Public Policy* (Cambridge: Cambridge University Press, 2005), https://doi.org/10.1017/CBO9780511610332.

28. D. M. Cain, G. Loewenstein, and Don A. Moore, "The Dirt on Coming Clean: Perverse Effects of Disclosing Conflicts of Interest," *Journal of Legal Studies* 34, no. 1 (2005): 1–25, https://doi.org/10.1086/426699.

29. Fyodor Dostoevsky, *The Brothers Karamazov* (New York: Random House, 2011).

30. Mich Ross and F. Sicoly, "Egocentric Biases in Availability and Attribution," *Journal of Personality and Social Psychology* 37 (1979): 322–36.

31. Eugene M. Caruso, Nicholas Epley, and Max H. Bazerman, "The Good, the Bad, and the Ugly of Perspective Taking in Groups," in *Research on Managing Groups and Teams: Ethics and Groups*, ed. Elizabeth A. Mannix, Margaret A. Neale, and Ann E. Tenbrunsel, vol. 8 (Greenwich, CT: JAI Press, 2005).

32. Claire Cain Miller, "Nearly Half of Men Say They Do Most of the Home Schooling. 3 Percent of Women Agree," *New York Times,* May 6, 2020, https://www.nytimes.com/2020/05/06/upshot/pandemic-chores-homeschooling-gender.html.

33. Jennifer M. Logg, Uriel Haran, and Don A. Moore, "Is Overconfidence a Motivated Bias? Experimental Evidence," *Journal of Experimental Psychology: General* 147, no. 10 (2018): 1445–65.

34. Nicholas Epley, Eugene Caruso, and Max H. Bazerman, "When Perspective Taking Increases Taking: Reactive Egoism in Social Interaction," *Journal of Personality and Social Psychology* 91 (2006): 872–89.

35. Eugene Caruso, Nicholas Epley, and Max H. Bazerman, "The Costs and Benefits of Undoing Egocentric Responsibility Assessments in Groups," *Journal of Personality and Social Psychology* 91 (2006): 857–71.

36. Updated Statement Moves Away from Shareholder Primacy and Includes Commitment to All Stakeholders, "Business Roundtable Redefines the Purpose of a Corporation to Promote 'An Economy That Serves All Americans,' " August 19, 2019, https://www.businessroundtable.org/business-roundtable-redefines-the-purpose-of-a-corporation-to-promote-an-economy-that-serves-all-americans.

37. John Branch, "The Awakening of Colin Kaepernick," *New York Times,* September 7, 2017, https://www.nytimes.com/2017/09/07/sports/colin-kaepernick-nfl-protests.html.

Chapter 9. Nudging toward Better Leadership

1. Thaler and Sunstein, *Nudge: Improving Decisions about Health, Wealth, and Happiness.*

2. Max H. Bazerman, Jonathan Baron, and Katherine Shonk, *You Can't Enlarge the Pie: The Psychology of Ineffective Government* (New York: Basic Books, 2001).

3. U.S. Department of Health and Human Services, "Organ Donation Statistics," OrganDonor.gov, April 10, 2018, https://www.organdonor.gov/statistics-sto ries/statistics.html.

4. Eric J. Johnson and Daniel G. Goldstein, "Do Defaults Save Lives?," *Science* 302 (2003): 1338–39.

5. Richard H. Thaler and Shlomo Benartzi, "Save More Tomorrow: Using Behavioral Economics to Increase Employee Saving," *Journal of Political Economy* 112, no. 1 (2004): S164–87.

6. Bazerman and Moore, *Judgment in Managerial Decision Making.*

7. John Beshears et al., "Active Choice, Implicit Defaults, and the Incentive to Choose," *Organizational Behavior and Human Decision Processes* 163 (March 2021): 6–16.

8. Greg Iacurci, "Here's Why Americans Are Contributing More to Their 401(k) Plans," CNBC, January 7, 2020, https://www.cnbc.com/2020/01/07/heres-why-americans-are-contributing-more-to-their-401k-plans.html.

9. Thaler and Sunstein, *Nudge: Improving Decisions about Health, Wealth, and Happiness.*

10. Cass R. Sunstein and Richard H. Thaler, "Libertarian Paternalism," *American Economics Review* 93, no. 2 (2003): 175–79.

11. Eric P. Bettinger et al., "The Role of Application Assistance and Information in College Decisions: Results from the H&R Block Fafsa Experiment*," *Quarterly Journal of Economics* 127, no. 3 (August 1, 2012): 1205–42, https://doi.org/10.1093/qje/qjs017.

12. George Loewenstein and Nick Chater, "Putting Nudges in Perspective," *Behavioural Public Policy* 1, no. 1 (2017): 26; David Hagmann, Emily H. Ho, and George Loewenstein, "Nudging Out Support for a Carbon Tax," *Nature Climate Change* 9, no. 6 (2019): 484–89.

13. Shlomo Benartzi et al., "Should Governments Invest More in Nudging?," *Psychological Science* 28, no. 8 (June 5, 2017): 1041–55, https://doi.org/10.1177/0956797617702501.

14. HBS Working Knowledge, "The Cost-Effective Power of Psychological Nudges," Forbes, accessed April 20, 2021, https://www.forbes.com/sites/hbsworking knowledge/2017/07/19/the-cost-effective-power-of-psychological-nudges/.

15. Bettinger et al., "The Role of Application Assistance and Information in College Decisions."

16. DellaVigna and Linos, "RCTs to Scale: Comprehensive Evidence from Two Nudge Units."

17. Hunt Allcott, "Social Norms and Energy Conservation," *Journal of Public Economics* 95, no. 9–10 (2011): 1082–95.

18. Heather Long, " 'This Is Not Controversial': Bipartisan Group of Economists Calls for Carbon Tax," *Washington Post*, January 16, 2019, https://www.washington post.com/business/2019/01/17/this-is-not-controversial-bipartisan-group-econo mists-calls-carbon-tax/.

19. Hagmann, Ho, and Loewenstein, "Nudging Out Support for a Carbon Tax."

20. Barry Schwartz, "Why Not Nudge? A Review of Cass Sunstein's Why Nudge," *Behavioral Scientist* (blog), April 17, 2014, https://behavioralscientist.org/nudge-review-cass-sunsteins-why-nudge/.

21. Ibid.

22. Sunstein, *Sludge: What Stops Us from Getting Things Done and What to Do about It*.

Chapter 10. Designing a Better Decision Factory

1. Jennifer S. Lerner and Philip E. Tetlock, "Accounting for the Effects of Accountability," *Psychological Bulletin* 125, no. 2 (1999): 255–75.

2. Gary Klein, "Performing a Project Premortem," *Harvard Business Review* 85, no. 9 (2007): 18–19.

3. Hoffman, *Red Teaming*.

4. E. T. Anderson and D. Simister, "A Step-by-Step Guide to Smart Business Experiments," *Harvard Business Review* 89, no. 3 (2011); Thomas H. Davenport, "How to Design Smart Business Experiments," *Harvard Business Review* 87, no. 2 (2009): 68–76.

5. Fernando P. Polack et al., "Safety and Efficacy of the BNT162b2 MRNA Covid-19 Vaccine," *New England Journal of Medicine* 383, no. 27 (2020): 2603–15.

6. http://scholar.google.com is often a pretty good place to start.

7. Bock, *Work Rules!*

8. " 'Winning Just 52% of Your Points Is Your Goal' Says Djokovic Tactician," *Tennishead* (blog), March 31, 2020, https://tennishead.net/expert-analysis-winning-just-52-of-your-points-should-be-your-goal-says-novak-djokovic-tactician-craig-oshannessy/.

9. Maria Konnikova, *The Biggest Bluff: How I Learned to Pay Attention, Master Myself, and Win* (New York: Penguin, 2020).

Appendix: Decision Biases

1. Daniel Kahneman and Amos Tversky, "On the Reality of Cognitive Illusions," *Psychological Review* 103, no. 3 (1996): 582–91.

2. Tetlock and Gardner, *Superforecasting: The Art and Science of Prediction.*

3. M. K. Lindell and R. W. Perry, "Household Adjustment to Earthquake Hazard: A Review of Research," *Environment and Behavior* 32 (2000): 461–501; Risa Palm, "Catastrophic Earthquake Insurance: Patterns of Adoption," *Economic Geography* 71, no. 2 (1995): 119–31; Howard Kunreuther, *Disaster Insurance Protection: Public Policy Lessons* (New York: Wiley, 1978).

4. Uri Simonsohn et al., "The Tree of Experience in the Forest of Information: Overweighing Experienced Relative to Observed Information," *Games and Economic Behavior* 62, no. 1 (2008): 263–86.

5. Amos Tversky and Daniel Kahneman, "Extensional versus Intuitive Reasoning: The Conjunction Fallacy in Probability Judgment," *Psychological Review* 90, no. 4 (1983): 293–315.

6. Jeff Orlowski, *The Social Dilemma*, Documentary (Netflix, 2020), https://www.netflix.com/title/81254224.

7. Christopher A. Bail, *Breaking the Social Media Prism: How to Make Our Platforms Less Polarizing* (Princeton: Princeton University Press, 2021).

8. G. B. Chapman and E. J. Johnson, "Anchoring, Activation, and the Construction of Values," *Organizational Behavior and Human Decision Processes* 79, no. 2 (August 1999): 115–53, https://doi.org/10.1006/obhd.1999.2841.

9. G. B. Northcraft and Margaret A. Neale, "Expert, Amateurs, and Real Estate: An Anchoring-and-Adjustment Perspective on Property Pricing Decisions," *Organizational Behavior and Human Decision Processes* 39 (1987): 228–41; Thomas Mussweiler, Fritz Strack, and Tim Pfeiffer, "Overcoming the Inevitable Anchoring Effect: Considering the Opposite Compensates for Selective Accessibility," *Personality and Social Psychology Bulletin* 26, no. 9 (2000): 1142–50.

10. Rüdiger Pohl and Ulrich Hoffrage, *Hindsight Bias* (Hove, UK: Hove Books Psychology, 2003).

11. Nate Cohn, "A 2016 Review: Why Key State Polls Were Wrong About Trump (Published 2017)," *New York Times*, May 31, 2017, sec. The Upshot, https://www.nytimes.com/2017/05/31/upshot/a-2016-review-why-key-state-polls-were-wrong-about-trump.html.

12. Roy F. Baumeister et al., "Bad Is Stronger than Good," *Review of General Psychology* 5, no. 4 (2001): 323.

13. Geoffrey L. Cohen, "Party over Policy: The Dominating Impact of Group Influence on Political Beliefs," *Journal of Personality and Social Psychology* 85, no. 5 (2003): 808–22.

14. Scott Highhouse, "Stubborn Reliance on Intuition and Subjectivity in Employee Selection," *Industrial and Organizational Psychology* 1, no. 3 (2008): 333–42.

15. Don A. Moore, "How to Improve the Accuracy and Reduce the Cost of Personnel Selection," *California Management Review* 60, no. 1 (August 7, 2017): 8–17, https://doi.org/10.1177/0008125617725288.

16. Tversky and Kahneman, "Extensional versus Intuitive Reasoning: The Conjunction Fallacy in Probability Judgment."

17. Anthony King, "BAD Science: Homeopathy—Can the Undetectable Cure?," *British Dental Journal* 224, no. 3 (February 1, 2018): 128–29, https://doi.org/10.1038/sj.bdj.2018.94.

18. "About Homeopathy," accessed February 23, 2021, https://homeopathy-uk.org/homeopathy.

19. Joseph Patrick Byrne, *Encyclopedia of the Black Death* (Santa Barbara, CA: ABC–CLIO, 2012).

20. John M. Last, ed., "Miasma Theory," in *A Dictionary of Public Health* (Westminster College, PA: Oxford University Press, 2007).

21. Lynne Peeples, "Face Masks: What the Data Say," *Nature* 586, no. 7828 (October 6, 2020): 186–89, https://doi.org/10.1038/d41586–020–02801–8.

22. Luca and Bazerman, *The Power of Experiments.*

23. Terrance Odean, "Are Investors Reluctant to Realize Their Losses?," *Journal of Finance* 53, no. 5 (1998): 1775–98.

24. At least not if you have infinitely sensitive utilities.

25. Christopher K. Hsee, "The Evaluability Hypothesis: An Explanation for Preference Reversals between Joint and Separate Evaluations of Alternatives," *Organizational Behavior and Human Decision Processes* 67, no. 3 (1996): 247–57.

26. Daniel Kahneman, Jack L. Knetsch, and Richard H. Thaler, "Experimental Tests of the Endowment Effect and the Coase Theorem," *Journal of Political Economy* 98, no. 6 (1990): 1325–48.

27. Kahneman, *Thinking Fast and Slow.*

28. Michael Lewis, *The Undoing Project: A Friendship That Changed Our Minds* (New York: W. W. Norton, 2016).

29. Richard H. Thaler, *Misbehaving: The Making of Behavioral Economics* (New York: W. W. Norton, 2015), https://books.google.com/books?id=xQedBAAAQBAJ.

30. Annie Duke, *How to Decide: Simple Tools for Making Better Choices* (New York: Penguin, 2020).

31. Bazerman and Moore, *Judgment in Managerial Decision Making.* Other sources include John S. Hammond, Ralph L. Keeney, and Howard Raiffa, *Smart Choices: A Practical Guide to Making Better Decisions* (Cambridge: Harvard Business Review Press, 2015); David Hardman, *Judgment and Decision Making: Psychological Perspectives*, 1st ed. (Malden, MA: BPS Blackwell, 2009).

Index

Table references are indicated by *t* following the page number.

academia. *See* universities and colleges
accountability: of advisers, 72–73, 80, 81, 186; deception decreased through, 139; delegation and, 159–60; dissent and, 87; McKinsey and, 99–100
Adidas, 147
admissions processes, 27–28, 149–51, 173
advice and feedback: accountability to, 72–73, 80, 81, 186; conflicts of interest and, 160–63; diverse perspectives in, 88, 93–94, 156; experimentation and, 115–16; importance of, 71, 86–88, 186–87; leading others to provide, 96–100, 186–87; at Netflix, 85–88, 103–4; prediction markets and, 100–103; weighting of, 88–91; wisdom of groups and, 25, 86, 91–96
Airbnb, 105–9
Airbus, 73–74
algorithms for expected value, 25, 27–28, 43. *See also* artificial intelligence and machine learning
Alibaba, 52
Amazon: advice and feedback and, 88; experimentation and, 115; George

Floyd murder and, 147; incentivization in, 186; one-click buying feature of, 13
ambiguity. *See* uncertainty
ambition in goal setting, 74–78, 82, 185–86
American Airlines, 73–74
anchoring biases, 200
Anderson, Cameron, 66
Ant (bike sharing company), 48
Ardern, Jacinda, 63, 68
Arpey, Gerard, 73–74
Arthur Andersen (accounting firm), 55, 110
artificial intelligence and machine learning, 28, 138–39
athletes and athletic performance, 30, 60, 164, 204
auditors and auditing: Enron and, 110; of ethics, 159–66, 190–91; of intuition, 14–15, 28–29; U.S. system for, 54–55, 110
autoplay features, 172
availability heuristic, 29, 195–99, 196*t*

Banaji, Mahzarin, 148
Baron, Jonathan, 167
Barr, William, 159

Bay of Pigs invasion (1961), 87, 88

Bazerman, Max: BIG and, 9–10, 120–21; Covid-19 ethics experiment of, 154–56; El-Tek negotiation simulation and, 128; on ethical slippery slopes, 56, 57; experimentation and, 41, 116–17; on intuition, 32; on joint decision making, 40, 41; *Judgment in Managerial Decision Making* (with Moore), 23, 209–10; *Negotiation Genius* (with Malhotra), 134; Rabin and, 34, 38; risk assessment and, 36, 38; *You Can't Enlarge the Pie*, 167–68

Beane, Billy, 60

Beech Tree restaurant, 45–46

behavioral economics, 16, 110–11, 113, 170

Behavioral Insights Group (BIG), 9–10, 120–21

Behavior Change for Good project (BCFG), 117–18

Behavioural Insights Team (BIT), 113–14, 170–71, 174–75

Ben and Jerry's ice cream, 147

Benartzi, Shlomo, 168, 172–73, 175

Benchmark Capital, 52–53

Bennis, Warren, 58

Bentham, Jeremy, 144

Berkshire Hathaway, 98

Beshears, John, 172–73, 175

Best Buy's TagTrade market, 101

betting and bids: contingent contracts and, 84; expected value and, 39, 68, 192; prediction markets and, 100–103; risk assessment and, 34–35; testing confidence through, 77–81, 84. *See also* forecasting

Bettinger, Eric, 173

Beyond Meat, 7

Bezos, Jeff, 68–69, 115, 206

biases: academic publication and, 175; bounded ethicality and, 152; confidence and, 83–84; conflicts of interest and, 161–63; deliberation and, 42–43, 195–202, 196*t*; expected value and, 78; from first opinion, 94–96; framing and, 205–9; heuristics leading to, 195, 196*t*, 197, 200–201, 205, 207–8; incentives for accuracy vs., 81; intuition and, 14, 29–31; overclaiming credit, 163–65; representativeness and, 202–5; in weighting of advice, 88–90, 93. *See also* heuristics

Biden, Joe, 9

bike sharing, 48

Black Lives Matter, 146

Black Lives Matter protests, 2

Blecharczyk, Nathan, 105

Bluebikes (bike sharing company), 48

Bock, Laszlo, 5

Boeing, 73–77

Bohnet, Iris, 40, 157

Bolsonaro, Jair, 63, 82, 84

bounded ethicality, 152

Bower, Marvin, 98

Boyer, Nate, 1

Boy Scouts, 54, 61

Branson, Richard, 20–21

Brees, Drew, 1, 2

Bridgewater Associates, 71, 88

Brion, Sebastien, 66

British Petroleum (BP), 140

Buffett, Warren, 98

Business Roundtable, 165–66

Cain, Daylian, 48, 162

California and Airbnb, 108

calorie labeling, 4

Cameron, David, 112–13
carbon emissions, 176
Carlyle, Thomas, 3
casinos and gambling, 31, 34. *See also*
    betting and bids
Castro, Fidel, 87
Catholic Church, 54, 60
Center for Applied Rationality, 70
Center for Behavioral Decision
    Research, 4
Center for Public Leadership at the
    Harvard Kennedy School of
    Government, 9–10
Chabris, Chris, 22
Chambliss, Saxby, 7–8
Chang, Edward, 42
Chesky, Brian, 105–6, 108
chief executive officers (CEOs):
    cooperation and, 136; George Floyd
    murder and responses of, 146–47;
    noticing responsibilities of, 58–60;
    oversight of, 52–54; risk aversion
    and, 38. *See also* corporations;
    leadership
child labor, 26
China: Covid-19 pandemic and, 62,
    65; free-trade agreements and,
    125–26; McKinsey and, 100
choice architecture. *See* decision
    architecture
Churchill, Winston, 66, 81
Coffman, Lucas, 159–60
colleges. *See* universities and colleges
Collins, Jim: *Built to Last* (with
    Porras), 74–77
Comcast, 147
comparative decision making, 40–42
competition: optimism and overlook-
    ing, 47–48; trade-offs between
    cooperation and, 139–42, 189

confidence: calibrating to reality,
    16–17, 69–73, 81, 185–86; honesty
    and, 67, 69–70; optimism and,
    66–67, 81–84. *See also* overconfi-
    dence
confirmation, 30, 184–85, 196*t*,
    199–202
conflicts of interest, 26, 110, 149,
    160–64
Congressional Black Caucus, 108
conjunction fallacy, 203
consensus, 87, 93–94
conservation efforts, 7
consultants and advice professionals,
    91, 96–100, 110, 116, 160–63, 176.
    See also advice and feedback
contact tracing, 83
contingent contracts, 80, 84
cooperation: joint decision making,
    40–42; negotiating terms of, 128,
    139–42; overclaiming credit and,
    163–65; sociobiological accounts of,
    144–45; trade-offs between
    competition and, 139–42, 189; value
    creation through, 136, 142
coping mechanisms, 209
Copperfield, David, 56–57
corporations: barriers introduced by,
    13; boards' oversight role in, 52–54;
    ethical leadership of, 165–66;
    Friedman on, 143–45; George Floyd
    murder and, 146–48; internal
    conflict within, 127–29; nudges
    and, 171–72, 180–81; oversight and
    noticing within, 52–54; profit
    maximization and, 144, 146–51;
    risk-neutral policies for, 35–39
Covid-19 pandemic: Bolsonaro and,
    82; ethical dilemmas of, 154–56;
    experimentation and, 188; face

Covid-19 pandemic *(continued)*
mask usage and, 63, 64, 204;
Lukashenko and, 82–83; nudges
during, 167; overconfident
leadership and, 62–65, 82–84;
representativeness heuristic and,
204
credibility, 67, 68, 71, 82, 84

Dalio, Ray, 88
Dalkey, Norman, 94
decision architecture: calibrating to
reality, 71–73; empowerment
through, 183; leadership examples of,
5, 9–11; noticing threats and
opportunities in, 60; nudges in, 5,
17, 111, 169–70, 181, 190; power of
situation in, 11–13; wisdom of crowds
and, 92, 103–4. *See also* nudges
declining marginal utility, 206–7
Deepwater Horizon oil rig explosion
(2010), 139–41
defaults in decision making: as
element of decision architecture,
182, 191–92; experimentation and,
188; in government policy, 9, 168;
organ donation and, 168, 179–80;
retirement savings and, 9, 176;
status quo bias and, 208; YouTube
and, 172. *See also* nudges
de la Villehuchet, René-Thierry
Magon, 50, 208
deliberation: benefits of, 42–43; on
ethical challenges, 151–58; intuition
vs., 21–22, 28–29, 43, 158, 170, 184;
joint decision making and, 40–43;
leadership through, 31–38, 42–43;
nudges and, 180–81; scientific
perspectives on, 22–29; System 2
thinking and, 26–27

DellaVigna, Stefano, 174–76
Delphi method of group decision
making, 94–96
deontology, 154
dependent measures, 58, 77, 81–82,
118–19
dictator games, 159–60
discrimination and Airbnb, 105–9. *See
also* diversity; gender stereotypes;
racism
dispositions vs. situations, 11–13
diversity: corporate commitments to,
147; of feedback, 88, 93–94, 156;
joint decision making and, 40, 42;
prediction markets and, 101; Uber
and, 109
Dostoevsky, Fyodor, 163
Douglas Aircraft, 74
Downs, Julie, 4
Duckworth, Angela, 117
Duke, Annie: *Thinking in Bets,* 77
Dunlevie, Bruce, 53
Dwan, Tom, 77

Edelman, Ben, 107, 109
effective altruism movement, 155
Ellison, Larry, 52
El-Tek intraorganizational case study,
128–30, 135–36
endowment effect, 207–8
Enron, 55, 61
Enron Corporation, 99, 100, 110, 141,
162
entrepreneurship: contingent
contracts for, 80; failure to analyze
competition and, 47–49; goal
setting and, 77–78; optimism and,
47–48, 66–67, 77–80, 82; uncertainty and, 68–69
epistemic principle, 178

ethical fading, 55–56, 58–60
ethics: advice and, 100; auditing
leadership in, 159–66, 190–91;
deliberating on challenges of,
23–24, 151–58; of experimentation,
119–23, 178–80; insurance industry
and, 138; of nudges, 120–21, 176–81,
191–92; profit maximization and,
143–46; random assignment and,
119–20, 122
evidence-based decisions. *See* advice
and feedback; experimentation
Ewing Kaufmann Foundation, 79
expected value: betting on, 39, 68, 192;
confidence and, 70, 73; as essence
of decision making, 21–22;
free-trade agreements and, 125–26;
goal setting and, 38, 76, 186; joint
decision making and, 43; maximization strategies for, 31–38;
outcomes vs., 39; start-up
investment and, 78
experimentation: Airbnb and, 108–9;
applications of, 112–15, 188; ethics
of, 119–23, 178–80; features of,
118–20; history of, 110–11; importance of, 17, 109; intuition vs., 109,
115–17, 122, 123; leadership
perspectives on, 109, 115–18, 122–23;
Netflix and, 104; nudges informing,
171–72; reasons for, 115–17, 123
external vs. internal attributions, 59

Facebook, 199
face mask usage, 63, 64, 204
failure: Bezos on, 69; premortem
discussions of, 84, 86, 187–88;
stretch goals and, 39, 76–77, 82
farm animals, 6–7
Farm Sanctuary, 6

Federal Aviation Administration, 76
feedback. *See* advice and feedback
Feinman, Jay: *Delay, Deny, Defend,*
138
financial crisis of 2008, 99
fixed-pie mindset, 17, 127, 130, 134, 135
Floyd, George, 2, 146–48, 152, 166
footbridge dilemma, 152–54
forecasting: accountability to, 71–73,
84, 186; availability heuristic and,
194–95; expected value and, 70;
Kahneman on, 91; overconfidence
and, 72–73, 79–80; prediction
markets for, 100–103; weighting of
advice in, 89–90; *WSJ* competition
in, 91–93. *See also* betting and bids;
goal setting
Foundations for Evidence-Based
Policymaking Act (2018), 114
framing, 30–31, 33, 36, 196t, 205–8
free-trade agreements, 124–25
Friedman, Milton, 143–46, 165
Friedrich, Bruce, 6–7, 11

Gaertig, Celia, 67
Galef, Julia: *The Scout Mindset,* 70
Galton, Francis, 91–92
game theory, 60
Gebbia, Joe, 105–6
Geisinger Health System, 117
gender stereotypes, 40, 42, 148, 157
General Electric, 127–28
generalizability of results, 115–16, 118
Germany and Covid-19 pandemic, 62
Gino, Francesca, 56, 90–91
Gladwell, Malcolm: *Blink,* 21–22
goal setting: advisers' role in, 96–97;
ambition in, 74–78, 82, 185–86;
ethics of, 158–60, 166; expected
value in, 38, 76, 186; negotiation

goal setting *(continued)*
and, 130; purpose in, 143–46; scout
mindset for, 70; utilitarianism and,
154, 177, 179. *See also* forecasting
Goldstein, Dan, 168
Goodell, Roger, 2
Good Food Institute (GFI), 6–7
Good Judgment Project (GJP), 102–3
Google: confirmation heuristic and,
199; experimentation and, 115;
incentives at, 189; People Operations unit of, 5–6; prediction
markets and, 101
great man theory, 3
Greene, Joshua, 157
Greenwald, Anthony, 148
group meetings, 94–96, 187
groupthink, 87, 93–94. *See also* advice
and feedback
group wisdom. *See* wisdom of crowds
gut: deliberation vs., 152, 183–84;
leadership perspectives on, 13–15;
oversight and noticing of, 53;
System 2 thinking vs., 26–27. *See
also* intuition

Halliburton, 140
Halpern, David, 112–14, 119
harm principle, 177–78
Harvard Business Review (HBR), 110
Harvard University admissions
lawsuit, 149–50
Hastie, Reid: *Wiser* (with Sunstein),
100
Hastings, Reed, 85–88, 103–4,
186–87
Hayek, Friedrich, 100–101
hedge funds, 72, 98, 208
Helmer, Olaf, 94
Henriques, Diana: *Wizard of Lies,* 50

heuristics: availability, 29, 195–99,
196*t*; biases resulting from, 195,
196*t*, 197, 200–201, 205, 207–8;
confirmation, 30, 184–85, 196*t*,
199–202; framing, 30–31, 33, 36,
196*t*, 205–8; intuition and, 29–31;
representativeness, 30, 196*t*, 202–5
Hidden Brain (radio program), 107–8
hindsight bias, 201
hiring processes, 19–20, 40–42, 95,
132–33, 202–3
honesty: confidence and, 67, 69–70;
leaders' responsibility to, 66–67,
69; self-conceptions of, 161
Hony Capital, 52
Humu, 5–6
hydroxychloroquine, 82

Iger, Robert: *The Ride of a Lifetime,*
65, 66
IKEA, 26
Immigration and Customs Enforcement, 100
Implicit Associations Test (IAT),
148–49
Impossible Burger, 7
incentivization: for advisers, 161–63;
for auditors, 54–55; ethics of,
140–41, 145, 161; goal setting and,
77, 166; of good decisions vs.
performance, 186, 189; nudges
compared to, 171, 173, 176;
unintended consequences of, 13, 59
information sharing, 129–33, 136,
184–85
insurance industry and insurtech,
38–39, 116–17, 137–39
interaction within groups, 94–96
Intermediation Game, 159–60
internal vs. external attributions, 59

internships, 190
intuition: bounded ethicality of, 152,
   158; deliberation vs., 21–22, 28–29,
   43, 158, 170, 183–84; emotional
   reactions and, 41–42; experimentation vs., 109, 115–17, 122, 123;
   heuristics and biases of, 14, 29–31;
   inability to audit, 14–15, 28–29;
   leadership perspectives on, 13–15,
   21–22, 43; oversight and noticing
   of, 53, 59; reliance on, 19–21, 209;
   representativeness heuristic and,
   203–5; risk assessment and, 32–33;
   scientific perspectives on, 22–29;
   siren song of, 21–22, 183–84. *See also*
   heuristics
Ivey, Phil, 77

Janus, Irving, 87
Jobs, Steve, 20–21, 66
Johnson, Boris, 63
Johnson, Eric, 168
joint decision making, 40–42

Kaepernick, Colin, 1–4, 10–11, 166
Kahneman, Daniel: on business
   forecasting, 91; experimentation
   and, 110–11; on Gladwell's
   arguments for intuition, 22; on
   reactions to social and environmen-
   tal issues, 41–42; representativeness
   heuristic and, 30; risk assessment
   and, 32–33; *Thinking, Fast and
   Slow*, 209
Kalanick, Travis, 109
Kennedy, Jessica, 66
Kennedy, John F., 87
Kennedy, Reed, 106
Kerr, Steve, 68
Khosrowshahi, Dara, 109

Kmart, 48–49
Knight, Rebecca, 66
Komisar, Randy, 66
Kors, Michael, 6

Laibson, David, 10
Larrick, Rick, 89, 90, 92
lawyers and risk aversion, 37–38
leadership: advice, 88–91, 96–100;
   ambition in goal-setting and,
   74–77, 82–84; assessing information and, 72–73; behavioral science
   and, 9–11; deliberation and, 31–38,
   42–43; ethics and, 159–66;
   experimentation and, 109, 115–18,
   122–23; honesty and, 66–67, 69;
   intuition and, 13–15, 21–22, 43; joint
   decision making and, 39–42, 165;
   negotiation and, 126, 127, 134–36;
   nudges and, 181; optimism and,
   65–66, 68, 81
legacy admissions, 149–51
Lewis, Michael: *Moneyball,* 60; *The
   Undoing Project,* 111, 209
Lime (bike sharing company), 48
linear models, 25, 27–28. *See also*
   expected value
Linos, Elizabeth, 174–76
Loewenstein, George, 4, 110, 162
López Obrador, Andrés Manuel,
   62–63
loss aversion, 35, 168–69, 196*t,*
   205–6
Luca, Mike, 107, 109
Ludtke, Rick, 74
Lukashenko, Aleksandr, 63, 82–83

Ma, Jack, 52, 53
machine learning and artificial
   intelligence, 28, 138–39

Madoff, Bernie, 49–51, 53, 55–56
Malhotra, Deepak: *Negotiation Genius* (with Bazerman), 134
Mandery, Evan, 150
maneuvering characteristics augmentation system (MCAS), 76
markets. *See* forecasting; incentivization; prediction markets
masking during Covid-19 pandemic, 63, 64, 204
Maxwell, Robert, 44–47
McDonald, Duff, 99
McDonnell Douglas (aircraft manufacturer), 74
McKinsey, James, 98
McKinsey & Company, 98–100
McLean, Bethany, 99
McNerney, James, 74–75
meat consumption, 6–7
MERS (Middle East Respiratory Disease), 64
Microsoft, 147
Milkman, Katy, 117, 172–73, 175
Mill, John Stuart: *On Liberty*, 177
misdirection, 56–58, 183
Moon Jae-in, 63
Moore, Don: on conflicts of interest, 162; as consultant, 59; forecasting and, 72, 102; Good Judgment Project and, 102–3; *Judgment in Managerial Decision Making* (with Bazerman), 23, 209–10; on optimism, 66; *Perfectly Confident*, 69–70, 90–91; on reference group neglect, 48; Wisdom and, 4
Morse, Gardiner, 110
motivated blindness, 54–55

NASCAR, 147
Nazis and Nazism, 120, 121

negotiation: asking questions in, 130–31; building trust and sharing information in, 129–31; experimentation and, 116–17; fixed-pie mindset in, 17, 127, 130, 134, 135; lowering costs of dispute resolution in, 136–39; of multiple issues simultaneously, 131–33; post-settlement settlements in, 133–34; role of leadership in, 126, 127, 134–36; trade-offs between cooperation and competition in, 139–42; value creation through, 126–31, 135–36, 189–90
Netflix: advice and feedback processes of, 85–88, 93, 103–4, 187; experimentation and, 114–15
Neumann, Adam, 51–54, 58, 79
New Zealand and Covid-19 pandemic, 62–64, 68
Nike, 2
Nisbett, Richard: *Human Inference* (with Ross), 15–16
Nosek, Brian, 148
noticing: action steps toward, 58–60, 184–85; causes of failures in, 54–57; leaders' responsibilities for, 49, 51–54, 58–60, 65; of suspicious details, 49–54; of threats, 60, 64–65
nudges: cost-effectiveness of, 172–74; Covid-19 pandemic and, 167; in decision architecture, 5, 17, 111, 169–70, 181, 190; ethics of, 120–21, 176–81, 191–92; in government policymaking, 8–9, 112–14, 120–21, 170–71, 178; hype surrounding, 174–76; leadership perspectives vs., 10–11, 170; in retirement savings, 9, 10, 168–69, 173–74, 176–78, 191; retirement savings and, 168–69; Sunstein and, 8–9; Wisdom and,

5–6. *See also* defaults in decision making

Nuremberg Code (1947), 120

Obama, Barack, 8–9, 125
Obrador, Andrés Manuel López, 84
Office of Information and Regulatory Affairs (OIRA), 8
Ofo (bike sharing company), 48
optimism: calibrating to reality, 69–73; entrepreneurship and, 47–48, 66–67, 77–80, 82; goal setting and, 74–78; honesty balanced with, 65–69; noticing vs., 55
ordinary prejudice, 148–49. *See also* biases; racism
organ donation, 113, 167–68, 177–80
outcome bias, 39–41, 186
outcomes: cause and effect heuristic, 30; confidence in, 67, 69; default options and, 191; evidence-based decision making and, 114; framing, 33; goal setting and, 186; nudges and, 175, 176; probabilities for, 70, 184, 196; tracking of, 72
outsiders' perspectives, 28, 59
overclaiming credit, 163–65
overconfidence: calibrating to reality, 16–17, 69–73, 81, 185–86; of consultants, 97; Covid-19 pandemic and, 62–64; familiarity and, 14; optimism and, 66–67, 81–84; weighting of advice and, 90
OxyContin and opioid sales, 99–100

pandemic. *See* Covid-19 pandemic
paternalism, 8, 9, 178
PayPal, 147
Penn Medicine and vaccination rates, 117–18

Penn State, 54, 60–61
People for the Ethical Treatment of Animals (PETA), 6
PepsiCo, 147
personalities. *See* dispositions vs. situations
persuasion: behavioral science vs., 10; experimentation and, 111, 204; intuition's vulnerability to, 184; negotiation and, 131; status quo bias and, 208. *See also* nudges
planning. *See* forecasting; goal setting
policing and police reform, 146–48
Porras, Jerry: *Built to Last* (with Collins), 74–77
Posner, Richard, 22
post-settlement settlements, 133–34
prediction markets, 100–103. *See also* betting and bids; forecasting
premortems, 84, 86, 187–88
presidential election of 2020, 69
profits and profit maximization: Friedman on, 143–45; racism and moving beyond, 146–51
prospect theory, 33
Purdue Pharma, 99–100

Quaker Oats, 147
quality-adjusted life years (QALYs), 154–56
Qwikster, 85–88, 103

Rabin, Matthew, 31–33, 34, 36, 38
racism: Airbnb and, 105–9; bad apples accounts of, 151–52; corporate commitments against, 146–48; implicit and ordinary prejudices of, 149–51; Kaepernick and, 1; Singer on, 145
Raiffa, Howard, 28–29, 133, 134

random assignment, 118–20, 122
rational decision making: assumption of, 111, 205; steps for, 23–25
Rawls, John, 155
red teaming, 187–88
reference group neglect, 48–49
regression to the mean, 204
Reid, Eric, 1
representativeness heuristic, 30, 196t, 202–5
restaurants and restaurant industry, 44–48, 124, 209
retirement savings, 9, 10, 168–69, 173–74, 176–78, 191
Rhône Group, 52
risk assessment: framing heuristic and, 206; leadership in, 31–34; neutrality policies for, 34–39; outcome bias and, 39–41; prospect theory of, 33; uncertainty and, 68
Ritov, Ilana, 41
Rosenberg, Michael, 3
Rosenzweig, Phil: *The Halo Effect,* 48
Ross, Lee: *Human Inference* (with Nisbett), 15–16
Ross, Michael, 163

Samuelson, Paul, 34
Sarbanes-Oxley Act (2002), 162
Save More Tomorrow, 168–69, 172
Schlesinger, Arthur, 87
Schwartz, Barry, 178
scout mindset, 70–71, 202
Sebenius, James and Isaac, 65
select-crowd strategy, 92
selecting on dependent variable, 58, 77, 81–82
self-interest: availability heuristic and, 197; conflicts of interest and, 163; costs of, 189; incentivization and,

141; nudges and, 176–77, 180; sociobiological accounts of, 144–45; veil of ignorance and, 155. *See also* cooperation
separate decision making, 40–42
Severino, Roger, 157–58
shareholders, 38, 143–44
Shonk, Katherine, 167
Sicoly, Fiore, 163
Simmons, Joe, 67
Simons, Dan, 22
Sinclair, Upton, 50
Singapore, 121
Singer, Peter: *The Expanding Circle,* 145
situations vs. dispositions, 11–13
Slice Insurance, 139
slippery slope, 55–56
sludge (exploitative nudges), 180–81
sociobiology, 144–45
SoftBank, 51, 52
Soll, Jack, 89, 90
Son, Masayoshi, 51–54
South Korea: Covid-19 pandemic and, 62–64; MERS and, 64–65
Spin (bike sharing company), 48
stakeholders, 4, 165–66
Stanovich, Keith, 25
start-ups. *See* entrepreneurship
Statue of Liberty's disappearance, 56–57
status quo bias, 112, 153, 207–8
steps for rational decision making, 23–25, 40
stereotypes, 148–49. *See also* biases; racism
stock investments, 35, 38
stretch goals, 74–77, 82
Sunstein, Cass: Behavioral Insights Group and, 10; *Nudge* (with

Thaler), 8–9, 111, 113, 167, 169–70, 176; on nudging ethics, 180–81; as OIRA chief, 8–9, 11; on rights of animals, 7; *Simpler,* 9; *Wiser* (with Hastie), 100

Surowiecki, James, 91–92

Svirsky, Dan, 107, 109

System 1: bounded ethicality and, 152; characteristics of, 25–26, 42; experimentation and, 122; joint decision making vs., 40–41; nudges and, 170; risk assessment by, 32

System 2: characteristics of, 26, 42; ethical thinking and, 145–46, 151, 157, 158; joint decision making and, 42; linear models for, 27–28; nudges and, 170

TagTrade prediction market, 101

taxes and tax delinquency, 112, 113, 119, 177

Thaler, Richard: on consultancy firms, 97–98; experimentation of, 111; *Misbehaving,* 111, 209; *Nudge* (with Sunstein), 8, 111, 113, 167, 169–70, 176, 180; on retirement savings, 9

Toronto Underground Food Market, 44

Transocean, 140

Trans-Pacific Partnership, 125

tribalism, 145, 149

Trivers, Robert: *The Folly of Fools,* 82

trolley problem, 152–54

Trump, Donald: *The Art of the Deal,* 69; census citizenship question and, 121; Covid-19 pandemic and, 62–65, 67, 69, 73, 82–84; on Kaepernick protests, 1–2; pandemic special unit disbanded by, 65; presidential election of 2020 and, 69; protesters tear-gassed for, 159; United States–China trade relations and, 125–26

Tuskegee syphilis study, 120

Tversky, Amos: experimentation and, 110–11; representativeness heuristic and, 30; risk assessment and, 32–33

Uber, 109

uncertainty: acceptance of, 67–70, 81; betting on, 78–79; optimism in face of, 55; outcome bias and, 39; wisdom of crowds and, 25

unethical behaviors. *See* ethics

United States: auditing system, 54–55; Covid-19 response in, 62–65; free-trade agreements and, 124–26; organ donation policy in, 168; Social and Behavioral Sciences Team, 114

universities and colleges: admissions processes of, 27–28, 149–50, 173; competition and cooperation among, 141–42; hiring processes of, 19–20, 95

University of California system, 150

U.S. Census, 121

U.S. Department of Housing and Urban Development, 108

U.S. Olympic gymnastics, 54

utilitarianism, 144, 146, 153–54, 156, 158, 177–79

vaccination rates, 117–18, 174, 188

Valeant, 99

value creation: deliberation and, 152; information sharing and, 133–34, 142; leadership and, 4, 126–31, 135–36, 166; from lower costs of

value creation *(continued)*
dispute resolution, 136–39; through cooperation, 136, 142; trade agreements and, 124–26; utilitarianism and, 144, 154
van Geen, Alexandra, 40, 157
veil of ignorance, 155–57, 179–80
venture capitalists, 77–80

Wall Street Journal (WSJ) economic forecast competition, 91–93
Walmart, 49
weight-on-advice (WOA), 89–90
Welch, Jack: *Winning: The Ultimate Business How-To Book,* 13–15, 21

Welsh, David, 56
West, Richard, 25
WeWork, 51–54, 58, 60, 79
Wilson, E. O., 144
winner's curse, 78–80
Wisdom, Jessica, 4–6, 11
wisdom of crowds, 25, 86, 91–96, 103, 186–87

YouTube, 172, 199

Zagster (bike sharing company), 48
zero-based budgeting, 208
Zillow, 24
z-scores, 27